Mothers of the
Disappeared

LEGE

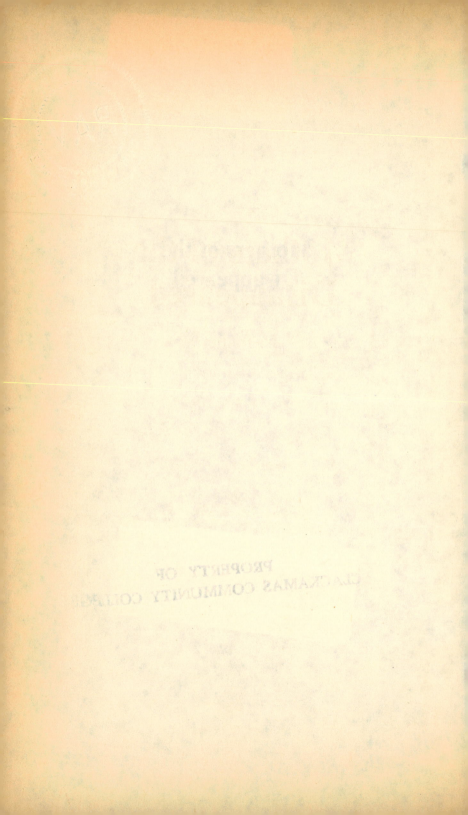

Mothers of the Disappeared

Jo Fisher

South End Press
Boston

Mothers of the Disappeared was first published in the United Kingdom by Zed Books Ltd, 57 Caledonian Road, London N1 9BU, UK and in the United States of America by South End Press, Institute for Social and Cultural Change, 116 St Botolph St, Boston, MA 02115, in 1989.

Cover designed by Andrew Corbett.
Cover photograph by Jorge Martinez (detail).
Typeset by EMS Photosetters, Rochford, Essex.
Printed and bound in the United Kingdom
at Bookcraft (Bath) Ltd, Midsomer Norton.

British Library Cataloguing in Publication Data

Fisher, Jo
 Mothers of the disappeared
 1. Argentina. Pressure groups
 I. Title.
 322.4'3'0982

 ISBN 0-86232-804-7
 ISBN 0-86232-805-5 pbk

Library of Congress Cataloging-in-Publication Data

Fisher, Jo (Josephine), 1954–
 Mothers of the Disappeared.

 Bibliography: p.
 Includes index.
 1. Madres de Plaza de Mayo (Association)
2. Disappeared persons–Argentina. I. Title.
HV6322.3.A7F57   1989   323.4'9'0982   89-11583
ISBN 0-89608-371-3 cloth
ISBN 0-89608-370-5 paper

Contents

For Las Madres de Plaza de Mayo
and for my mother

Acknowledgements

My thanks go first to the Madres and Abuelas de Plaza de Mayo who were so generous with their time and affections and whose strength and courage made it a great privilege for me to work with them. I am especially grateful to Juanita de Pargament – her patience, interest and remarkable energy have contributed so much to making this book a reality – and for the support and assistance shown to me by María del Rosario and Hebe de Bonafini. Special thanks too for Nora, Rita and Pedro Krichmar for all their help and encouragement, for María and Osiris Domínguez and Elsa and Ciro Becerra for the kindness they showed me in Mendoza; to Graciela de Jeger, Marina de Curia, Rita de Ponce, Nellie Bianchi and Sara in Tucumán; and to the Mothers of Mar del Plata and La Plata.

Many friends and associates have offered me much appreciated support throughout. I am indebted to Inés Kuguel, Nora Krichmar, Sandra Forerro, Ramón Ruíz, Ulrica Thynne, Jo Gilbert and Jaime Flórez for help with transcribing and translating the interview material; and to Sandie Alden, Richard Brown, Maggie Roy, Jo Gilbert, Louise Orrock, Jenny Cole and Eddie Toman for their careful readings of the manuscript, their invaluable insights and suggestions and for the many hours they spent discussing the work with me. Many thanks to Jorge Martínez for keeping me up to date with events during the period of writing, to Ernesto Tiffenberg, whose research on the subject was an excellent source of additional material and to Dra di Lonardo for giving me her time to explain her department's role in the scientific identification of disappeared grandchildren. Thanks also to Ana Carmargo-Rizzo and Mercedes Loaiza for their secretarial assistance. I am especially grateful to Dr Colin Lewis of the Institute of Latin American Studies of the University of London, not only for contributing so many valuable ideas, but also for inspiring my interest in Latin America in the first place.

And lastly, a special thank you to my family and to Jorge whose support has never faltered and for which I am deeply grateful.

Jo Fisher

Preface

The sole aim of this book is to give a voice to the Madres de Plaza de Mayo. It is written on the basis of interviews with over forty Mothers and Grandmothers during two visits to Argentina between May and December 1985 and March and June 1987. It is intended as a history of a collective struggle rather than as a series of testimonies of individual women. This reflects the priority expressed by the Mothers who, while always willing to discuss their own personal cases, believe the emphasis should be on their collective action against a state-organized system of repression designed to eliminate all opposition or potential opposition, not a series of unrelated individuals. Nevertheless, it seems inevitable that readers will also be interested to follow the stories of individual women, and an index of the Mothers who appear most frequently in the text is located at the end of the book.

The material is organized in a roughly chronological order, based on events the Mothers raised most often in the interviews and in their publications. I have seen my role as one of facilitating an understanding of the context of these events and have tried to leave interpretation and analysis to the women themselves and to avoid intruding into a history which is not my own. This book is, however, written out of a profound sense of solidarity with the objectives of their struggle.

The Introduction is intended to provide a background to the events covered in the book. It examines briefly Argentina's recent history and the role of women in the country's development.

In Chapter 2 the testimonies of women from all over Argentina show the systematic and co-ordinated nature of the plan of repression implemented after the coup of 1976, under the pretext of the 'war against subversion'. The country's democratic and progressive sectors proved incapable of providing an answer in the face of state terrorism, and the Mothers found themselves alone and powerless in the search for their children. This chapter shows how their growing desperation led them to organize the first public protest against military rule and to their emergence as the voice of opposition to the dictatorship.

Chapter 3 looks at the backgrounds of those women who were brought together by the disappearances. It comprises the testimonies of nine of the Mothers, chosen to demonstrate the varied backgrounds from which they originated. What emerges through the class differences are very similar life stories. The Mothers' shared experiences and concerns were traditionally female, and their only resources in what for many was their first entry into public and political life. This chapter also helps account for the kind of problems they were to face later and serves as a basis of comparison for demonstrating the extent to which their lives were transformed by their participation with the Mothers of Plaza de Mayo.

In Chapter 4 we see how what is normally considered a conservative force in society, was converted into a force of opposition to military rule. It follows the process by which the women became more conscious of the dimensions of the repression and how this made them more confrontational, stronger and determined. It was also a process that opened the way for their own personal politicization. This chapter shows how their participation with the Mothers forced them to modify their traditional role as mothers and changed their perceptions of their roles within the family and society. By characterizing themselves as mothers of all the disappeared they were challenging the traditional ideology of individual families and motherhood, an ideology most commonly found in the moral discourse of the military and the church. In this chapter we see how the women turned the discourse against its authors and how they managed to survive their first year together.

Chapters 5 and 6 illustrate the extent to which the Mothers created what has been called 'new ways of making politics'. With normal political channels closed to them, both as a result of the repression and their past isolation from the political system, the Mothers improvised a new political style that was non-bureaucratic, direct, uncompromising and successful. We see in Chapter 5 how this style, together with a demand that transcended any one ideology, the fundamental assertion of the right to life, enabled them to secure international support for their struggle. Beginning with the episode of the World Cup in 1978, designed as a propaganda exercise by the military rulers, it shows how the Mothers turned international attention to their advantage. It covers their first trips abroad, their expectations of foreign governments and how they achieved the international solidarity and financial support which helped them to continue their struggle.

With the establishment of the legal association, described in Chapter 6, the Mothers formalized both the non-negotiability of their demands and their non-party political status. The Association was also an attempt to co-ordinate their struggle within Argentina where the public were still largely unaware of the Mothers and where the military were intensifying their campaign against the women. Women from the isolated provinces of the interior of Argentina explain how they came to join the Mothers of Plaza de Mayo and the specific difficulties they faced in their areas. Chapter 6 also introduces the struggle of the Grandmothers who, by the end of 1977, had already organized themselves into a separate group to fight for the return of their disappeared grandchildren.

Chapter 7 opens with the crisis of the economic programme imposed by the military regime and traces the breakdown of military rule from 1980 to 1983, culminating in the debacle of the Falklands/Malvinas war. It traces the role of the Mothers in the growing protest movement against the military and in the events leading up to the election of 1983. As the election approaches and the political parties begin to reconstitute themselves, we see more clearly the contrasting positions of Argentina's new and old political actors. This chapter shows the difficulties the Mothers faced in obtaining a place for themselves and their demands inside the traditional political system and the beginnings of the tensions that were to characterize the period following the restoration of constitutional rule.

Chapter 8 deals with the period of 'democratic' rule until the end of 1987. It sets the Mothers' principal demands against the policies implemented by the new government on the issues of human rights and the military. The testimonies at the end of the chapter demonstrate the extent to which the Mothers have evolved from a single issue campaign to a concept of human rights and democracy which incorporates economic, as well as political, demands. Chapter 8 shows how this, together with the women's refusal to modify their demands to suit the 'political realism' of the traditional political process, has led to their progressive isolation from formal politics.

The last word goes to the Mothers and Grandmothers, who in the final section of the book consider how the struggle has changed them personally and the significance of the Mothers for Argentine women and society. In particular, they discuss how they have come to redefine and reaffirm the concept of the maternal role in terms which imply a radical transformation of social relations and ultimately the socialization of motherhood. The testimonies also reveal the determination of the women to continue their struggle into the future.

Jo Fisher
Argentina, 1988

Glossary of Terms

Abuelas de Plaza de Mayo: The Grandmothers of Plaza de Mayo.

Aparición con Vida: Literally, 'reappearance with life', this slogan represented the principal demand of the Mothers for the return of their children alive.

Arsenales: An extermination camp set up in the premises of a munitions company under the Fifth Infantry Brigade in Tucumán.

Asamblea Permanente de los Derechos Humanos: Permanent Assembly of Human Rights, an Argentine human rights organization, established in 1975.

Campo de Mayo: An army garrison in the province of Buenos Aires and site of a secret detention centre.

Capucha: The hood most prisoners were forced to wear for the duration of their detention.

Casa Rosada: Literally, 'The Pink House', the name given to Government House, the seat of the federal government of the nation.

CGT, Confederación General de Trabajadores: The main national trade union organization.

CONADEP, Comisión Nacional Sobre la Desaparición de Personas: The Commission established by President Alfonsín in 1984 to investigate the disappearances which took place under the military governments.

Cordobazo: The name given to the urban uprising which took place in the city of Córdoba in 1969.

Desaparecidos: Disappeared people. The term is used where there are reasonable grounds to believe a person has been taken into custody by, or with the connivance of, the authorities who subsequently deny any knowledge of their whereabouts.

Detenidos: Detained people.

Dos demonios: Literally, 'two evils', this refers to an interpretation of recent Argentine history which sees the military coup of 1976 and subsequent events as the result of a confrontation between the evils of two terrorisms, that of the state and that of the guerrillas.

El Banco: A secret detention centre in the province of Buenos Aires.

Enfrentamiento: Literally, 'armed confrontation'. It became the standard military explanation for the appearance of dead bodies.

ERP, Ejército Revolucionario del Pueblo: The People's Revolutionary Army, created in the late 1960s as the armed wing of the Workers' Revolutionary Party (PRT).

ESMA, Escuela Superior Mecánica de la Armada: The Navy Mechanics School in the Federal Capital and site of a secret detention centre.

Famaillá: La Escuelita de Famaillá was the first secret detention centre to go into operation. It was set up by the army in 1975.

Famaillá: La Comisión de Familiares de Desaparecidos y Prisioneros por Motivos Políticos: Families of *Desaparecidos* and Political Prisoners, the first human rights group to emerge which was composed of the relatives of those directly affected by the disappearances.

Golpistas: A term used to describe those military officers who see a permanent role for the military in government (from *golpe*: coup).

Juventud Peronista: The Peronist Youth, on the left of Peronism and very strong in the universities in the years before the 1976 coup.

La Cacha: a secret detention centre located in the city of La Plata in the province of Buenos Aires.

La Noche de Los Lápices: The Night of the Pencils, refers to the night of 16 September 1976 when 16 young people between the ages of 14 and 18 who had taken part in a campaign in favour of school subsidies were kidnapped and disappeared. Only three survived.

Ley de Fuga: Law of Escape, frequently used by the military to justify the murder of political prisoners.

Liga de los Derechos del Hombre: The League for the Rights of Man is one of Argentina's oldest human rights organizations.

Locas: Madwomen.

Madres de Plaza de Mayo: Mothers of Plaza de Mayo.

Marcha por la Vida: March for Life.

Marcha de Resistencia: March of Resistance, the name the Mothers gave to their 24-hour demonstrations which began in 1981 as a show of civil resistance to military rule and which continue today.

Milicos: A derogatory term used to describe military officers.

Montoneros: The Peronist left's principal armed wing.

Movimiento Ecuménico por los Derechos Humanos: Ecumenical Movement for Human Rights, a religious, but independent organization which never received the co-operation of the official Catholic Church.

Multipartidaria: The coalition of the major political parties which was formed in July 1981 in response to the resurgence of mass protest and to General Viola's proposal for a dialogue on a political transition.

NN, Non nombre: Identity unknown.

Nunca Más: 'Never Again', the name given to the report produced by CONADEP, q.v.

Obediencia Debida: The Law of Due Obedience was enacted in April 1987, exonerating military officers who had not committed specified crimes during the rule of the juntas on the grounds that they were executing orders from a military superior.

Partido Comunista: The Communist Party.

PEN, Poder Ejecutivo de la Nación: PEN prisoners were those held at the disposal of the Executive Power. The Argentine constitution places no time limit on such detentions.

Peronist Party: The political party created by General Juan Domingo Perón in 1947 which came to represent the political identity of Argentina's working classes.

Picana: An electric cattle prod, used in the secret detention centres as an instrument of torture.

Plata dulce: Literally, 'sweet money', the term used to describe the period when, under José Martínez de Hoz, the junta's Minister of the Economy, Argentine currency was set at an artificially high level relative to foreign currencies, enabling the moneyed classes to indulge in a spending spree on imported goods and foreign travel.

Proceso: The Process of National Reorganization, the name given to the economic and political project imposed by the military after the coup.

Punto final: Literally, 'Full stop', the name given to the Radical government's law introduced at the end of 1986 which put a time limit on the presentation of new prosecutions of military officers for human rights abuses.

Radical Party: Emerged in the early part of the twentieth century in response to the growth of the middle-class component in the population.

Rodrigazo: The name given to the general strike which followed the attempt to impose a drastic austerity programme by Isabel Perón's Economy Minister, Celestino Rodrigo, in 1975.

Submarino: The name used to describe torture by immersion in water.

Triple A, Alianza Argentina Anti-Comunista: The Argentine Anti-Communist Alliance was the name given to the death squads which operated from the Ministry of Social Welfare during the government of Isabel Perón.

Vesubio: A secret detention centre in the province of Buenos Aires.

Villas miserias: Shanty towns.

Introduction – Historical Background

Until the early 1950s Argentina ranked among the richest of Latin American nations, with rates of economic growth, levels of urban and industrial organization, a per capita income, and health and medical facilities that compared favourably with many European countries. The demand from the industrializing countries of Europe for Argentina's cheap beef and wheat had stimulated rapid growth of the economy and provided the foundation for the development of the nation's own industrial and urban base. With labour in high demand and wages which were relatively high, even by European standards, Argentina came to represent a land of opportunity and attracted a flood of immigrants, chiefly of Italian and Spanish origin. Between 1857 and 1941 over six-and-a-half million people emigrated to Argentina and nearly three-and-a-half million stayed permanently, largely concentrated around the capital, Buenos Aires. The male members of the new middle and working classes were incorporated into the political system with the introduction of universal male suffrage in 1912 and despite periods of military rule beginning in 1930, politics remained relatively open and the political parties retained a level of influence. Argentina's labour movement was already the strongest in the continent by the early 1900s and after a history of militant, often violent struggles with the authorities had won a place for the working class in the political process. By the 1940s Argentina had established the beginnings of a welfare state. The media, too, retained a level of freedom throughout periods of authoritarian rule and the country was renowned for its high level of artistic and cultural development. The Argentine people saw themselves as a sophisticated society, distinct from other Latin American nations and more like Europe in their levels of development. Argentina's economic and social record supported a spirit of optimism for the future.

From 1955, however, Argentina embarked on a period of severe economic and political instability culminating in the brutal repression that followed the military coup of 1976 and which was to identify the country more closely with the rest of Latin America. Many of the problems Argentina was to face in the post-1955 years had their origin in the earlier period. The nation's economic prosperity had relied on the export of agricultural products to Europe and on European capital. It was largely British investments which had financed the construction of the railways and commercial facilities which had made possible the exploitation of the country's vast agricultural wealth. The depression of 1929 drew attention to the vulnerability of pursuing a model of development which depended so heavily on external markets. The depression was foreshadowed by a sharp fall in demand for primary products on the world market and a sudden exodus of foreign capital, which drastically curtailed Argentina's ability to sustain its levels of economic growth. Agriculture stagnated, severely affecting the interior regions of the country, provoking unemployment and a large scale movement of population to the capital in search of work. While the 1930s saw a considerable increase in the rate of domestic industrial growth, primarily the manufacture of goods previously imported, industrialization itself depended on imported technology and increasingly on foreign capital. It was only the exceptional circumstances created by the onset of World War II which led to the renewal of world demand for Argentine grain and meat and provided resources for the continued expansion of national industry and for the establishment of the rudiments of a welfare state.

The years following the Great Depression also saw growing restrictions on political participation, and the intervention of the military in political affairs. In 1930 the civilian government was overthrown by a military coup and for twelve years the country was ruled by a series of governments which maintained themselves in power on the basis of fraudulent elections. The new industrialist class had failed to displace the traditional agricultural oligarchy who still retained much of their economic power, but neither group was either unified or strong enough to gain control of the state apparatus. Moreover, both groups had to contend with the demands being made on economic resources by the organized labour movement. It was in this context of political stalemate that a populist alliance was cemented around the charismatic figure of General Juan Domingo Perón. His anti-oligarchy and anti-imperialist rhetoric was combined with specific appeals to the working classes aimed at winning their support for the implementation of a national industrial project for Argentina. As Minister of Labour in the new military government that seized power in 1943, Perón had introduced a number of reforms which had improved the pay and conditions of the working class. With their votes, the support of industrialists producing for the home market and a 'nationalist' sector of the army, Perón was elected president in 1946. He ensured the loyalty of the working-class element of the alliance by creating a central Peronist trade union organization and by displacing the existing socialist, syndicalist and communist leaders who threatened his project of unifying labour under the Peronist banner. Although labour was to benefit from a 20% increase in real wages and from the introduction of a social security system, this was achieved during a period of general prosperity and with little real cost to the traditional elites.

By the 1950s, however, a change in international and internal conditions sharply exposed Argentina's underlying economic and political problems. From 1953 a severe deterioration in the terms of trade led to balance of payments crises and a shortage of capital. The United States was beginning to invest heavily in Argentina, undermining local industrialists with its superior technology. Faced with economic collapse and the growing militancy of the working class, the national industrialists deserted the alliance of interests that had supported the Peronist government and joined the US-backed coalition. From 1953, in an attempt to restore his political position, Perón conceded to foreign capital and approved a law favouring foreign investment in industry and mining on terms beneficial to US companies. At the same time, he introduced austerity measures, the effect of which was to drastically reduce the standard of living of the working class. Before the labour movement had time to resist these policies Perón was swept from power. In September 1955, with the country on the verge of bankruptcy and faced with the violent opposition of sections of the business community, the Church and the armed forces, Perón was toppled by a military coup which brought the fiercely anti-Peronist General Aramburu to power.

The policies adopted by successive governments after 1955 consolidated the trend towards an increased foreign presence in the economy and the decline of working-class living standards. These years witnessed a steady inflow of foreign capital which overtook the most dynamic sectors of the economy. The growing dependence on international capital markets was reflected in the instability and short term crises which wracked the country from 1955.

At the same time long term factors were conspiring to weaken Argentina's position in international markets. As world prices for agricultural products fell relative to those of industrial goods, Argentina had to produce and sell more to earn the foreign exchange that would pay for the imports of machinery and capital goods essential for the industrialization process. It also had to compete with the new giants in agricultural production, the United States, Australia and Canada, at a time when demand was shrinking as new trading communities closed off their markets. Agriculture failed to adapt to these new conditions and entered a long period of stagnation. Imports outstripped exports and there were regular balance of payments crises which fuelled inflation, recession and unemployment.

While it is possible to argue that until the early 1950s economic expansion had benefited most sectors of the population, in the subsequent years the beneficiaries were more specific. From 1955 there was a long term deterioration in the share of national income going to the poorest 60% of the population while the richest 10% experienced a substantial increase. Real wages declined steadily and from the late 1950s Argentina experienced substantial open unemployment for the first time since the depression. The per capita standard of living, although still higher than most Latin American nations, was falling behind Brazil and Mexico and was no longer comparable to that of Europe. The division between Buenos Aires and the rest of the country also sharpened. During the 1960s three-quarters of a million migrants from the poor interior provinces of Argentina settled in the Buenos Aires area, where most economic activity took place. In 1970, while Buenos Aires represented only 0.1% of Argentine territory 35% of the population and almost 38% of the labour force were concentrated there. Housing shortages and the lack of industrial employment created the conditions for the growth of shanty towns. For the first time a level of poverty of the kind characteristic of its Latin American neighbours was appearing around Argentina's major cities.

In the absence of a popular consensus for their economic programmes, governments increasingly came to depend on the exclusion of certain sectors by force and intimidation. On seizing power in 1955 the military regime set about repressing the movement which had come to represent the political voice and unity of the working class. Perón was forced into exile, the Peronist Party was proscribed, and its leaders, together with the leaders of the trade unions, were subjected to arbitrary arrest. For the next eighteen years the military stood guard over the prohibition of Peronism. Between 1955 and 1973 there were only seven years of civilian rule and with Peronism banned, neither of the two elected governments was recognized as legitimate by large sectors of the population. When the civilian presidents Frondizi, Illia and Guido attempted to broaden their popular support by offering concessions to the working class and to Peronism, the military stepped in to reverse the policies and ultimately to remove the civilians from power. General Onganía's coup of 1966 represented a new attempt by the armed forces to resolve Argentina's political stalemate. For the first time the military openly stated their intention to maintain an indefinite presence in government in order to achieve the complete economic and social transformation they believed Argentina required.

The clampdown on peaceful political expression by a series of military governments failed to prevent the emergence of an organized resistance to military rule, based in the working class and Peronism. After the removal of the Peronist leadership, the labour movement reconstituted itself into factory committees, organized at grass-roots level, and launched a campaign to undermine the military regime through industrial unrest and sabotage, culminating in the general strike of 1959. By the end of 1963, however, a right-wing faction which advocated collaboration with the state, industrialists and the US multinationals gained the leadership of the Peronist union movement. The trade union bureaucracy was among the first to publicly justify General Onganía's coup of 1966 and to co-operate with the military authorities. Both the Peronist and non-Peronist Left responded by regrouping around a rival national organization composed of the more radical and combative unions. By the late 1960s opposition to military rule had spread to a wide range of society. Small businesses protested about the damage being done to national industry by foreign competition, the student movement became more politicized and a large sector of the young middle classes were attracted to the left of Peronism. Students joined workers in strike actions which culminated in a series of urban insurrections, such as the 'Cordobazo' that took place in the city of Córdoba in 1969. Against the background of general discontent, small guerrilla groups began to emerge inside and outside Peronism. By 1973, unable to contain the political violence, the military government was forced to contemplate the unthinkable, the return of Perón.

Perón assumed the presidency in 1973 with the support of 62% of the electorate. He proved unable, however, to resolve the contradictory elements contained within Peronism and bring economic and political order to Argentina. Elected with the support of the armed left of Peronism, whose actions he had endorsed in the years before his return, he quickly joined forces with the right in the battle for control of the Peronist Party. The disintegration of the movement intensified with Perón's death and the succession of his wife Isabel to the presidency in 1974, and culminated in the increasingly violent political conflict that preceded the military coup of 1976.

In the particularly acute and frequently violent struggle for resources that takes place between social classes in Latin America, the specific concerns of women may appear secondary. When male workers are paid starvation wages, calls for equal pay become irrelevant and a struggle for equal political rights is redundant in a country in the grip of an authoritarian regime that prohibits all political activity. Nevertheless, women, regardless of class, remain a severely oppressed group in Argentina, suffering the dual exploitation of dependent capitalism and patriarchy.

Machismo is the name given to the Latin American brand of sexism which contains some features unique to Latin America and others recognizable by women the world over. It has its origins in the particular conditions of dependent development, a blend of ideas deriving from indigenous cultures, the Spanish colonial church and imported patriarchal ideas of a more 'Western' variety. Machismo emphasizes a division of functions, capacities and qualities between male and female that seeks to confirm the superiority of the male. The relationship of domination–subordination established between men and women, and the specific characteristics ascribed to each have come to be regarded as 'natural'. The 'natural' role for a woman is that of wife and mother and her proper place is in the home. Work outside the home is not considered appropriate for married women. These traditional ideas dominate the educational system and the teachings of the Church and are disseminated at a popular level through contemporary literature, television and cinema. Women's subordinate position in society has been consolidated by civil and family law which was strongly influenced by the Spanish legal system that stipulated the dominance of the husband over women and children. Excluded from the Sáenz Peña laws of 1912, women could neither vote nor stand for public office until 1947.

Machismo seeks to represent the unpaid labour performed by women inside the home as somehow 'natural' extensions of femininity and not as productive work which contributes any value to the wider economy. In reality, tasks such as the preparation of food, maintenance of property, and childcare are essential to the survival and reproduction of economic systems, and women in Argentina have always been integrated into the economy. The failure to recognize women's contributions to economic development is reflected in the official statistics. Measurement of the 'economically active population' excludes domestic labour carried out by women or their contribution to family businesses and includes only the work women do through the market, that is paid work. Nevertheless, the statistics indicate that a substantial proportion of women have been represented in the paid workforce. The confinement of women to the home and their exclusion from paid employment has not been an option for many working-class families. While work outside the home was considered demeaning for Argentine women of the higher social classes, for the working class, women's wages were often a necessary contribution to the family income.

It is a widely held belief that economic development will provide increased employment opportunities for women, allowing them to enter into direct relations with other members of the workforce, greater independence from the family and greater possibilities for political participation. Contrary to generally accepted notions, Argentine women have participated in the paid labour force on a large scale since the development of an urban and industrial base in the late nineteenth century. The 1895 census recorded 30% of the entire labour force as female, primarily working as day labourers, artisans, domestic servants, and in the sewing and cooking trades. 'Economic development', however, did not lead to any modification of traditional ideas about the role of women in society. Rather, traditional ideas defined the terms on which women could participate in the economy and led to fewer, not increased, job opportunities for female labour. As factories replaced the traditional craft industries which women had been able to perform inside the home, they found it increasingly difficult to combine housework and child-rearing with paid employment. By 1914 the percentage of females in the paid labour force declined to 22%, reflecting this difficulty together with the fall in agricultural employment. It was also an effect of the massive numbers of immigrants who arrived from Europe. During 1870–1930 almost three-quarters of immigrants were male. Since the 1920s the percentage of females in the work force has steadily increased. Argentine women today have one of the highest economic participation rates in Latin America, although this figure still represents only about half that of Europe and the United States. The low proportion of married women in paid employment reflects the continued difficulty of combining work inside the home with outside employment. Moreover, it is highly questionable whether access to paid work has freed women from their traditional constraints. Their household work has not diminished accordingly and they have simply had to add outside work to their traditional duties, in what has been called the 'double-day'.

Traditional ideas about women have also formed the basis of the sexual division of labour that exists in paid employment and accounts for their disadvantaged entry into the job market. Their role in the home not only restricts mobility, but also defines the kind of work for which they are considered suitable, normally social extensions of the kind of work they perform in the home. Education was not considered a priority for women. Since the approved role was motherhood, girls were socialized for their responsibilities as wives and mothers, rather than for the labour market. With the growth of the middle classes some single, educated women were able to take advantage of the increased professional opportunities in areas considered compatible with femininity, such as medicine and teaching. The view that work outside the home was the primary responsibility of men also served to justify women's low wages. On average women were paid half the wages paid to men. From the beginning women were concentrated in the areas of work with the worst pay and conditions. Early reports of the National Labour Department found women suffering the most intense discrimination and exploitation, and documented long hours, dangerous and unhealthy conditions and low pay, which characterized female paid employment. Women's subordinate status in the labour market was underlined in periods of recession when female workers lost their jobs at a higher rate than their male counterparts. This occurred at the time of the world depression of 1929. While 43% of unemployed male workers had previously been in full-time and permanent employment, the figure for women was 61%.

Women were also subjected to periodic attempts to curb their participation in the paid labour force. Sections of Argentine society reacted with horror at the increased presence of women in the workforce, claiming it would lead to a fall in the birth rate and a collapse of the family. There was also concern that it would change the balance of power within the family, leading to the decline of the father's authority in the family structure. One study in the 1930s proposed that women should be officially barred from paid work and confined to motherhood; and a reform of the civil code proposed in 1935 was intended to reduce women to the status of minor. It failed to get the approval of Congress, partly due to a campaign waged by women's organizations such as the Union of Argentine Women, but the campaign against female employment continued, particularly in the Catholic press and in the churches. Sections of the military who together with the Church, represented the most vocal defenders of 'traditional womanhood' proved responsive to demands to reassert traditional ideas about women. With the increasing role of the armed forces in political affairs these ideas were reaffirmed. When the military seized power in 1943, industry, commerce and government offices were encouraged to stop employing women; the employment of female staff above the rank of clerk in government administration was prohibited.

At the same time the industrial capitalists who used women as a supply of super-cheap labour were quick to detail the dire consequences of their withdrawal from employment for the national industry. It was in their interest to defend female labour, from which they could make two or even three times the profit they could make from men. Despite the opposition of the Church and the attempts by military governments to restrict women's employment outside the home, the proportion of women working increased with the growing demand for industrial labour in the 1930s and 1940s. Women were entering the labour force in Buenos Aires faster than men. In the period 1914–47 twice as many women as men migrated to Buenos Aires from the poorer interior provinces where the stagnation of the agricultural and livestock market had resulted in severe unemployment. The proportion of females in the paid workforce in Buenos Aires rose from 24% in 1920s to 31% in 1947. They were concentrated in food, tobacco, clothing, chemical and textile industries where they earned between one-third and one-half of the average male wage. The expansion of work opportunities also affected areas of work requiring some education and considered suitable for middle-class women, such as clerical and sales work, teaching, administration and the growing state bureaucracy. By the 1940s, 84% of primary school teachers and 50% of secondary teachers, for example, were women.

Perón's appointment as Minister of Labour in the military government of the early 1940s brought about a reversal of the policies designed to curb the employment of women outside the home. In speeches designed to appeal to female workers, women's contribution to the development of Argentina was recognized and praised for the first time. In 1943 Perón said, 'More than 900,000 Argentine women are part of the paid workforce, in all kinds of jobs and professions . . . it is our duty, morally and materially, to dignify their efforts.' He established the first Women's Division of Labour and Assistance within the Ministry of Labour and called for the improvement and implementation of existing protective legislation and for equal pay. In 1944 piece-work was declared illegal in all branches of industry, and women who worked in their own homes came under minimum wage regulations. In 1945 protective legislation was extended, legislation governing domestic service was introduced and a minimum wage established in the food industry at a rate 20% below that of men. In 1949 women in the textile industry were awarded equal pay and this affected more than 15,000 female workers.

Perón also set about the political mobilization of women on a mass scale. Until the 1940s women's increased economic participation had not been matched by their greater involvement in political affairs. Some political groups, including the Socialist Party, had supported women's suffrage and civil equality. There were also exceptional autonomous women's currents, such as the anarchist feminists of the late nineteenth century who identified the family as the source of women's subordination and attacked marriage and the Church. Their limited popular appeal was a result of their failure to deal with the real concerns of working-class women. Many of the women's movements established in Argentina also failed to take account of these concerns. Most were composed of women from the more affluent sectors of society and their priorities were issues that largely reflected their class base. Organizations such as the Argentine Feminist Party, founded in 1919, and the Union of Argentine Women, founded in the 1930s, worked to promote equal civil status and political rights. These organizations were important in the campaign that in the 1920s led to legislation improving the civil position of women and in defending it against attempts in the 1930s to reverse these legislative gains. Many of these groups also called for women's suffrage, in particular the Argentine Association for Women's Suffrage, established in the 1930s, which claimed a membership of 80,000. In addition, many campaigned for equal pay, improved conditions of work, greater access to high income jobs and maternity benefits but they failed to appeal to the broad mass of women.

Perón quickly recognized the political value of supporting female suffrage. In 1945, as Vice-President, he pledged his support for equal political rights and, as President, began organizing women in the poorer districts, effectively dislodging the old feminist leadership. He sponsored centres at a local level which were designed to offer training in new work skills and medical and legal advice. In 1947 women won the right to vote and to be elected to public office. Two years later married women obtained constitutional guarantees of equality with their husbands and equal authority over their children, which was a significant departure from their previous status. In the same year he formed the Peronist Women's Party under the leadership of his wife, Evita, herself from a poor family from the interior of Argentina and who received massive support from the Argentine working class. While never holding elective office, she worked energetically to secure the vote for women and for the political mobilization of women within the Peronist Party.

The election in 1951 was the first in which Argentine women were able to vote and they voted overwhelmingly in favour of Perón. A majority of women from all constituencies, and more particularly from the working-class districts, voted for the Peronist ticket. In addition, all the women who had stood as Peronist candidates, seven for the Senate and twenty-four as Deputies, were elected. Moreover, in 1953 Deputies elected a woman as Vice-President of the National Congress. This represented a level of female political participation unequalled elsewhere in Latin America. It was followed in 1954 by two pieces of legislation also unique in the region. The first, personally supported by Perón, gave children born out of marriage the same rights as those born in marriage; the second legalized divorce.

While Perón's government of 1945–55 offered women unprecedented gains in some areas, it never fundamentally challenged the ideology of the primacy of motherhood. Evita Perón called on women to fight to improve their position and linked their struggle with that of the working class in general: 'Just as only the workers can wage their own struggle for liberation, so too can only women be the salvation of women', but she never questioned the primacy of women's role as housewife and mother. Many of her calls for women to mobilize were expressed in terms of their duty to family and home: 'The home is the sanctuary of motherhood and the pivot of society. It is the appropriate sphere in which women, for the good of their country and for their own children, fulfil their patriotic duty daily.' She saw her own role in terms of love and loyalty to her husband, 'He the figure, I the shadow'. These contradictions may have accounted for the widespread appeal of Peronism to women in Argentina during these years, but in the end it failed to address itself to the real source of women's oppression and it posed no threat to the source of the oppression of the working class in general.

Calls for a return to 'Christian and family values' accompanied the military seizure of power in 1955. Once again, traditional ideas about women were reinforced by the military rulers in close association with the conservative elements of the Church which spoke out against married women working. Perón's divorce laws were repealed in 1955 and women's role in the family and their subjugation to their husbands was reaffirmed. While there has been some increase in the proportion of married women in paid work, the majority of the female workforce is composed of single, separated and divorced women. Married women tend to work on an irregular basis, closely associated with the number and age of the children in the family, reflecting the conflict that still exists between the traditional role and economic participation.

Despite this, there had been a big fall in the number of women with no education and an explosion in the numbers entering higher education. While the economic participation rate of females over the age of eleven years rose from 21.2% in 1950 to 24.5% in 1970, almost the entire increase is accounted for by new employment for educated women in the state sector, in such areas as teaching, nursing, public administration, and community and social services. For working-class women who possess the educational requirements to work as wage labourers, the employment picture is not promising. Women have dominated in labour-intensive industries, such as textiles and food-processing, and these are precisely the areas which have declined with increased foreign competition. Women's work opportunities have not been replaced in the modern, capital-intensive industries and their employment has declined in all areas of manufacturing. Work in the dynamic sectors of the economy, until the 1970s, such as cars and petrochemicals, over which the multinational companies have gained a stranglehold, is dominated by men. Women have come to depend increasingly on marginal sources of employment.

After the coup of 1955, opportunities for political participation were severely restricted for both men and women. Nevertheless, women have made a significant contribution to the movements of protest and resistance to military rule. In union struggles and general strikes women have played a primary role in the plants themselves and in the wider community. Women were also among the generation of young people who were mobilized into political action in the years following the coup of General Onganía. Young women were active in the student protest movements, youth political organizations and church groups which, together with the militant unions, formed the basis of opposition to the economic, political and social projects of successive military governments. They were also integrated into the high commands of the small guerrilla armies that emerged in the late 1960s. It was the participants of these popular struggles who became the principal victims of the repression imposed on Argentina after the coup of 1976. The illegal and clandestine methods employed by the new military regime were designed to eliminate all opposition and to create a terror which would silence all protest. The silence was broken when a group of women whose children were among the estimated 30,000 people who 'disappeared' during almost eight years of military rule went to the streets to demand justice. They were women who had taken little part in the popular struggles of the preceding years. For the vast majority theirs had been the lives of traditional Argentine women. The challenge they mounted to one of the most brutal regimes Latin America has witnessed was to be their first experience of politics.

1. The Kidnappings

On the night of 18 June 1976 Marina, who was then eleven months old, appeared in the doorway of our block of apartments. It was a terribly cold night. My husband and I weren't at home and the doorman took her in and called the police. We didn't know what had happened but we knew that our daughter and her husband must have been kidnapped: first, because the baby was left at the door and second, because that night they were going to visit her husband's parents and they didn't arrive. We don't know where they were taken from but we calculate it was after they had left the baby at the nursery, when they were driving back, because their car also disappeared. We never saw them again.

Rita de Krichmar

On 24 March 1976 President Isabel Perón was helicoptered from the presidential palace to a country retreat and a military junta composed of the three commanders-in-chief of the armed forces, General Jorge Rafael Videla for the army, Admiral Emilio Eduardo Massera for the navy and Brigadier Ramón Agosti for the air force, installed itself as the government of Argentina.

The coup surprised few people. For weeks there had been strong rumours that it was imminent and some senators and deputies had already packed their bags and left the country. The press had done more than predict the coup; many newspapers had been calling for the takeover for months. Nor was it a particularly unusual occurrence in the nation's recent political history. Of Argentina's twenty-four presidents since 1930, eleven were serving military officers and there had been more years of military rule than civilian. Only one elected government, that of General Perón in the 1940s, survived to complete its full term of office.

Some Argentines were surprised the military had waited so long. It had been two years since the death of Perón and the transfer of power to his wife María Estela, 'Isabel', who had proved totally incapable of resolving the in-fighting which was tearing the Peronist movement apart. Sections of the trade unions had begun to withdraw their traditional support for the Peronist Party and the left wing of the movement, led by the Montoneros, was driven underground and adopted a stand of armed resistance against the ruling Peronists. Only six years earlier they had led an armed campaign against the military regimes of the early 1970s for the return of the exiled Perón. Factions within the government had responded to the dissent inside and outside its ranks by creating the Argentine Anti-communist Alliance, the brutal and notorious Triple A, co-ordinated from the offices of the Ministry of Social Welfare. In addition, the State of Siege declared in November 1975 had suspended constitutional guarantees and given the army a free hand to deal with a rural guerrilla campaign being waged by the People's Revolutionary Army (ERP) in the northern province of Tucumán.[1]

Nor was the government able to exercise any control over an economy crippled by inflation and deficits. The attempt to introduce an austerity programme was met with a wave of massive strikes throughout the country's industrial centres. By 1976 the annual inflation rate was approaching 500%, with projections that by the end of the year it would reach 1000%, there was a huge public sector deficit and the balance of payments was in a desperate condition. As the country stood within days of defaulting on payments of the international debt which amounted to more than $8 billion, the International Monetary Fund refused the government further credits.[2]

Against this background of economic and political turmoil the new regime's claim that they had intervened in order to restore 'order and decency' to the nation was met with relief by large sectors of the population. Their language, like that of their predecessors, was deliberately moderate, designed to pacify anxieties on both internal and external fronts. Their declared objectives were the eradication of subversion and the stabilization of the economy and they promised a speedy return to constitutional normality. The extensive powers which they confiscated from Argentina's democratic institutions on 24 March were, they said, necessary for the success of their mission: they required complete control of the machinery of the state to rescue the country from chaos and anarchy. Federal and provincial parliaments were closed down, political parties and meetings banned and all trade unions declared illegal. The junta sacked the members of the Supreme Court and the Attorney General and replaced them with their own appointees. They shut down several universities and took control of television channels and the radio and every newspaper report containing political comment had to be submitted to the junta for approval before publication.

In terms of Argentine coups there seemed nothing extraordinary in the measures outlined in the junta's Process of National Reorganization or the *proceso* as it came to be known. General Videla, who led the three-man junta, assured the public that the nation would be governed by the values and morality of Christianity, patriotism and the family. 'The common good,' he said, 'is achieved by the resolution of conflicts and by the energetic protection of the human rights of all members of the community.'[3] While many expected the military takeover to be followed by a period of repression, few people predicted the unprecedented savagery which was to follow.

The Victims

Workers

Workers in industrial centres throughout the country did not have to wait until 24 March to discover that the armed forces had seized power. On the eve of the coup, the industrial belt of Buenos Aires and the provinces suffered a wave of abductions by armed men, identified as members of the armed and security forces, often with the collaboration of factory proprietors and management. In the Ledesma sugar-cane factory in the province of Jujuy, 2,000 kilometres north of Buenos Aires, this co-operation was undisguised. The morning after the coup hundreds of people were detained in an operation co-ordinated by the army and company police. The raids continued in the following months.

> **Olga de Arédez:** There was someone knocking at the door at half past three in the morning. My husband was a factory doctor and thought it might be a patient, so he opened it. I went to find out what was happening and I saw soldiers and policemen bundling my husband into a lorry. This lorry was from the factory, and was driven by an employee of the company. In a single night, soldiers and the company police, using company vehicles, rounded up three hundred people and took them away.[4]

In the months to follow, these raids were extended into the homes of working-class families throughout the country.

> **Aída de Suárez:** On 2 December 1977 at four o'clock in the morning, twenty armed men broke into our house with rifles and pistols pointed at us. They were nervous. They opened and closed the cupboards, the fridge. They were looking for things, guns apparently. They took everything of any value they could carry, the few things of value that a working-class family has in their home, sentimental things. But that wasn't important to me. They could have taken everything, but my son, no. He was sitting on the bed, trying to get dressed. One man shouted, 'There's one in here!' and then two huge men with guns in their hands told me not to move. They asked only if he was Hubo Héctor Suárez and that he had to go with them.
>
> 'Who are you?' I screamed. 'We are the security forces.' They were in civilian suits but underneath they were wearing army fatigues and boots, and green bullet-proof vests, the colour of the army. I saw that one of them was wearing a bullet-proof vest because he caught his jacket on the door handle and it tore open. So it was the army. I said, 'Why! My son has done nothing, he's not a criminal. Why have you come in like this, frightening the children with guns pointed at everyone?' – twenty armed men for a child of twenty-one years, an old woman like me and two young children. 'We've come to take him away for questioning.' 'Why?' I asked and they pushed me and threw me against the wall. They took my son. That was the last time I saw him.

Carmen de Guede: I wasn't at home at the time they were kidnapped. I had gone to the province of Mendoza with my husband and the youngest one to look after my mother. He returned early to go back to work. I don't know how they disappeared but, according to a neighbour, my son, who was nineteen, had gone to the police station to pay a fine and he never came back. My husband went to look for him and he disappeared as well. My husband had gone in the car and later the police came back in his car, opened the door of our house with his keys and took everything, machines, electrical things, everything. When I came back from Mendoza the house was empty. This is the only information I have about how they were kidnapped.

The paralysis of working-class reaction was the essential precondition for the implementation of the military government's long-term plan for the complete restructuring of the Argentine economy. The project, similar to those imposed under military regimes in Chile in 1973 and Uruguay in 1974, was based on a monetarist diagnosis of the country's economic problems. The prescription, as articulated by the new Minister of the Economy, José Martínez de Hoz, involved freeing the market from the restrictions imposed by successive governments. All tariffs which favoured industry and all taxes which discriminated against agricultural exports were removed in order to promote the expansion of agriculture, which was where Argentina's comparative advantage was seen to reside. Financial and foreign exchange markets were liberalized to attract foreign capital, government expenditure was cut and real wages halved.[5] The international banking community signalled its approval and the military government quickly raised over $870 million in loans. The junta also earned the congratulations of both the national and foreign business communities. The local subsidiary of Ford placed a full-page advertisement in the press for the New Year of 1977 which read, '1976: Argentina gets back on the right track. 1977: New Year of Faith and Hope for Argentines of good will. Ford Motor Company and its staff pledge their participation in the efforts to fulfil the nation's destiny. Again Ford gives you more'.[6] It was Ford which supplied the security forces with the Falcon cars which became the sinister trademark of the *proceso*.

The success of this exercise in free market economics depended on inflicting a decisive defeat on working-class organizations and politics. On seizing power the military had attempted to immobilize any resistance by intervening in the Confederación Nacional de Trabajadores, the national trade union organization, and by freezing trade union funds. An 'Industrial Security' decree prohibited strikes with the penalty of five years' imprisonment and ten years for the strike leaders. There were massive purges of the militant members of agricultural and industrial unions.

Students
General Vilas provided the confirmation that the military's concept of 'subversion' referred not only to the guerrilla organizations or even the factory

militants when he announced, 'Until now only the tip of the iceberg has been touched in our war against subversion. It is necessary to destroy the sources which feed, form and indoctrinate the subversive delinquent and this source is in the universities and secondary schools themselves.'[7]

Elsa de Becerra: My son was a student in La Plata but at the time of the coup, because of all the problems in the university, he was living here in Mendoza. On 15 December 1976 Jorge was riding home from work on his bike when a lorry crashed into him and he was taken to hospital with serious injuries. He was discharged on the 22nd and a friend went to collect him in a van. His legs were in plaster with a double fracture, he had a fractured hip, multiple injuries. On the way home they drove into the middle of a police and army operation. He didn't have his identity card with him so they arrested him, took him away with the van and everything. Someone called us and told us what had happened. We were told that he was taken to police headquarters and when we went there to ask for him they denied all knowledge of him. We went to the army and they said they didn't have him. No one had him. Effectively he had disappeared. Later they came to our house and searched everything.

A month after his kidnapping they returned to the house. At that moment our daughter Violeta, who was a student in La Plata, was staying with us and Ana María, the youngest who was at secondary school. It was 22 January 1977. They arrived at eleven or twelve at night in a number of cars, masked and with rifles. They invaded the house from the front and back, kicking in the doors. They didn't say who they were, but even though it was dark we could see that one of the cars was a police car. They were talking about drugs.

They tore down the curtains and ripped up sheets to tie us up with and they threw us to the floor, threatening and insulting us, more than anything else about our jobs as teachers. They took away our two daughters aged sixteen and eighteen. They were both crying desperately. I suffered a nervous attack and, I don't know by what miracle, but they brought back the youngest. They tied her to a chair by the front door and set an alarm clock. All this time the others were taking out everything from the house, anything they could carry. And they took Violeta. Before they left they told us if we moved before the alarm clock went off they would shoot Ana María, tied to a chair by the front door which was open.

We heard our daughter weeping as they took her away. It's something I'll never forget. When we heard the cars leaving my husband untied us. The alarm clock went off and we ran to untie our daughter at the door. Ana María was all right but they'd taken Violeta.

After all this my husband and I began to keep guard in the house. He slept a few hours and I kept guard and then he slept. One night, a week later, my husband heard a noise and looked out of the window. He had a stick ready to defend himself against anyone who tried to get in. It was Violeta. She was naked, crawling on all fours, don't ask me in what condition – infections in her eyes, covered in bruises and with a terror on her face . . . but she was there. She told us they had taken her to a place outside the city and kept her inside a car all the time, crouched up, with her hands tied, and blindfolded. She said she heard other people there. She could hear the screams of people being tortured. They tortured her too. That night they said nothing but they took her in a car, making a lot of turns so she wouldn't know where she was, stopped suddenly and threw her to the ground, telling her to stay there until she'd counted to a hundred.

Dora de Bazze: My daughter was eighteen, recently married and in her second year of medical school in La Plata. She had come to stay a few days with me in Buenos Aires because I wasn't well. That day, 14 April 1976, she went to visit her sister-in-law who was about to have a baby and who she hadn't been able to contact by phone. She'd called her and it seemed that someone had answered and then hung up, but she didn't think for one minute that anything was wrong and she went off to see her. She didn't come back. I spent the whole night waiting. We didn't know where the sister-in-law lived so the next day we went to her mother's house in La Plata. She knew nothing. Her daughter had disappeared the week before so we came to the conclusion that some security men had stayed inside the house waiting to see who came and by chance my daughter went and they kidnapped her. They'd also got her husband.

My son was in his fifth year of medical school when he was kidnapped, married with a young child. The day after he was taken, 21 October 1976, was his daughter's third birthday. We were driving in the car when, three streets from my house, we stopped at some traffic lights and three or four cars surrounded us. One went up on the pavement at the side of us. Hugo only had time to say 'Mamá . . .' and stopped. There was a man pointing a machine gun at his head through the car window and on my side another one with a machine gun pointed at me. They pulled out my son and I shouted like a madwoman and they dragged me out and threw me on the ground, stamping on my glasses and one of them holding me down with his boot, an army boot, and a machine gun at my face. From the ground I saw them tie my son's hands and put a hood over his head.

It was one in the afternoon, in the middle of a street at the side of the hospital in Palermo where there was always a lot of people. It all happened very quickly. They put Hugo in the back seat of a car and one of them got into my son's car and drove it away with three or four others following behind. One, a Ford Falcon, went on ahead down the wrong side of the street with its sirens going.

I stood there in the street shouting and a young woman came running up to me. Apparently she was a doctor. She had a badge with her name on which said Dr somebody, but at the time it didn't occur to me to remember it. She said, 'Don't run after them because they'll kill you too.' I just stood there, three streets from my house, but so shocked and confused I felt like I was in another world.

Control of communications, education and the arts was shared out on the basis of one third to each section of the armed forces and serving officers were installed in almost every public office or institution. Universities were closed down and departments placed under the control of military men. One of the government's first measures was to facilitate the dismissal of staff considered 'dangerous'. In the University of Buenos Aires alone these numbered 1,500. Entry requirements were tightened up, the curriculum was rewritten, books withdrawn and subjects discredited. The social sciences came under the fiercest attack. The psychology department was forced to teach without the works of Freud and Jung, political and economic sciences without the works of Marx and the biological sciences without the benefit of Darwin. All student political activity was banned and student activists rounded up. This included secondary school students. On 16 September 1976 in La Plata sixteen were kidnapped in one night in an operation which became known as the 'Night of the Pencils'.[8]

Pregnant Women and Children
While General Viola was justifying the decision of the armed forces in terms of their obligatory responsibility 'to reaffirm the values of the family as the base of our society',[9] entire families, including pregnant women and children, were falling victim to the kidnappers.

Elsa de Oesterheld: One day I went out with my nineteen-year-old daughter. I remember she told me that she'd decided to study medicine because she wanted to work in the provinces with deprived children. She was very idealistic. That same day we said goodbye she disappeared. This was 19 June 1976. That day she was supposed to go to a *villa* [*villa miseria*: shanty town] where she worked as a teacher and she never arrived. One month or so later I received news from Tucumán that my daughter, who was living there and who was six months pregnant, her husband and their one-year-old child had disappeared. The parents of my son-in-law later traced the baby to an orphanage. On 21 April 1977 they took my husband from La Plata. Soon after an officer from La Plata brought me my three-year-old grandson. There had been a raid on my oldest daughter's house and everyone had been taken. This officer had been in the operation and had taken the child to his grandfather in a secret detention centre. He spent the whole afternoon with my husband who gave this man my address and he brought me my grandson. He was bringing him against orders and he was very frightened he'd be found out. Then they kidnapped my last daughter, who was seventeen, the only one unmarried. Later I found out she was pregnant. I've never heard any news about her. So I lost my four daughters, my husband and I possibly have two grandchildren who may have been born in captivity.

Estela de Carlotto: The two little Britos sisters disappeared in October 1977 after they had been kidnapped together with their parents. Tatiana was four years old and Laura was just three months. The rest of the family had hidden the truth from the grandmother at first but as time went by and she heard nothing from her son and her grandchildren she began to suspect that something was wrong. She stayed alone in her house, very depressed. She couldn't go out and look for them because she was old and very ill.

Institutional Roles

The similarities of detail in the wave of abductions being reported throughout the country were the hallmarks of concerted and co-ordinated planning. Kidnappings had been used as a method of disposing of opposition by Isabel's government and this method was to be refined and elaborated by top military officers at a series of secret meetings in the run-up to the coup. In one of these meetings General Videla was quoted as saying, 'In order to achieve peace in Argentina all the necessary people will die.'[10]

The sweeping powers the military government had awarded itself under the State of Siege, including extensive powers of detention and the use of the death penalty, were only the legal façade of repression. Their control over Argentina's institutions was a preliminary measure to obtain the collaboration and guarantee of impunity they required to implement a parallel system of repression based on manifestly illegal methods. There would be none of the evidence of mass slaughter which followed Pinochet's seizure of power in Chile and none of the international outcry which it provoked. There would be no mass imprisonment as in Uruguay, where left-wing suspects had converted other prisoners and even prison guards to their cause, and there would be no possibility of such prisoners being released under a general amnesty only to start their campaign again, as happened in Argentina under Perón's predecessor, President Cámpora. There would be no evidence and no one would be able to prove who was responsible. The murderous campaign would be concealed from Argentina and the world.

The Police and Armed Forces

Aída de Suárez: I had a neighbour who was a doctor and after they took my son I went to him and he gave me an injection to calm me down. They come into your house and they take your child like that – you think you've gone mad. The injection didn't calm me at all. At seven in the morning I was in the police station. A guard at the entrance asked me what I wanted. I said my son had been taken away and I didn't know by who or why. I cried so much he let me in. They took my statement. As I was leaving a policeman at the door said to me, 'Señora, there's no point in coming here. Go to the military regiments, they're the ones who are taking people. Don't waste your time here. We have orders to keep out of the zones of their operations.' I went straight to the regiment. They didn't want to see me. They said that they didn't know anything and that I should go to the Ministry of the Interior. Then one man told me to try the regiment at Ciudadela. I went there and they said I'd come to the wrong place and that I had to go to the First Army Corps in Palermo. That day I went to all those places but I didn't find out anything.

Dora de Bazze: I went to the police station nearest to my house. They said it was nothing to do with them and as they hadn't any evidence they refused to take my statement. They didn't want to take statements because the police were in contact with the military and they knew what was going on. After two or three months of going backwards and forwards I walked into one military headquarters and I had the proof it was them. Behind the desk I saw the face of one of the men who had taken my son, it was a face which had stuck in my mind. He saw me, lowered his head and walked off into another room.

The role of the police within the illegal structure of repression was to clear the path for the activities of the security forces. Immediately after the coup 'anti-subversive' operations were made the direct responsibility of each regional army commander. Task forces or commando units were set up, drawing men from all the services. Each compiled lists of those considered subversive which they jealously guarded. They rarely informed the others of an intended raid, not only for prestige in numbers but also for the profits which could be made from the theft of family property. In order to avoid the interference of the police in a raid, or to avoid armed confrontations between the task forces themselves, the raiders would ask for a 'green light' from local and central police stations. In this way the police relieved themselves of any responsibility in the attacks, often refusing to take statements from the victims or referring them to military authorities. Military personnel throughout the country closed ranks, denying any involvement and subjecting relatives of disappeared people to obstructions, intimidation and threats designed to halt their search for information.

Margarita de Oro: I used to travel from Mendoza to Buenos Aires by train and begin going round all the military barracks and headquarters, the army, the navy, the air force, asking if they had my son. Everyone said they knew nothing. I went to one in La Plata when for a moment I really thought I'd found him because they asked me my name, when he disappeared, questions to involve you and give you hope and that make you think they were going to do something, and then they asked me to wait and you believed you were going to see him and later they came back and said no, he's not here.

In another place I had to wait from the early morning until five in the afternoon before I could see someone, with men with machine guns standing on either side of me. Then they called me to an office and I had to speak through a little window. They asked me what I wanted and I told them I was looking for my son and there, in front of my little grandson they told me I was another subversive. They told me to stop looking, that I should watch out for myself because I was just another subversive.

Nellie Bianchi: After my son was kidnapped I went to Famaillá to ask for him. I didn't know anything about it being a secret camp then. For me it was a police headquarters and I went there to speak to the chief. I spoke to a colonel, I think. He told me, 'I don't have any bad news for you, if I had I would tell you. I have the young Bianchi and I'm going to take a statement from him and after that he'll be released. Go home and be calm. If he hasn't done anything nothing will happen to him.' I didn't believe him. I left that place with a feeling of death inside me.

A bit later the father of another boy who had been kidnapped the same night as my son came to tell me some bodies had been found in the south of Tucumán and did I want to go with him to identify them. I went. There were five bodies, two boys and three girls, completely naked but unrecognizable. They had shot them so many times they were completely disfigured. When I saw them I went into a state of shock. I couldn't tell if my son was one of them. I didn't think my son was there. I spoke to a military officer and I was crying and shouting – I don't know how nothing happened to me – and he said, 'But your son wasn't there.' 'So you know where he is, you are responsible, why are you lying?' I shouted. He said nothing. Every time I went to the army they always said come back tomorrow, next week. Once one of them told me, 'Your son is being held under PEN [see Glossary]. Be calm and come back next week. I'll have more information.' I went back the next week and he denied that he'd ever said it and said they knew nothing about a Bianchi.

Estela de Carlotto: I managed to get to see General Bignone who became the last president of the dictatorship but who then was a secretary to the junta. It was in December 1977. We were alone in his office, with a desk between us and across the desk he had laid a huge rifle. I pleaded for Laura, for them to free her or at least not kill her. He told me terrible things. He said they didn't want to have prisons full of 'subversives', as he called them, because they only get stronger and that if they're allowed to go abroad they all conspire against the government from outside the country and that they had special prisons, and that they had to do what was necessary, by which it was clear he meant to kill them. I was now certain that Laura was dead so I asked please, would he at least return the body because I didn't want to search cemeteries amongst the anonymous graves for the body of my daughter. I think it was because of this that nine months later I was given the body of my daughter. They said she'd been killed in an *enfrentamiento* [armed confrontation].

The Judiciary

Enfrentamiento became the military's established explanation for the appearance of dead bodies on the outskirts of cities and around the countryside, even when these bodies appeared naked and showing evidence of torture and even when the victims had been previously registered as detainees in official prisons. This explanation was not challenged by the courts, even though there were clear violations of the legal procedure which required a criminal judge to investigate the circumstances of a violent death. The Criminal Appeals Court stood by in silence as the judicial morgue and cemeteries throughout the country buried those killed in '*enfrentamientos*' in unmarked graves while at the same time judges were rejecting thousands of habeas corpus writs in favour of missing people.

Carmen de Guede: Someone told me I should file writs of habeas corpus. I'd never heard of it before. It was very difficult to find a lawyer. I went to see one who a friend of my husband had recommended, a very old lawyer, and he drew it up but he didn't present it for me. I should say he sold me the piece of paper. He sold it for half a million pesos. With that money we could have lived for a month. I went to La Plata to present it without a lawyer's signature. They accepted it because they never did anything with them anyway. You could take it signed or unsigned because they never went anywhere. After a week I went to get the reply but there wasn't any reply. It was just a piece of paper which was passed from one person to another, nothing more.

Rita de Krichmar: You couldn't find a lawyer. You had to file the writ by yourself or get help from a lawyer who didn't put his name to it. This was because many lawyers were themselves kidnapped for helping the families of disappeared people. I went to hand in a writ at the court early one morning. The official looked at me and said, 'Señora, I already have seventy writs of habeas corpus on my desk.' Seventy had already been filed that morning. We never got a reply.

Elsa de Becerra: We drew up our own habeas corpus because we couldn't find a lawyer who would do it and we presented it to the courts. They never replied. About six weeks after Jorge's disappearance we saw in the newspaper a list of prisoners being held under PEN.[11] The name Jorge Becerra was there. His detention had been legalized. We wrote letters and after a few months we were able to visit him in a prison in La Plata, forty-five minutes every two months. Then, soon after a visit, one of our letters was returned with '*Not known at this address*' written in big letters across the envelope. We contacted the prison and they said they knew nothing of a Jorge Becerra. How could it be possible that he'd disappeared again?

Somehow my son managed to get a message to us that he had been transferred to a prison in Córdoba. He'd been taken there secretly with twenty-nine others because General Videla was making an official visit to Tucumán and – they were so brave – if anything happened to Videla they were going to shoot all thirty prisoners. They denied Jorge was there but after a fortnight, through a group of families of political prisoners in Córdoba, we managed to get proof and they were forced to admit it. With them admitting it we thought he would be in less danger. It was four years before they released him. I've kept the release papers. It says he was imprisoned under the orders of the Eighth Infantry Brigade for the crime of . . . and these lines have been scratched out. Four years without being charged with anything.

The judiciary failed to locate one single kidnap victim during military rule. After replacing the most senior legal officers on the first day of the coup the junta required all other judges to swear to uphold the Articles and Objectives of the *proceso*. Those who remained in post had effectively agreed to surrender their role as guarantors of the constitutional rights of citizens and to collaborate in a system which gave the appearance of legality to the legal aberrations being committed and which maintained the impunity of those responsible. In the cases of '*enfrentamientos*', habeas corpus and the indefinite detention of prisoners held under PEN the judiciary failed to question the military version of events. Those who did try to fulfil their responsibilities, and particularly lawyers who attempted to defend the families of missing people, were liable to find themselves on the lists of the disappeared.

Margarita de Oro: I had filed ten writs of habeas corpus and then I decided to go to prisons all over the country. I went to Devoto, Caseros, Santa Fe, Córdoba, taking clean clothes and food in case I found him there. Caseros was a terrible place. I asked for my son and they let me in these huge doors with enormous keys and then through more doors and they took out a book where a Barerra was registered but it wasn't my son. Later I realized that even if my son had been there they wouldn't have told me anyway because the disappeared didn't have names, only numbers. I went to a reformatory in La Plata which is a big place and when you enter there's an office and you could see all the offices on the upper level where they used to keep the prisoners and down below a garage full of Falcons. I went to psychiatric hospitals. I went to El Borda [a mental institution in Buenos Aires] where all the patients were lying on the floor and I had to turn them over to see if one of them was my son.

The Church

Many families went to their priests and bishops believing that the church would offer a condemnation of the activities of the security forces and support them in their search for relatives. Roman Catholicism is the official religion of Argentina and historically the church has always enjoyed a close relationship with the state. If the church spoke out, the families believed, the military would have to listen.

Rita de Krichmar: Then I wasn't so disillusioned with the church. I thought there were priests who were really concerned about people. But the church was the worst of all. They were more terrible than anyone could imagine considering that they say they believe in the good of humanity. People told me to go to see Mgr Grasselli, the naval chaplain. I had to wait in line because there were a lot of people who wanted to see him. I told him that I had a granddaughter who was nearly one year old and that I needed to know what to tell her. He said, in a very weary, very tired way, 'These children, what trouble they give us. Sometimes they take the wrong paths . . .' He said he had no information but I believe that what he was doing was taking information from us because he asked me what we talked about at home, what political ideas our children had, what our political ideas were. He had a file in which he took down notes. He told me to come back in ten days.

The next time I went I told him that I had information that my daughter was being held at a military headquarters, because we had received a telephone call from a journalist friend who told us that he had information that they were being held in Campo de Mayo, but he couldn't tell us any more than that. Grasselli told me to come back in ten days. When I went back again he told me, 'No, they're not there.' That was a terrible day for me. Imagine, you get some information, you build up your hopes and they tell you no . . . Then I went to see Primatesta [Archbishop of Córdoba and later President of the Episcopal Conference]. He wouldn't see me but I received a letter from his secretary. The church was very false. Very false. There were some priests who really tried to help, but I never met them. Never.

Margarita de Oro: I went to the Navy to see Grasselli. When you went in they put a card on you and made you sign a piece of paper and you had to wait in long queues and then he looked through huge piles of files. They had files on our children. They knew exactly what was happening. Then he told you, 'No, he's not here,' and then you had to show your card to get out again.

I went to the First Army Corps where I saw this Padre Monzón who was very understanding and patient so I went back another time to see him and when I got there they told me he was in retreat but as I'd come all the way from Mendoza I said I'd wait anyway. It was a terrible shock for me when hours later he walked in wearing military uniform. He'd been on a military operation in a *villa miseria*. He said he was sorry to have kept me waiting and he would see me in a moment, like that, as if it was completely normal.

The families never got the condemnation they were expecting from the Catholic church. The ecclesiastical hierarchy had never hidden its identification with the social and political vision of the Argentine military and its close relationship with the state remained untroubled by the events following the coup of 1976. As an institution it reserved any criticisms of the activities of the military regime to mildly worded letters which it refused to make public. It remained silent even as its own members became victims of the *proceso*. During the late 1960s and early 1970s the traditional conservatism of the Argentine church had been challenged by the growth of progessive sectors within its ranks, such as the group of Third World priests who expressed concern about social justice and the worker priests who lived and worked amongst the poor. At least 30 of these priests and nuns, together with those individuals who dared to speak out against the kidnappings, disappeared in the months following the coup.[12]

By contrast, within days of the military takeover Mgr Tortolo, President of the influential Argentine Episcopal Conference, had announced that 'the hour of the great rebirth has begun' and urged all Argentines to 'co-operate positively' with the new regime.[13] They continued to supply the military with chaplains, invited leading military figures to church ceremonies and provided their services at military functions. On 29 March 1976, when Videla was confirmed as President, both Tortolo and Mgr Aramburu, Archbishop of Buenos Aires and primate of all Argentina, had been present. In addition, leading Catholics accepted influential posts in the junta's Ministry of Education and used this position to impose a more rigid Christian orthodoxy. One consequence of this was the prohibition placed on the public practice of the faith of the Jehovah's Witnesses. The moral legitimacy the Argentine church conferred on the regime played a crucial role in consolidating public acceptance of military rule.

Jewish Organizations

The representatives of Argentina's large Jewish population were also slow to act. Families of kidnapped Jews went to the offices of the Delegation of Argentine Jewish Associations (DAIA) but they too failed to obtain a vigorous denunciation of the activities of the military government. Apart from outspoken individuals, the Jewish authorities preferred to work behind the scenes, believing this put the Jewish community as a whole at less risk. The climate had become increasingly hostile towards Jews. Military rule was accompanied by an increase in anti-Semitic propaganda and in acts of violence against synagogues and Jewish centres.[14]

Renée Epelbaum: We tried to get help from what you could call the 'establishment' of the Argentine Jewish community. We felt very disappointed and alone. The behaviour of the organized community as a whole was not emphatic enough. On the contrary, some community leaders even tried to improve the image of the military. The dictatorship was being criticized all over the world and these leaders said there was no discrimination, religious or racial. There is a lot of proof, statements by Jewish and non-Jewish people, that the Jews were treated infinitely worse.[15]

Neighbouring Countries

In their desperation families sought out influential people from all sectors of society to assist them in their search for information on the whereabouts of their children. Some paid out large sums of money to people claiming to be in a position to help but saw neither their children nor their money again. After the kidnapping of one of her sons Renée Epelbaum believed that by sending her two remaining children to neighbouring Uruguay she would be securing their safety.

I have three children disappeared. All my children. The eldest Luís who was a medical student was kidnapped from the street. I sent the two younger ones, it must have been a month after Luís disappeared, to Punta del Este in Uruguay. I did this to protect them because here, in Argentina, we lived in terror. They were kidnapped in Punta del Este three months later by an Argentine commando unit with the help of the Uruguayan army.[16]

With the collaboration of the security forces of neighbouring countries which had also fallen under authoritarian governments, including Brazil in 1964, Bolivia in 1971 and Chile and Uruguay in 1973, the Argentine military were able to extend their operations across national frontiers, unobstructed by considerations of national sovereignty. By reciprocal and clandestine arrangements which were blatant violations of the conventions of political asylum to which Argentina subscribed, Argentine security forces kidnapped and assassinated foreign exiles or transferred them to secret detention centres in their own countries. In the months which followed the coup, three prominent Uruguayan politicians and the former Bolivian president, Juan Torres, were kidnapped and murdered in Buenos Aires.

The Media

None of these incidents was reported in the press. On 24 March the junta had issued the following instruction:

'Anyone who through any medium whatsoever defends, propagates or divulges news, communiqués or views with the purpose of disrupting, prejudicing or lessening the prestige of the activities of the Armed Forces will be subject to detention for a period of up to ten years.'[17]

This was followed by a system of self-censorship under the guidance of principles and procedures drafted by the junta's press director. The press was to comply enthusiastically with this form of self-censorship. The publication *Gente*, for example, which before the coup had supported the Peronist government, ran the headline 'We were wrong!' on 25 March 1976. The respected newspaper *Clarín* reported on the same day 'Everything is normal'. The tortured bodies which were appearing on the outskirts of cities or being washed up on the shores of the River Plate and the kidnappings were not reported. On 22 April 1976 the military introduced a more stringent control of information:

As from today it is forbidden to comment or make references to suspects connected with subversive incidents, the appearance of bodies and the deaths of subversive elements and/or members of the armed or security forces in these incidents, unless they are reported by a responsible official source. This includes the victims of kidnappings and missing persons.[18]

Most newspaper proprietors were to earn General Videla's praise for their 'objective reporting'. Those which did not conform were closed down and their staff kidnapped. An estimated 100 journalists disappeared during the *proceso* and a further 100 were imprisoned without ever being brought to trial.[19]

The clandestine nature of the operations reduced the possibility of witnesses. Most were carried out at night after first diverting the traffic with roadblocks and cutting off the electricity supply and were executed with the maximum display of violence designed to instil a terror which would paralyse public reaction and ensure the silence of neighbours and friends.

Elsa de Becerra: The military's propaganda was put out constantly in the newspapers, on the radio, on television. You switched on the TV and it said things like 'Do you know where your child is at this moment? Do you know what he's doing?' and they showed sinister figures and blown up cars and then 'Denounce him because here is a subversive who is about to plant a bomb.' People believed this, so when they heard that your child had been taken they asked what they had been involved in, that they must have done something. So people distanced themselves. When they broke into my house and took my daughter, in spite of the violence of the attack and in spite of the cars and the noise, my neighbours acted like they saw and heard nothing. They considered it dangerous for their own children to associate with us. Most people avoided speaking to us.

Carmen de Guede: After the kidnappings I was told that one of our neighbours had gone to the police station with my husband to find our son. I went to see him and he said, yes, he had accompanied him but that nothing had happened. He didn't want to tell the truth. People were afraid.

The family distanced themselves completely. They didn't offer to help me and they never came to see me because they were afraid. One sister who was here in Buenos Aires came to see me sometimes, but very rarely. My husband's mother never came and she's never spoken about what happened to her son and grandson. My other son, who is sixteen now and was just five when it happened, went to see her recently after all this time and she didn't mention his father or his brother. I was completely alone with the children.

Friends were like this too. The people we most expected to help us turned out not to be our friends. They never came to see what had happened to my husband. After he disappeared only one of his friends from work came to see how we were and this man died soon after. But his other friends from work, the ones he thought were his friends, never came. Until today. I suppose they were afraid they would lose their jobs. I don't know. Apart from two families who have always helped us my other neighbours didn't want to know us any more. There were some neighbours who had children the same age as mine and they didn't want them to play with mine. The television was making everybody afraid. It used to say that the people who had disappeared were all terrorists, that the army was cleaning the country of terrorism. They showed horrendous films of people blowing up cars or putting bombs in colleges and blamed it on our children. People saw that and believed it was true, that everyone who had disappeared was a terrorist. The only people who really knew what was happening were the people it was happening to.

Mothers Meet in the Search

The military government's 'war against subversion' had divided the country in two. One was the Argentina which saw, heard and knew nothing of the Ford Falcons and their armed occupants and the other an Argentina which had fallen victim to their sinister mission. It was a world which was becoming a reality for the growing numbers of families and friends who found themselves drawn into the search for people who had disappeared. Increasingly, it was the women who persisted with the long, time-consuming task of searching for their children. On the endless circuit of military headquarters, courts, prisons and government offices they had begun to come across other women whose faces reflected their own desperation.

María del Rosario: My son was kidnapped from my house on 10 May 1976. The next day I went to the army headquarters in Palermo, because the kidnappers had told me that I would get some information there. In that place I met two other mothers whose children had disappeared two months earlier. We agreed to meet again to go to the headquarters together. Wherever we went we met women asking for information about their children. By July 1976 there were already thirty of us, mothers, fathers, families in general, and every week we went together to different places. We went to the church as well. Twenty-seven of us were allowed in to see the three bishops who were the heads of the episcopate. They didn't give us any information. They recommended that we pray to the Virgin.

Beatriz de Rubinstein: In the middle of 1976 the Ministry of the Interior opened an office to receive complaints about the disappearances. I used to come from Mar del Plata and they would tell me to come back in thirty or forty days. If you came late they would close the case. Anyway, they always said the same – that they had no information. They played with us. It was a form of psychological torture. Sometimes they would tell us not to continue because it would endanger our other children. They tried to paralyse us in this way. There I met mothers who had come from all over Argentina, women of all ages and backgrounds. Someone would come in every now and then to tell us not to speak to each other so we all sat there in silence holding the number that gave us an appointment with some official. That piece of paper was the only thing we had which gave us some hope that we would find our children.

Dora de Bazze: Four months after my daughter and son-in-law were kidnapped, and after all those months of searching, they admitted they were holding them. Their detention was legalized. When I went to visit them in prison I met other mothers who'd also been lucky enough to find their children. I also met others, who like me, were still looking for a child. I was still looking for my son, Hugo. I hadn't been able to find any information about him. Three or four of us went to the Ministry of the Interior where they told us we had to come back the next day to take a number and they would see us at ten o'clock. You had to be at the door at seven in the morning to get a number because they only saw the first ten. Every day there were more and more people waiting and we had to start going at night to be sure to get a number. We arranged a place to meet and we went with vacuum flasks and blankets because it was the middle of the winter and we had to spend the whole night there. We used to sit in the warmth from the underground station. At ten o'clock they let in the first ten.

The *milicos* [a derogatory term for military officers] were all called González or Diego – they never gave their real names and they always told us we would be seen by some lieutenant or captain but we didn't know who we were really speaking to because they were all liars. They always said there was no news and they asked a lot of questions, like what were our children like, who were their friends, who was their girlfriend or boyfriend. They took information from us. They didn't give us any. Out of desperation we began to shout 'What have you done with our children?' We began to lose our tempers and this anger helped to make us stronger.

It was in the Ministry of the Interior that the scale of the horror was first revealed to the families of its victims. For many, this realization, together with the recognition that the kidnappings were taking place with the co-operation of neighbouring countries, industrialists, the legal system and with the blessing of the church authorities brought with it a sense of powerlessness and terror. It seemed inconceivable that these groups of women in the waiting room of the Ministry of the Interior could offer any real challenge to this powerful alliance.

María del Rosario: In April 1977, after a year of going in groups from one place to another, one of the mothers, Azucena Villaflor de Vicenti, said, 'Let's go to Plaza de Mayo and when there's enough of us' – a thousand she said – 'we'll go together to Government House and demand an answer.' We chose Plaza de Mayo because it's in front of Government House which was where they'd moved the office of the Ministry of the Interior which was responsible for enquiries about the disappearances. Also, we needed to meet in a public place to make it more difficult for them to kidnap us and where we could make sure that our protest could be seen. We arranged to meet in Plaza de Mayo on 30 April at eleven in the morning.

We arrived separately. We wore flat shoes so we could make a run for it if they came after us. To demonstrate in front of Government House was very dangerous. That day was a Saturday. Nobody was at work. We found ourselves in the middle of an empty square with no one around to see us. We agreed to return the next week on a weekday and to prepare a letter together to send to Videla. 'What time?' we asked each other . 'Well, after cooking for the family, after cleaning the kitchen, before they close the banks' – Plaza de Mayo is in a banking area so the streets are always full of people when the banks are open. 'Half past three next Friday afternoon.' That Friday we prepared the wording of the letter to Videla in our heads and decided to meet the next week to sign the letter and deliver it to Government House. One of the Mothers said, 'Let's not make it Friday, Friday's an unlucky day' – they say it's the day of the witches – 'let's make it Thursday.' 'Okay. Thursday at half past three.' That Thursday we went back and delivered the letter. We arranged to meet the next week to discuss the reply.

We came back every week until one Thursday, two months later, an under-secretary saw us and told us he'd arranged for three Mothers to speak with the Minister of the Interior, General Harguindeguy. I was one of the Mothers who went, with Azucena and Beatriz de Neuhaus. We went in about six o'clock and a group of about sixty Mothers waited for us outside. We left about seven. Harguindeguy pointed to a file which contained the names of disappeared people. He said that in that file were the names of members of his own friends' families and that if he knew who was responsible he would do something, but that he didn't know. He said that they couldn't know everything, that there were para-military groups out there who couldn't be controlled. He passed the responsibility to other people. Then he said that perhaps our sons had run away with a woman, that perhaps our daughters were working as prostitutes somewhere. So we told him that they were cowards, because even a cruel dictator like Franco had signed the death sentences with his own hand, that making people disappear was cowardly. We told him everything we felt and we told him that we would come back every week until they gave us an answer and that we would walk in the square every Thursday until we dropped. 'But it's illegal to hold public meetings under a State of Siege!' 'Then we'll stay here until you give us an answer.' It was a challenge.

Aída de Suárez: In the Ministry of the Interior I met another mother looking for her child. When I left the building she was waiting for me outside and she called me over. She asked me if they'd taken my child too. I told her what had happened. She said, 'Come to the square on Thursday and join the Mothers. We meet every Thursday.' I said yes, that I'd already heard something about the Mothers. She said, 'Come, they won't ask you any questions. We're all women together.' Within a few days of my son's disappearance I was in Plaza de Mayo.

The first Thursday I got off the bus and just stood there in the street. I saw some women but I didn't know what to do. There was one here, two there. They weren't allowed to be in a group so they were all dispersed around the square. I asked myself, 'Is that a Mother? Is she a Mother?' I felt afraid, like you always do when you do something for the first time. Then I saw the woman who had waited for me outside the Ministry of the Interior. What luck she was there! I walked straight towards her, without looking to either side, without looking at the police. At first you feel afraid, but when I got to the Mothers they all seemed so strong . . . and how can you feel afraid when you are fighting for a just cause? I cried a lot, but they were tears of relief. I felt like another person. Because looking at the faces of other mothers who had experienced the same as me gave me the strength to fight.

Elisa de Landín: I went to the military headquarters, to the courts, to prisons and then to the Ministry of the Interior, where I met the Mothers and really it was the best thing that could have happened to me. To meet this group of women who all had the same pain, spoke the same language and who understood each other better than our own families. Because my family closed their doors on me. I've got a brother who told me, 'You can bring mamá, but you can't come in.' So what could be better than to be with the Mothers? I remember the first time I went to the square, no one asked me what religion are you, what race, what are your politics. The only thing they asked me was 'Who has disappeared?' and then you found out that other mothers had lost two, three children and that their children were just as excellent as your own and the pain gets worse all the time. At first we cried a lot but then we realized we had to fight for them all. It's a love we learnt, that every child has the same value. That's what we learnt from being together.

Hebe de Bonafini: We began to realize we had to move outside our own families and struggle for all the people who had disappeared, that the explanation for the disappearance of our own children could only be found in the explanation for all the disappearances.

Together they became known as the Mothers of Plaza de Mayo. They were a group of women whose paths would probably never have crossed in any other circumstances but who were now united in the collective search for their children. There had been little in their previous experience to prepare them for the central place they were to occupy in Argentine politics in the coming years.

Notes

1. For more information on the growth of an anti-bureaucratic, militant current in the unions and on the guerrilla organizations, see Torre, Juan Carlos, 1974; Jelin, Elizabeth, 1979; Munck, Ronaldo, 1984; James, Daniel, 1976; Gillespie, Richard, 1982; Hodges, D. C., 1976; 'Urban Guerrillas in Argentina: A Select Bibliography', *Latin American Research Review*, Vol. IX, No. 3, 1974.

2. Canitrot, A., 1981.

3. Quoted in the monthly newspaper, *Madres de Plaza de Mayo*, No. 16, March 1986.

4. This account was given indirectly to the author.

5. For an analysis of the economic policies of the military government, see Canitrot, A., 1980. For an overview, see Ferrer, Aldo, 1980.

6. Latin American Bureau, 1982.

7. Quoted in Gillespie, Richard, 1982.

8. For a full account of the 'Night of the Pencils', see Seoane, María and Ruiz Núñez, Héctor, 1986.

9. *Madres de Plaza de Mayo*, No. 16, March 1986.

10. *Clarín*, 24 October 1975.

11. 5,182 people were put at the disposal of PEN from March 1976, added to the 3,443 already detained before the coup under the State of Siege.

12. See Catholic Institute for International Relations 1980, compiled by a group of priests in

Argentina on the disappearance of members of the clergy. Also the National Commission on Disappeared People, 1986, pp. 337–55 and Simpson, John and Bennett, Jana, 1985, pp. 176–83.

13. *Madres de Plaza de Mayo*, No. 16, March 1986.

14. According to some of the most extreme anti-Semitic literature, three Jews, Marx, Einstein and Freud, were responsible for the evils of modern society. See National Commission on Disappeared People, 1986, pp. 67–72 and Timerman, Jacobo, 1982.

15. Quoted in *Las Madres, The Mothers of Plaza de Mayo*, the film documentary by Susana Muñoz and Lourdes Portillo.

16. Renée Epelbaum, as above.

17. Amnesty International, 1977.

18. As above.

19. The English-language *Buenos Aires Herald* and *La Opinión* were the only two major newspapers to defy the press censorship. See Simpson, John, and Bennett, Jana, 1985, Chapter 13.

2.   The Mothers

The women who organized the first public protest against the government's repressive strategy seemed an unlikely source of opposition to military rule. There was little which united them in terms of their geographical origins, social and economic backgrounds or religious and political beliefs. Despite their diverse backgrounds, they were to find they shared much more than the tragedy which had affected their lives. Like the majority of other women in Argentina, the Mothers had seen their role in life as almost exclusively that of housewife and mother to their children and it was in this role that they went to the streets to protest. These testimonies tell the stories of the lives of nine of the women until the coup of 1976.

Aída de Suárez: We lived in the province of Tucumán. It was the kind of house that working-class people in the country used to live in with big patios and a garden with plants. My mother loved plants and flowers. It was very beautiful. My mother wanted all of us girls to be good housewives and when I finished secondary school she sent me to the *Escuela Profesional de Mujeres* [Professional School for Women]. I wanted to go there too. They tried to teach us to be perfect housewives, to learn about the house and children, how to sew, cook. I was very close to my father. He was a railway worker, all the men in my family worked on the railways and he was political. Sometimes I used to go with him when he travelled around the province, but I wasn't interested in politics. My mother neither. She was the perfect housewife. She used to sew, knit and embroider everything for us and she was very religious. The rest of the family wasn't interested in politics either. The first time Perón was President he gave women the vote, well, I think it was because of Evita really, and I voted. At that time there was a complete change. It wasn't so much Perón but Evita. Most of the people I knew supported the Peronists and most of the women too, because of Evita Perón.

I got married when I was twenty-two years old. It wasn't possible for a woman to live independently then. The people from the provinces especially were more attached to the home. My parents brought up their children as they were brought up. Now girls are more independent. My daughters are more independent. My husband was a wonderful man and a hard worker and he loved his children very much. We had six children. Every time we had another one it became more difficult so I used to knit or work as a seamstress to help my husband with the family income, doing work that I could do in the house. We worked hard to try to give our children a better life. He used to help in the house too. When I was very tired after making clothes all day, he would help me in the kitchen and look after the little ones. I used to work on individual things, sewing clothes or knitting a jumper for local people, and I charged what they could pay. They were as short of money as us.

When we got married we went to live in our own house in the city. Then my mother became ill and as we were all married and she was living alone it was decided that I should go and live with her and take care of her. By the time I moved back with my mother we already had four children. We stayed with her until she died and afterwards, because I didn't have a house of my own, we all agreed that I should stay on.

We used to suffer a lot every time the military were in power. I understood that every military coup put the country back ten years. In Tucumán, after the coup of Onganía, they closed down eleven sugar mills in one go. You can imagine that left a lot of people unemployed, it was almost half the factories in the province and you could see how people were suffering. The men had to leave their families and go away to find work. If they were used to working in sugar they went north to Jujuy, or they went to Chaco for the tobacco harvest, to Río Negro for the apples or to Mendoza for the grapes. Young people found all their hopes frustrated, they couldn't get work and they couldn't study and this is why the unrest started there and why the government moved in the troops there first.

My husband had to work away for many years at the sugar mill in Ledesma. He used to get contracts from a private company and he would spend a couple of years in one factory and a few years in another to repair the damage done to the machines used during the sugar harvest ready for the next harvest. He used to come home at the end of every month and spend three or four days with the family. This went on for twelve years so I spent many years living alone with the children. He didn't want to take all the children there because it wasn't a very good place for them and there wasn't a school nearby and the oldest were already at secondary school and it would have been a big disruption. I had to make decisions about the children alone, be responsible for them when they were ill and for their education. My husband was so far away I couldn't just call on him. So in this way I grew up too.

Ever since he was very young my son Hubo worried about people around him who had less than he did. Once he came home from school and told me he had a friend who didn't have a uniform and that as he had two and only needed one, he had given the other one to his friend. He didn't realize that we had difficulties too. Between my husband and myself we always managed to provide for the necessities of the children but it worried him that he had things that some of the other children didn't have, and we lived in a place which was very poor, where we were surrounded by people in need.

When my husband fell ill the economic situation in my home became desperate. We had to come to live in Buenos Aires because my three older children were already married and in Tucumán I had no money coming in and I had to stay at home with the youngest ones. Hubo was fifteen when his father died and he had to leave school and go out to work to support the family.

He started work in a ceramics factory and he was put in the basement and he used to get ill because of the dust. They had no masks to protect them and there wasn't any ventilation in the basement so it was very bad for their health. And they were only given cold water to wash their hands and all their tools. In the mornings in the winter the water was frozen and they had to break the ice. So he argued with the owners because it was terrible to work all day and then wash in cold water. He became a union delegate in the factory. He was very popular with his workmates because he would always work their shifts for them if they had problems at home. He managed to get masks for the workers in the basement and warm water, but he had to fight for these things. After this he started a campaign to get free milk. If you drink milk it helps protect you against the poison in the enamel dust and he managed to get thirty litres of milk a day for the workers in the basement.

He was about eighteen when Perón returned to Argentina and he wanted to change things. It's what all young people wanted at that time. He used to come home and tell me everything. He said they treated them worse than animals in the factory. He said they had to work twelve hours a day for a starvation wage. It was like this in all the factories. There were strikes and workers' protests every day because of the economic policies of Isabel Perón. It all began with the *Rodrigazo* [see Glossary]. My son used to say they were negotiating away the working class and that nobody was doing anything about it. He wasn't on good terms with the union. Here the unions are very bureaucratic so he had to fight against the company and the unions at the same time. The union leaders would say, 'There are some things you have to leave alone', but the young people spoke out, they wanted to make their voices heard. He used to say that the young people loved their country and wanted to live in peace but they wanted to live with dignity.

One day he came home and told me he was going to resign from the union. He said, 'People are disappearing.' I said, 'What do you mean they're disappearing? How can they disappear?' I told him it couldn't be true. This was in 1976 under the government of Isabel, when the Triple A had already started to kidnap and kill people. He said the leadership of the union was very bad and that one day he might disappear himself. So he resigned from the union.

Then, with the coup, things got much worse. He came home one day and said his friend hadn't come to work for three days and his body had been discovered in the Riachuelo riddled with bullets. He told me that he was going to speak to me very honestly. He said that he was going to continue working and continue fighting, but he said he would have to leave home, for the security of the family. He said that he could be seen as a subversive for what he had been doing in the factory. Already they were beginning to publish things in the newspapers. Bodies were appearing in different places and they were saying they were subversives. I couldn't understand how he could be called a subversive. Since the death of my husband it was him that supported the family. He did his best to make sure that his brother and sister didn't need anything and he was the one who paid for their education. I told him that he must never think of leaving his home, that we were all together and that if we had to confront anything we would all confront it together.

Josefa de Mujica: My father came from Italy when he was young and set up a business in the province of Córdoba, which was where I was born. I was lucky enough to be brought up in a house where, without knowing about politics or political parties, I knew what it was to be able to express things freely. We never felt restricted in what we could say at home. I began to study literature at the university in Córdoba. It was more unusual then for a woman to go to university, especially in the provinces, but in Córdoba it wasn't that uncommon because it was always one of the more advanced provinces. I was lucky to have access to the university. I had relatives living in the city who I could stay with. Girls couldn't stay in boarding houses because people thought this was terrible. The boys could, of course, like my husband, but we had to stay in the house of a relative or a very good friend of the family, otherwise we wouldn't have been allowed to study.

My husband was in my brother's circle of friends which was how we met. He was from the province of Buenos Aires and had gone to Córdoba to study dentistry. My brother introduced us and we started courting. My husband was always political. Córdoba was the centre of political activity for young people. Around this time, in 1938, the local government was very liberal and lots of young people wanted to study there. If you studied in Córdoba it was difficult not to be aware of what was going on.

We got married in 1944 and went to live in the south, in Neuquén, so I never finished my studies. Two years later Irene was born and three years after that Susana. There wasn't a university in Neuquén at that time so I couldn't continue studying. There was one in Bahía Blanca, about 500 kilometres away, but I couldn't go because I was already married, I had my house to look after. It would have been something extremely unusual for a married woman to leave home and study. Most women left their professions when they got married to concentrate on their families. The society was very conservative and women especially were conservative. After they got married they didn't leave their home. Now it's different because there are a lot of women who work in all sectors, but it took a long time to get to this.

I had some consciousness of politics through my husband. His political involvement meant the coups had a big effect on our lives. Between the coups, when political activity wasn't illegal, Miguel left his dental surgery and went into politics. He was a deputy for the Radical Party in the Neuquén state parliament and he worked under both President Frondizi and President Illia and both of them were overthrown by the military. Every time there was a coup they closed down the parliament and he had to pack up his bags and go back to the surgery. It wasn't dangerous for him then and at the dangerous moment, after the coup in 1976, he had already died. Our life was very unstable but as he was an independent professional and didn't depend on an employer he could always go back to being a dentist. Even during periods of military rule he was working with some group to restore democracy. So I lived in this kind of environment and the children too. I was never involved myself. I don't know why I never thought of getting involved. But even now I find it difficult to talk in public.

When Miguel died I received a monthly pension from the Neuquén legislature and while we had a constitutional government I could manage. When the military took power again in 1976 they reduced it to a pittance so that it wasn't possible to survive. Because I hadn't finished university the only work I could get was manual work. I used to make children's clothes and do other bits of sewing and my daughters both helped out.

By 1976 we'd already seen examples of the way the police and military dealt with protest. We saw what they did in Córdoba in 1969 after the famous *Cordobazo*. Córdoba had always been revolutionary because it had the important university and a large concentration of workers in the car industry. And we heard about the activities of the Triple A in the north.

Susana studied political science in the university in Buenos Aires. At that time many young people from the provinces went to the big centres like Buenos Aires and La Plata to study. They weren't necessarily all rich people. Many of the students had to work as well as study so you could have the son of an industrialist living with the son of a worker, whose family wanted him to improve his position because in their day it wasn't possible to study. They formed student unions. There was a big student movement which was concerned about the serious social and economic problems the country was facing. Susana was involved in all this, in all the groups and demonstrations, because politics was her ambition, she wanted to be a politician. It was in the family.

There was no talk of 'subversion' then. They began talking about subversion with the events in Tucumán in 1975 [see pp. 39]. We took this as something isolated, an armed confrontation between the guerrillas and the army. It wasn't a war because such a small group could never make war against the entire armed forces of a nation, with all its troops and weapons. It's a lie when they say it was a war. It was a pretext for attacking all the young people all over the country, accusing them of subversion and breaking into their homes. They put up blacklists in the universities and it didn't matter which group you belonged to, to the military they were all communist subversives.

Susana had come back to Neuquén to work in the university. I was living in Buenos Aires at the time, looking after my mother, and I'd gone to stay with Susana because she'd just had her second baby who was just two weeks old. Susana was one of those who didn't keep quiet. She always spoke out and said what she thought and, of course, she was on a blacklist. We found this out later. We didn't know at the time.

Rita de Ponce: I only went to primary school. It was mostly the boys who went to secondary schools. If girls went it was to learn how to sew and cook while the boys went to the technical schools to learn a career like engineering. So when they left school the boys went to the big, modern factories because they had the skills to use the new machines and we got the lower-paid jobs in the older factories, like clothes factories or food. Girls didn't go to university like today. They used to call it the factory of spinsters. Under Perón's government it was easier for working-class people to get into university because it was made free. Before you had to pay one peso for each course and thirty-six to enrol. Then a worker earned about five pesos a day so it was impossible. They made primary education compulsory but there were many children from the country where I lived who didn't go anyway. There weren't many schools in the country.

Food was always cheap but when they started to build the factories with Perón there was a terrible shortage of houses. People used to go to the cities and there was nowhere to live so they had to build their own houses from boxes and corrugated iron and there wasn't any sanitation or water. There was a lot of disease and people couldn't afford to pay for medicines. If you want people to work in the factories you have to give them somewhere to live. There wasn't the terrible inflation then when you had to spend everything you earned as soon as you got it because by the end of the month it wasn't worth anything.

Girls spent most of their time with the family, with aunts and parents and grandparents. We didn't have many expectations. It was considered very bad to wear your hair short then, and you couldn't wear trousers because people would be shocked and it wasn't even considered proper for a woman to drive a car. It was difficult to meet any men because you spent so much time at home with the family. On Saturday nights there might be a dance and we had to be accompanied by our parents or a member of the family. We used to dance the bolero, slow and smoochy, and if your parents were there it was okay, but they didn't like to see you in the street with a boy.

On Sundays the family used to have a party in the house and the women would prepare the food and the men would bring the wine. In the evenings we used to go to the cinema or for a walk or to visit people. I used to listen to the radio a lot because you can do the housework and listen at the same time. We didn't have television here until 1966.

After I got married I always worked in my husband's tailoring business and looked after the house and the children. He didn't help with that, not like my son. Men never did the cooking except for making the *asado* [traditional barbecue] and they believe that women don't know how to do that. I looked after the house and the workshop, I hardly went out at all. I hardly knew the streets of Tucumán until they took my son prisoner and I'd never been to Buenos Aires before. I only went to the shops and to church. I am very religious and our family was well-known at the church because Humberto used to be an altar boy.

Everything changed on 18 January 1975 when one of my sons was taken prisoner under the State of Siege. He was held under PEN which meant he didn't need to be accused of anything and we didn't know when they were going to let him out. We weren't allowed to visit them very often. They kept transferring them between prisons and we knew that they were being tortured and beaten. There were many of them, about seventy in Villa Urquiza. The conditions were very bad. They took them from Tucumán to Chaco, blindfolded and tied together in threes. Later they took them to Rawson [an official detention centre for political prisoners, in the south].

I'd met some of the mothers of other political prisoners in the prisons and the police stations and we formed a group to try and stop the ill-treatment and to find lawyers to defend them. There were five of us at first but we knew a lot of other families had been affected because seventy writs of habeas corpus had been filed in the courts in one day. We went out to look for them and we used to meet in a church, when they gave us the space, and then in the offices of the Radical Party until they were blown up. The lawyer Dr Pizarela defended the political prisoners and used to follow them around from prison to prison. My son Humerto Rubén was twenty-seven then and had never been involved in politics, but after his brother was taken he started to accompany Dr Pizarela and went with him to the prisons to visit the prisoners. The lawyer was always being threatened with death but he said he would never give it up because it was his mission and his country. After the coup the lawyer was kidnapped and his body appeared in another province. He had been mutilated, castrated and his mouth sewn up with wire. This was the punishment for lawyers who spoke out. After this, Humerto knew that something terrible might happen to him.

Graciela de Jeger: I am an exception amongst the *Madres de Plaza de Mayo* in the sense that I already had some political awareness. I was a primary school teacher and I was active in the union, and I also studied in the university, in the faculty of law. I knew what fascism meant. I am fifty and part of a generation which was born at the time of the Spanish Civil War. My family was Spanish and very Republican and I lived my youth through the events of World War II. Moreover my generation woke up with the Cuban Revolution which gave young people hope that things in Latin America could be different. All this was a part of my history that I couldn't avoid. But any experience I had wasn't to help me with what happened. What happened here was something completely different.

When the dictator Onganía took power in 1966 they began to close down the sugar mills in Tucumán. Many people were left on the street because although this is a very rich province – they call it the Garden of the Republic – where you can grow wheat, citrus fruits, grapes, most of the land has been converted into huge plantations for the cultivation of sugar cane. People depend on the work in the cane fields and in the big sugar mills, from the smaller producers who don't have enough land and who, when they finish harvesting their own crop, go to work for the big estates, to those who travel from the neighbouring provinces to cut the cane. The most important union in Tucumán is the *Federación Obrera Tucumana de la Industria Azucarera* which is the union for those who work in the sugar fields and factories. Here there was always a climate of combativeness, above all from the university which is the centre of cultural life in Tucumán and the focus of the big popular mobilizations against the military governments. The mass detentions had already begun under President Cámpora who appointed a police chief well-known for his repressive activities elsewhere. So we never had peace or public freedoms here.

Independently of this, a group from the People's Revolutionary Army [ERP] installed themselves in the zones where the factories had been closed down and where there was the most extreme misery. There was also a column of Montoneros, but fundamentally it was ERP. They had a plan similar to that of Che Guevara, to set up a *foco* in the mountainous jungle area to fight against the military. They say there were large numbers of them and that they were heavily armed but in truth it seems there were no more than about one hundred and fifty. This *foco* was very well known to the police who walked past them in the street because the order was not to intervene, to leave open the way for the army. After the death of Perón, when Isabel Perón declared the State of Siege and the death squads of the Triple A began operating throughout the country, here in Tucumán we got the *Comando Nacionalista del Norte*, a para-military group of military and police who began to intensify the terror by planting bombs in the universities, in the homes of the lawyers of political prisoners.

The *Operativo Independencia* [Operation Independence] began in February 1975 with the arrival of about 5,000 troops in Tucumán, theoretically to destroy the *foco* in the mountains. The soldiers were brought from Salta, Jujuy and Formosa because they didn't want to use the men from around here. The guerrillas were exterminated. Many died in battle and others were taken prisoner and shot. The people who lived near the area of the operation were the ones who suffered most. Everybody who lived there was considered to be suspicious. The army searched their houses, took them prisoner and forced many of them to act as their guides. The peasants used to leave out tributes to the army at night, a chicken or a cake, so that their houses wouldn't be completely destroyed. There is testimony from an ex-police officer from Famaillá who said that the area was bombed with napalm. Before bombing they removed the peasants to a series of little villages they had built, the sort they like, a lot of little houses all white, all the same. They put them there, a long way from their natural environment and means of livelihood, and closed off all contact with the outside world. They employed the methods used in Vietnam, to eradicate the rebellious population and leave the guerrillas without support.

The operation began on 9 February 1975. At that time I remember I was taking a summer holiday in the mountains and when I came back to the city I saw the army everywhere, roads cut off and sections of the city blacked out. Everything became militarized. A man couldn't wear his hair below his collar without being taken off to the police station to have it cut. If you had to stop your car at the traffic lights or somewhere you had to keep the window down and the light on inside so they could see who you were. People who lived near the main cemetery said that lorries used to come at night full of bodies. We thought these were exaggerations but we also knew there were times when they closed off the cemetery. I remember once, on the anniversary of the death of one of our relatives I was turned back with my bunch of flowers.

There were *operativos rastrillos* [raking operations] when the army arrived, generally at midday when the family was eating or Saturday or Sunday in the evening, closed off the zone and began a 'weeding out' operation, searching houses, asking for documents. It was done more or less in a correct way, but at night-time the bands of masked kidnappers used to operate.

In the time of Lanusse [General Lanusse, President from 1971 to 1973] a committee of families had already been formed to support the political prisoners. I began to work with them, knitting sweaters for the prisoners, collecting money and visiting them. With the *Comando Nacionalista del Norte* there were already kidnappings, but followed by murders where the bodies appeared. Every day bodies used to appear around the city. They also set off bombs. They blew up the office where the families of the political prisoners used to meet and one night they came to my house and on finding it empty they blew that up as well. Already by 1975 we were beginning to hear of cases of people disappearing but we never believed these stories. We thought they hadn't managed to get their lists up to date, we didn't believe that such a dreadful thing could be happening. We didn't know about Famaillá [the first secret detention centre].

At the end of September 1975 the commander of the operations, General Vilas, declared that the guerrillas were destroyed, left Tucumán and was replaced by General Bussi. The guerrillas were destroyed but the repression intensified. They had never been worried by what they called the crazy boys who ran around with a gun in their hand and Che Guevara's book under their arm. That was a game for them.

Once, many years later, I was obliged to go on an outing to the mountains with my schoolchildren to visit an army exhibition where they displayed the 'sophisticated' weapons captured from the guerrillas. In fact it was all very rudimentary, old rifles, grenades made from cans of tomato sauce, and the stripes on their uniforms had been painted on. What was important to them was the rest of society, the workers, the students, the intellectuals. It's not an accident that with the coup in 1976 almost all the militants in the sugar workers' union and the teachers' unions were killed or disappeared almost immediately.

My husband and I were separated but we maintained a very good relationship, above all for the children who he loved very much. He was a journalist and we had a bookshop that was a meeting place for many intellectuals in the city. He belonged to a small democratic progressive party, the equivalent of a European social-democratic party, but he was never a militant. He was a French Jew and used to work with a group in Buenos Aires which supported the victims of the Nazis. On 1 July 1975 a lawyer friend of ours was kidnapped. His dead body appeared the next day. We went to his funeral and they'd cut off the road and only let us through because we said we were family. That was the last time I saw my husband.

On the night of 4 November 1975 thirty men broke into my family's house, cut the telephone line and ordered us to turn off the lights. They blindfolded me with one of my own scarves, but they tied it only loosely so I could see everything. They took me to a place which I recognized as the police headquarters and put me in a room which in the day functioned as an office, but that night was empty. The furniture had gone. I saw the chief of police who was in combat gear with grenades hanging from his belt. Lots of people were coming in and out all night. Sitting next to me was a boy who couldn't have been more than fifteen years old and he was crying desperately. From another room I could hear someone crying out in pain, who they were obviously torturing with electricity because afterwards they took him out and he asked for water and they said, 'not yet'[1].

They interrogated me but it was something completely surreal. They were asking about people I didn't know, about my studies, about what I had read. The chief of police spoke to me in French. Then they took me to another office. They evidently didn't know what to do with me. I recognized a young student from La Rioja who was studying here whose face was completely destroyed and covered in blood. He was carried in by two men. I could see everything. It was clear that this wasn't very important to them. They then took me to another interrogation room. They never used electricity but they hit me and knocked me around.

When I returned to the room it was dawn and they were beginning to bring back the tables and chairs to return it to its original state. They took me outside and put me inside a car and I heard one of the policemen say, 'This one wouldn't hurt a fly but she's in the ideology and they're the worst.' They put me in the back of the car and the driver said, 'To Cadillal chief?' and he said, 'No. Before.' They left me in a deserted place and told me to count to one hundred before I took off the blindfold. Cadillal is the big artificial lake which supplies the city with water.

Carmen de Guede: We used to live in a beautiful house in the country, the old-fashioned kind with a long gallery and all the rooms going off from this. It was on a hillside on the edge of the Andes and down below there was a river. The garden was always full of flowers, trees and vegetables and we had many animals, cats and dogs and chickens and lambs. It was in an area of apple orchards, an area with few inhabitants. I didn't know my father very well because I was only eight when he died.

My family couldn't afford to send me to secondary school. I was twelve years old and I had to work. I studied too, but not the kind of things that women can study now because before careers were only for men. I learnt how to make clothes, to cook, knit, make toys, everything they thought a woman would need. I wanted to have a career but I couldn't because my mother was a widow and had little money and there were a lot of us. It wasn't possible. The only way we managed was because we all worked. My mother too, she used to work at home.

I worked in a sweet factory. People in the interior of the country aren't like people here in Buenos Aires where the young girls go out a lot. We stayed at home most of the time and anyway we worked from Monday to Saturday so we only had Sunday free. We were a lot of girls in the house. We never talked about politics or anything like that. We knew about Evita and we thought she was good. She did a lot of good things for women. We were living in the city at the time of the coup in 1955. We heard that they had bombed Plaza de Mayo to get Perón out.[2] We heard about the atrocities that were happening in Buenos Aires because I had a sister there. She had a child in hospital with polio – there was an epidemic of polio in Argentina and her child was in the Children's Hospital – and she said they bombed the hospital and the roof fell in. Some people said Perón was good and some people said he was bad but I didn't understand any of this and it never worried me. They got him out with a military coup but Perón was a military officer too, with the difference that he was elected by the people. But they were all the same to me.

I met my husband when he came to Mendoza for a holiday. He came back the next year and we got married. Afterwards we went to live in Buenos Aires. We went to live in an area which is nice now but before there were only two or three houses and people were buying pieces of land and building their houses. I used to feel very alone when my husband was out working all day. I never went out to work, I was never anything more than a housewife and a mother. Sometimes he was away for three or four days because he worked in a naval yard and if there was a damaged boat he had to stay there until the boat was repaired. So I stayed at home alone and I used to feel sad because I was used to a big family, with lots of people around. After I had my first child I was better and occasionally I would go to see my family in Mendoza. Most of the time I stayed at home. Sometimes friends of my husband from work would come and talk about political things but I never got involved.

I remember when Perón returned in 1973, my husband went to Ezeiza. He wasn't a Peronist but everyone went to see his plane come in. He spent the whole night there. When I heard on the radio about the massacre, that hundreds of people had been shot, I was very worried.[3] The next day he returned. I don't know how he managed to escape unhurt. I asked him, 'But why did you go?' and he said, 'If everyone thought like you nobody would ever leave the house. If there was another coup what would you expect us all to do, hide under the bed?' So as I didn't understand anything and didn't try to understand, when they disappeared I had to learn a lot of things very quickly.

It was the same with the coup in 1976. My husband said to me, 'Do you know what's going to happen now?' and I said 'Nothing's going to happen, the military have taken power so many times before,' and he said, 'But this is going to be terrible,' and my son said the same, that we were going to see a lot of hunger and a lot of suffering. When Videla took power I remember I was in the garage and my husband said to some of his clients, 'Now we're going to have to tighten our belts more than with Frondizi,' and after a while the persecution began and many of his friends began to disappear or to escape from the country. I don't know how they knew what was going to happen.

There were some disappearances before, under the government of Isabel, but I didn't know about this. My son used to say to me, 'But you should know what's happening in this country,' and I said, 'Yes, but how am I going to find out if nobody tells me?' He said I had to read, to open my eyes. I used to wait up for him when he came home at night from secondary school to cook his dinner and he used to tell me what was happening, that they were killing people, throwing people out of work and closing the factories. He used to tell me about the people from the *villas*. He used to go there and take them clothes and help them learn to read. Once he asked me to go with him but I never went. I used to make clothes at home and sometimes he took them to the people in the *villas*. Sometimes he brought people from the *villas* home, children of his own age. They were very nice children. They used to read and study together or listen to music. He was a very good person, very generous and he never saw any bad in anyone.

My son worked to be able to study in the engineering faculty. He worked in an optician's from six in the morning until two, then he came home to eat something and then, if he had a class, he would go to the university and when he got back he went to work with his father in the garage. It was incredible all the things he used to do. Apart from this he used to sing with a group on Saturdays and Sundays.

At the time he was studying there were many problems in the university between the students and the police. They were fighting the closure of the student refectories. Students who came from a long way away had to spend the whole day in La Plata without eating. They wanted to improve other things in the university too, like the courses, and to have more facilities in the college. He said that teachers who were good with the students were being forced out of their jobs and those who weren't stayed on, so the students got angry because they didn't want to study with those teachers.

My husband worked for the union where he was employed. At that time there were still some state workers who weren't unionized and he helped set one up. He believed that the national union leaders did nothing for the working class. They were always making deals while the wages of the workers got worse and worse. The wages were very low and they were sacking a lot of people and nobody did anything. Now I can understand what they were both trying to do, but I wish I could have understood it when they were here.

Elsa de Becerra: My husband and I were both teachers and we tried to bring up our children with some awareness of the society they lived in and with the social concern which we both shared. There was one year between each of them, Elsita the oldest, then Jorge, Violeta and Ana María. Elsita studied in the Faculty of Agricultural Sciences, here in Mendoza, Jorge studied for a doctorate in Natural Sciences in La Plata, Violeta studied in the Faculty of Arts in La Plata, specializing in cinema, and in 1976 Ana María was still at secondary school. We did the best we could to prepare the children for their future, to let them follow their vocations. Teachers are paid very low salaries in this country – to bring up four children and send them all to college is difficult and expensive. So my husband and myself in some way lived for this, for our children and for our responsibilities as parents. We were a close family. The children helped in the house and we tried to help support their studies and as far as they could they tried to support themselves. Elsita got some teaching work in the university and Jorge sold flowers and did odd jobs. We consider this to be important experience too.

With the military coup of 1955 we became aware of what the military were capable of, when they dropped the bombs on Buenos Aires and killed many people. After the coup in 1966 things got much worse. They stormed the university in Buenos Aires,[4] closed down factories, cut wages and began detaining people. Even then there were some cases of people disappearing. In 1968 or '69 two dentists from the neighbouring province of San Juan were detained by federal forces, their two children were taken to the grandparents and from then on nothing more was heard of them. Now, with the passing of time, we think these were trial runs to see what the public reaction would be like. People didn't notice because they were too involved in their own problems, the very low salaries, the unemployment, each fighting in their own little worlds. I had my world too, the house and the job, but I could see what was happening because I also worked in the teachers' union. I remember very clearly the *Cordobazo* in 1969 and then in 1972 the *Mendozazo* when Mendoza exploded as people went out to the streets to protest about the increases in electricity charges and low wages. The economic situation was very serious and people were fighting for their survival. The troops were sent in and there was a lot of violence.

We suffered the consequences of Isabel's government at close hand. We had a relative who was the administrative secretary of the University of La Plata, thirty-five and married with two very young children, who was being permanently threatened because he was against injustice. He denounced the way the *golpistas* [see Glossary] in the military were getting more power and he denounced the sinister people who were running the country, like López Rega[5] and the Triple A. One morning as he left his house for the university he was kidnapped and his body appeared at midday on a bridge in Buenos Aires with sixty bullets inside. So we knew from close hand what they were capable of.

And the children told us about the persecution in the universities. It was the same in all their different colleges. They were restricted in expression, they began to notice that friends didn't come and when they asked for them they were told they had been detained. So what do you do, in this narrow little world you live in? You ask your children not to get involved in anything, to avoid anything which could be dangerous. Perhaps if we'd supported the children in what they were doing none of it would ever have happened.

At the time of the coup in 1976 Jorge and Violeta were studying in La Plata. Jorge had lost practically a year through all the problems and he decided to return to Mendoza because he felt he was wasting his time at college. He came here with his wife who was pregnant and began to work, waiting for things to settle down in the university. Elsita worked with the students' union. She didn't have any political affiliation or belong to any political party but she was very concerned about the terrible social problems in the country. She was active in the students' centre where they met to discuss the problems in the university. Each course sent a representative to the centre and from these delegates they appointed advisers to sit on the advisory board which governs the university. They were involved in a protest against the high price of transport to the college which was a long way from the city centre. She was one of the main activists. This was one of the reasons they took her.

Dora de Bazze: I only had a primary school education because we were very poor and I had to go out to work to help support the family. My mother believed that a woman had to serve a man and the family so she taught me to cook and sew and knit to prepare me for that kind of life. I believed this too. I didn't know at this time that there could be any alternative. I wanted to study but we didn't have the money so I couldn't. I got married in 1953 when I was twenty-two and he was twenty-three and we started a little business, selling things.

We lived in Patagonia then, in the south. I didn't know about anything really. I never read the newspapers and there was no television then so I only listened to the radio. I wanted my children to read and study, probably because I'd never had the opportunity. When Hugo was ten and my daughter was just six I used to take them to a library in the town where we lived in the south. After school we used to go to the library together and when he was twelve my son started trying to teach me things. He told me that things weren't like I said, that people weren't free in Argentina and that when he was older he would study all this. My son opened my eyes because I'd never really thought about this. The coups never seemed to affect me. If you don't go out to the streets you don't see anything.

Hugo was very adventurous. He used to travel all over the country and everywhere he went he would send me a postcard. I kept them all. When he was fifteen he went to Europe. He got his father's permission to travel abroad and went off to Spain, France and England. He was mad about the Beatles. He had all their records and he wanted to go to their recording studio. He sent me a photograph of him with John Lennon. I don't know how he managed that. He sent me a telegram from London on my birthday and afterwards he told me that he'd used his last money to pay for it. He said he was sitting in a square near the recording studio on Christmas Day and he had nothing to eat and an English man walked by and gave him an apple and then someone else came and gave him some biscuits.

He was able to go because my husband got two free air tickets every year. Afterwards my son encouraged me to use the tickets because he said it was stupid not to use them and he didn't like to see me at home all the time. We'd never used them before because my husband didn't want to go abroad and I'd never thought of going away without him. I'd never been anywhere but I decided to take my daughter to Europe and we went everywhere, to Spain, France. Hugo arranged all the passports and took us to the airport. We didn't know anyone in Europe but we went everywhere and we managed perfectly well.

I remember I used to really enjoy smoking but I always smoked in secret because my husband didn't agree with women smoking. It was my son who taught me to stand up for myself. He said, 'You're an adult. If you want to smoke nobody can stop you.' For my birthday he bought me a small lighter and from then on I smoked in front of my husband. After that even my husband bought me cigarettes sometimes.

Hugo went to La Plata to study medicine in 1971 and got married and had a child. I felt bad being so far away from him so we decided to leave the south to be near him. Soon afterwards my daughter started at medical school as well. Hugo became involved in politics in the university. He didn't agree with the things the government was doing. He used to come and tell me about the people living in the *villas*. Student doctors then used to go and take medicines and treat all the people who didn't have the money to pay for prescriptions. I used to make up sheets and clothes and give him rice and pasta to take to the people who didn't have enough to eat. I suppose unconsciously I was collaborating with him, but I did it because he was my son, not because I understood what was happening in Argentina.

Hebe de Bonafini: I was brought up in front of the factory where my father worked, in a neighbourhood where the streets were made of earth and all the houses built of corrugated iron. At the back of my parents' house and at the front of the house where my children were born is the river, a part of the river where the sandboats used to dock. It was in this neighbourhood, with the club at the corner of our street, very near the YPF factory (the state-owned oil industry] that I grew up and my children were born. It was a very calm neighbourhood life where all week I would dedicate myself to the house and the children and on Saturdays and Sundays, if there was anything going on at the club, we would go there, to a bowls or a basketball competition or else to a dinner to celebrate something, or for a picnic. Sometimes at the weekends we used to drive out in the little old van we had to a nearby beach. These were our amusements. It was a completely quiet kind of life, without too many ups and downs and it was a life of hard work.

My mother and father were very hardworking and they taught me to do everything. I always enjoyed doing everything. I always used to say that if other people can do it, why shouldn't I be able to? So I would try to do everything everyone else did. When my son was about to be born I put in some windows in the hallway so the cold wouldn't come into the rooms. My husband had a small mechanics workshop and I used to help him clean the carburettors and adjust the valves at a time when women didn't do those kinds of things. But I said why should we pay someone when you can teach me and I can do it?

I only went to primary school. I liked school very much but we were very poor and the neighbourhood was very small, even today there's no secondary school, and to get to the nearest one you had to go by tram and there was no money to pay two fares. In those times if they had to choose between the boy and the girl studying, they chose the boy. The boy was always given the chance because they said a boy needs a career. So I had to stay at home and my brother was sent to school. In the end he gave it up anyway because he didn't like studying.

I always liked reading. I didn't have the money to buy books but I used to read the ones in the club library, but it was just a local club library which didn't have many books that you could learn from, just general knowledge books and short novels, nothing formative. It's only now, many years later that I realize this. At the time I didn't realize. We couldn't afford newspapers but I had an aunt who lived in Buenos Aires and who was better off than us and when she came to visit she always brought me the supplement from the newspaper. On Saturdays and Sundays *La Prensa* brought out this cultural supplement which at that time, I can still remember it, was in sepia. I was mad about them and used to collect them all in a folder.

I didn't have much awareness about what was happening around me because of this, because I didn't have access to information. As time went by and my brother began to spend more time outside the house, he brought back the problems which existed in the real world outside. From inside our house it always seemed to me that the military coups were always to do with other people, not me. We lived near the Naval Hospital and the Marine Infantry so every time there was a coup we had to leave our home and stay with relatives because someone always came to tell us there were bombs in the refinery and that we had to evacuate the area. So all the people in this little neighbourhood, with the refinery on one side and the gas works on the other, had to leave because if there was an explosion we'd have all been killed.

We used to listen to the radio at home. There was no television then. It came to Argentina in 1950 and in 1954 the club got a television, so I used to go there to watch it for the three hours in between giving the baby the breast. Sometimes it was all advertisements but I loved it anyway. I was fascinated by the television. It was many years before we got one in our house.

The newspapers and television never gave out much information about what was happening. In our neighbourhood there were Conservatives and

Radicals, that was when I was young. Then there were Radicals and Peronists. After they got rid of Perón in 1955 they said the Peronist Party was illegal. These things, yes, I saw, but I saw them as things which happened to other people, not to me. As we were never involved in politics I saw them as things which happened to people who were political. Terrible, but that's how it was. It never seemed to make any difference to us who was in power. As we were always poor, we always had to work a lot. My father in the factory, my husband in YPF and I used to make ponchos or knit or make up school uniforms. It didn't pay anything but I always had to work. For us it was work, work, work. But we were never unhappy working. We were so downtrodden that we worked happily. Very sad, but that's how it was.

When my sons were older we moved to the city. My youngest son Raúl started secondary school and one day he came home and said (because at this time we were a bit better off and we could afford newspapers), 'How do you read the newspaper?' I said, 'I read the deaths, the crimes and the jokes.' 'You're doing it wrong. First you should read national politics, then international politics, and then, if you've got any time left, the rest.' I said, 'Who told you this?' 'My teacher showed us today.' He was twelve years old then, a skinny little thing. So every day when he came home from school we used to read the paper together. It was him who taught me to read the newspaper.

My eldest son, Jorge, was the same. He was very concerned that I should read other things. He said I had the capacity and he used to bring me books, books of poetry, like Neruda, sometimes very ambitious books. For someone like me, who hadn't read anything, they were very hard to understand. I realized then that there had to be stages in reading and that you can't go from nothing to Neruda. I remember Jorge's girlfriend gave me *Demian* by Hermann Hesse as a present and I didn't understand anything so they explained it to me. I was always interested in learning.

I remember I wanted to get my secondary education when the children started secondary school but my husband didn't want me to. He was very *machista* and old-fashioned in his ideas and he said, 'How can you go to secondary school when you're thirty-seven years old?'

I noticed things getting worse in about 1975. In 1975 there was a big massacre in La Plata. In 1975 they killed one of my cousins and two students who were with him. Things got worse and worse. My sons used to come and tell me what was happening. It worried me, but in a way, let's say an egotistical way, because it worried me in the sense of what might happen to my children. It really began to hit me when they took two friends of theirs, but at the beginning when they told me they were taking students, due to my lack of consciousness, because of this deficiency in my development, I was worried for my own children, not as I should have been, for all our children. All I knew then was I didn't want it to happen to them.

Elisa de Landin: My father was an engineer and my mother a teacher. When I was seventeen I received my teaching qualification and to please my father, who came from a German family, I began to study German. I studied it for three years but the only thing I can remember now are the little songs the teacher used to sing at the beginning of the class. But this was the time of Perón when people were out in the streets fighting. I was conscious of this, but in my house they stopped me getting involved because they thought that a girl shouldn't be doing that kind of thing. How could a woman run in the streets with the mounted police hitting you across the back? At this time I was young and interested but after I got married I closed myself off. The rest of the world wasn't important to me.

We were so accustomed to coups we got used to having one president when we went to sleep and another one when we woke up in the morning. As there never seemed to be bloodshed we didn't worry, thinking this one might be better than the last one. Anyway I was a mother of five children, four sons and one daughter, and I had them all between 1950 and 1955 and with my work in the school, helping my husband in the shop and my work in the house I didn't have the time to think about politics. The rest of the world didn't interest me. We left all this for the young people. But now I think I was too wrapped up in my own affairs.

Martín was a law student and a political militant. When he was fifteen he joined a church youth group in our local parish and later he got more involved in political work. He joined the *Juventud Peronista* [Peronist Youth]. Horacio was a factory delegate from the age of twenty-one. At first he studied business but he left because he said he couldn't stand being stuck inside an office. He used to fight for better conditions in the factory, he was one of those delegates who didn't sell out. In 1975, when the Triple A already existed, they used to talk about the kidnappings and the torture. We didn't know anything about this because there was never much information. The young people, yes, they knew, but when they told me I couldn't understand it. You think that because they oppose the government they see everything as wrong, in spite of the fact that they were right about everything. When Martín told me they were torturing people I didn't believe him. I said to myself, 'This boy's mind's in the clouds, how can they be torturing people?' And when they started closing down the factories Martín told me that they would replace everything with imported products and it was true. Later we saw it, the *plata dulce* [see Glossary] – people without work, and even people with work who had to leave their homes because overnight the rents would double. Everybody bought from the USA and Brazil and all the factories here collapsed. And anyone who asked for a penny to support their families was a subversive.

It began with the government of Isabel, she was so inept, that woman. I always say that Perón left us with all his rubbish. We were never Peronists in our house and yet Martín turned out a Peronist. Every time I go to vote I say, 'Forgive me, Martín . . . but I can't.'

I always say that I didn't give birth to my children, they gave birth to me because it was Martín who really taught me to love people. In spite of the fact that I was a teacher and I loved my pupils, I wasn't really concerned about other people.

My husband had a chemist's near a *villa miseria* and all my children helped in the shop, but the only one who was concerned with how other people were living was Martín, the youngest. He used to say that it wasn't right that he shared a bedroom only with his brother when in the *villa* seven people slept, ate, washed and did everything in one room. He used to go on his bicycle and take medicines into the *villa*. I used to say, 'Where's all this social concern going to get you?' and he said that I was privileged because I had education, and these people came from the north with nothing and that before they'd been living without water and light, but that now they'd got electricity and water. He said you have to teach these people to defend themselves. When someone lost their job he used to write letters for them because many didn't know how to read and write. They rented a plot in the *villa* and they built a centre with three rooms and doctors from the hospital used to go and work as volunteers. As we had a chemist shop two streets away my husband complained that he was taking all his customers away, but it wasn't like this. When you go to the doctor's, they prescribe you four or five medicines, they don't consider your financial situation, and so the people from the *villas* used to come and ask which was the most important, because they didn't have the money for all of them. So the doctors who used to go to the centre would collect the prescriptions and take them to the public hospitals and bring the medicines from there.

I didn't have any consciousness about this. My father was an engineer, my mother a teacher and we always worked hard. There were no fortunes but as we all worked we didn't have to ask anyone for anything. I used to say that the people in the *villas* were all waiting to be given everything free. This was my consciousness . . . so terrible. Now I'm proud of what they did. My only regret is that we didn't understand them before. In that last year I was with Martín I learnt a lot of things from him.

At the time of the coup Martín was doing military service in the communications section of Campo de Mayo and one day he came home and said, 'I'm going to desert from the army.' I was horrified. I asked him why and he said, 'Because if I don't I'm going to disappear like the others.' One hundred and fifty conscripts had already disappeared and he said these people knew him well, they knew his name, address. I said, 'For God's sake, for the sake of your family, you can't do this,' and he said, 'Do you want them to kill me?' So he deserted and went into hiding. We used to talk by telephone and sometimes he would come to the house. They broke into my house five times looking for him and the sixth time they took us. But luckily they never found Martín there. They got him all the same though.

Notes

1. One of the after-effects of torture by electric shock is intense thirst. If water is drunk immediately, however, it can result in death.

2. The coup which swept Perón from power in September 1955 was preceded by a 'trial run' in June in which the air force bombed Government House, killing over 1,000 people.

3. As 3 million people gathered at Ezeiza airport to welcome Perón back from exile, an estimated 100 were killed after a column of Montoneros was fired on by the official platform marking the beginning of an intense campaign against the left by the right of Peronism.

4. On what came to be known as the 'Night of the Long Sticks' mounted police entered the University of Buenos Aires to remove students and staff protesting about the Onganía regime's new law which withdrew the right of students to participate in the government of the university.

5. José López Rega, the Minister for Social Welfare in Isabel's government, led the government offensive against the left of Peronism. He was one of the founders of the Triple A which he co-ordinated from his Ministry and which was responsible for a large proportion of some 1,500 assassinations which occurred in the 18-month period following Perón's death.

3. Las Locas de Plaza de Mayo (The Madwomen of Plaza de Mayo)

When Jorge disappeared my first reaction was to rush out desperately to look for him. I didn't cry. I didn't tear out my hair. Nothing mattered any more except that I should find him, that I should go everywhere, at any time, day or night. I didn't want to read anything about what was happening, just search, search. Then I realized we had to look for all of them and that we had to be together because together we were stronger. We had no previous political experience. We had no contacts. We knew no one. We made mistakes at first, but we learnt quickly. Every door slammed in our faces made us stop and think, made us stronger. We learnt quickly and we never gave up. Everything they said we shouldn't do, that we weren't able to do, we proved we could do.

Hebe de Bonafini

Becoming Visible

The decision to install a permanent weekly presence in Plaza de Mayo was an act of desperation rather than one of calculated political resistance. It was a sense of desperation which the women believed only other mothers who had lost their children would share.

Several other human rights groups in Argentina were already assisting relatives with the search for people who had disappeared and the Centre for Legal and Social Studies (CELS) was created to document and process legal cases involving disappearances and those arrested for political reasons. Of those already in existence just one was composed of people directly affected by the disappearances and this had been set up by the Argentine League for the Rights of Man which was legalistic in its approach to the problem: the Families of Desaparecidos and Political Prisoners recommended patience and moderation and discouraged illegal forms of protest. Under a law passed on 26 June 1976 the penalties for 'illicit association' had been increased from 3–8 years to 5–12 years, rising to 25 years for the leaders and organizers.

The Mothers, however, who had no legal or political expertise, recognized that their only weapon was direct action. They were committed to their illegal meetings in the square. Only by demonstrating their collective strength would they have any chance of breaking through the wall of silence erected by the authorities and challenging the appearance of normality conveyed in the media. With all means of communication responding totally to the interests of the government, and the police and security forces on the streets to enforce the ban on public meetings, the Mothers had to find ways of reaching other women in the same situation and of informing the wider public of their plight.

Dora de Bazze: Our first problem was how we were going to organize meetings if we didn't know each other. There were so many police and security men everywhere that you never knew who was standing next to you. It was very dangerous. So we carried different things so we could identify each other. For example one would hold a twig in her hand, one might carry a small purse instead of a handbag, one would pin a leaf to her lapel, anything to let us know this was a Mother. We used to go to the square and sit on the benches with our knitting or stroll about, whispering messages to each other and trying to discuss what else we could do.

Sometimes we met in churches. Most of us were very religious. At that time I was a believer too, so we went to the churches to pray together, 'Our Father . . .' and at the same time we would be passing round tiny pieces of folded paper, like when you're in school, cheating in a test. Then we hid them in the hems of our skirts in case we were searched later. Only the smallest churches, a long way out, lost in the middle of nowhere, would let us in. The rest closed their doors when they found out we were Mothers.

We tried to produce leaflets as well – we had to do it secretly because it was illegal of course – and little stickers saying the Mothers will be in such and such a place on such and such a day and '*¿Dónde están nuestros hijos desaparecidos?*' [Where are our disappeared children?] or '*Los militares se han llevado nuestros hijos*' [The military have taken our children]. We went out at night to stick them on the buses and underground trains. And we wrote messages on peso notes so that as many people as possible would see them. This was the only way we could let people know that our children had been taken, and what the military government was doing, because when you told them they always said, 'They must have done something.' There was nothing in the newspapers; if a journalist reported us, he disappeared; the television and radio were completely under military control, so people weren't conscious. In the beginning we had no support at all.

María del Rosario: At first we didn't march together in the square. We sat on the benches with our knitting or stood in small groups, trying to disguise the letters we were signing to send to the churches, to government officials, the military. We had to speak to each other quickly, in low voices so it didn't look as if we were having a meeting. Then, when the police saw what was happening and began pointing their rifles at us and telling us to move on, that we had to disperse, that we couldn't be more than two together, we began to walk in twos around the edge of the square. Two in front, two behind, because we had to keep moving but we also had to be able to speak to each other, to talk about what we were going to do next. Every time it got more difficult to communicate with each other because every week there were more police. Sometimes we met in parks as if we were having an office party and there were a few, very few, priests who let us meet in their churches occasionally and some of the press agencies helped us. France Press lent us their offices sometimes.

At first we walked around the outside of the square but because there were so few of us we were hardly noticed and we had to make sure the public knew we existed. We wanted people to see us, to know we were there, so we began to walk in the centre of the square, around the monument. Even if people supported us they stayed outside the square. It was very dangerous for them to approach us. We were very alone in the beginning.

Aída de Suárez: The headscarves grew out of an idea of our dear Azucena. It was at the time when thousands of people walked to Luján on the annual pilgrimage to pay homage to the Virgin. We decided to join the march in 1977 because many of us were religious and also because we thought it would be a chance for us to talk to each other and organize things. But as some of the Mothers were elderly and wouldn't be able to walk, and we would all be coming from different places, we thought, how will we be able to identify each other amongst all those people, because many thousands go, and how can we make other people notice us? Azucena's idea was to wear as a headscarf one of our children's nappies, because every mother keeps something like this, which belonged to your child as a baby. It was very easy to spot the headscarves in the crowds and people came up to us and asked us who we were. We'd managed to attract attention so we decided to use the scarves at other meetings and then every time we went to Plaza de Mayo together. We all made proper white scarves and we embroidered on the names of our children. Afterwards we put on them '*Aparición con Vida*' [literally 'Reappearance with life'] because we were no longer searching for just one child but for all the disappeared.

We used to go to the military regiments together to look for other women like us. The only way we could communicate was by word of mouth and we had to find a way to find other women, not just in Buenos Aires but women from all over the country. The press was silent. The only one which ever wrote anything about us was the English one, the [*Buenos Aires*] *Herald*. I went to ask for information at the *Herald*'s offices many times. It was very dangerous for journalists to show any interest in us.

A Woman's Place . . .

The structure of the family of a disappeared person was profoundly damaged by the experience. Many women had to concern themselves with the security and safety of other children and in some cases had to take on the responsibility for grandchildren. For some it meant assuming the role of head of the household at a time when the military's economic policies were causing severe hardship, particularly for the working class. In the midst of an acute inflationary spiral the government had announced a wage freeze and by the end of 1976 real wages stood at 50% of the pre-coup level.[1] The consumption of food is estimated to have dropped 40% after one year of military rule and as free hospitals were closed down the infant mortality rate in some parts of Buenos Aires reached 30%.[2] Cuts in government spending transferred much of the burden of social welfare back on the family. Amongst the working class, women's paid work became all the more crucial to the survival of the family at the same time as industrial unemployment was beginning to rise and the military and the church combined ideological forces to drive women back into their traditional place in the home. Those mothers who now believed their place was on the streets fighting for their children found themselves confronted by the obstacles which have traditionally restricted women to the home.

The Struggle for Subsistence

Aída de Suárez: When my son disappeared, my daughter was still studying and my youngest was still at primary school and we had no income. I felt desperate. I had to sell the few things of value we had left in the house. My first thought was to get money so I could go to all the places I needed to go to look for my son. It was the only thing we were all concerned about. Later one of my married daughters came to live with us to help with our expenses and my eldest son helped too. My family was always very united. I continued working as I'd always done, as I'd done as a single woman to help my parents, knitting and sewing at home. All that worried me was that I had enough to search for my son. All the Mothers felt the same. If we had a ring, we would sell it. Mothers came to Buenos Aires from all over the country because this is where the government is and this is where Plaza de Mayo is. Whatever way you could, you came here. We knew women who walked miles from the suburbs to be at the square on Thursdays.

Carmen de Guede: When my husband and son were taken the Mothers weren't yet organized and even when they were, I wasn't able to spend much time with them because I had been left with nothing. The military had stolen everything except the house itself and I was alone with two children, one fourteen years old and the other five. My husband had been sacked for not turning up for work, even though I took all the papers to show he had disappeared. We weren't entitled to any money from the state. To get anything from the state you had to register them as dead, but I wouldn't do that because I didn't know. My husband and his brothers had a business together, a shop which sold household goods, and when my husband died they were left with everything. They didn't help with my finances at all, even though they knew I was alone with my children and that a part of the business belonged to us. They have never helped, until now.

I had to go out to work. I'd never been anything more than a housewife looking after the children but then I had to work. I made some clothes for a shop in my neighbourhood. I worked from home for two years. We also made cardboard boxes, the children and I. Later I went out to work as an office cleaner. The pay was miserable. We only managed because my daughter, who was fourteen and in her third year of secondary school, left her studies and went out to work. At first she worked with me, knitting and sewing, and then she went out to work in a shoe factory. She was exploited in this factory. They made her work from six in the morning until six in the evening without a break. She used to take her food with her and eat while she was working. It was illegal for a minor to work such long hours. They paid her very little and deducted money which they said they were putting in a savings account for her and when I went to withdraw the money, after she left the job, the bank told me the money had never been deposited. They'd lied to her and we couldn't do anything about it.

When I began to look for work outside the home it was very hard because the government, or Martínez de Hoz, had closed a lot of factories and it was difficult to find work. For everyone, not just for me. But it was also difficult because I couldn't say I had a disappeared husband otherwise they wouldn't have given me a job. I had to say we were separated. All those lies we had to tell. My daughter had to lie too. If she went for a job and said her father had disappeared they wouldn't contact her again. The children had to suffer these kinds of attitudes from other people. She didn't trust anyone and she says how can she be friendly to people who turned their backs when her father disappeared?

I began to work with a group of families in the area where I live. We used to find out about women with the same problem as us and we went to their homes to speak to them. We would get a list of addresses from Mgr Novak, our priest, and on Saturdays and Sundays when I wasn't working I used to go with my children to visit these women, tell them what to do, go with them to the police stations or the Ministry of the Interior. Our priest was sympathetic. We used to meet once a week or fortnight in the church, in a room which Mgr Novak let us use, and there I met the *Madres de Plaza de Mayo*. I met Hebe and the other Mothers but I couldn't do very much with them because I was working all the time. It wasn't until 1979 that I could join them properly.

Margarita de Oro: We had serious economic problems. After thirty years of service they put my husband on the street. He was dismissed on 30 April 1976 because he was the union secretary. For them he wasn't a decent person any more. He worked in lots of different jobs for two or three months and when the authorities found out he was sacked. They said he was a subversive. We had no money coming in and we had our grandchild to look after as well. We only survived because our daughters paid our bills.

My grandson suffered a lot. Sometimes at night he woke up screaming and crying because he wanted his father and we didn't know what to do with him. Someone in Buenos Aires told me to tell him his father had gone away and I made the mistake of telling him this and one day he said to me,

'Grandma, if I haven't done anything wrong why doesn't my daddy call me?' So I had to tell him the truth, that his father had been kidnapped by the armed forces. He was always very close to his father. His mother had died when he was eight months old and the child stayed with me while my son studied in Córdoba, but they spoke to each other by phone every week. He wrote to Viola when he was President [from March to December 1981], a very pretty letter, a child's letter, which he wrote on Father's Day saying something like it made him want to cry because all his friends had fathers and he'd like to have his father with him and he asked please, could they give him back. He never got a reply. He wrote to Videla as well and to Mgr Calabrezzi in Buenos Aires. The bishop wrote back saying that it was a decision of God that his father had disappeared and that he should accept it as that. It's dreadful that he could have told a child such a terrible thing.

Because my son disappeared in Buenos Aires I went there to look for information. I went everywhere with my grandchild at my side. He was just three and a half then. I used to take a bag with food and things for him and we would arrive on the train from Mendoza and go to the army, and navy, the air force, police headquarters, places where you walked in between machine guns and everyone knew nothing. The boy had to suffer all this.

Prison Visits

Rita de Ponce: As well as searching for my son who had disappeared, every three months, or whenever I could, I used to visit my other son who was being held under PEN. At first we took out loans so I could go by plane but then we couldn't get any more credit so I had to go by bus. I had to travel eighteen hours to Buenos Aires and from there it was another twenty-seven hours on the bus to the prison at Rawson. There were many families who couldn't afford to visit their children but there was a lot of solidarity between the prisoners. One family would go and leave some money and they would put all the money in a 'bank' for those who needed something urgently. After the coup they stopped us taking them food and clothes.

I found it very difficult because I wasn't used to travelling. Before all this I'd hardly ever been outside my home. I remember it was very hard for me to go into a restaurant alone in the beginning. When I grew up it wasn't considered decent for a woman to go into a bar or a restaurant alone. I couldn't do it at first, I'd rather have starved, but then you realize you have to change.

The conditions in the prison were very bad. It's very hard to see your child living in conditions like that. Before the coup they could organize activities, they played chess and they started classes in history and philosophy and helped other prisoners with no education to learn how to read and write. After the coup things got much worse. The first thing they did was to take away the chess sets, so they used to make the chess pieces from the bread they were given in the morning and afterwards they played mentally, by memory. They took away their activities because they were trying to destroy their minds. After the coup some official prisoners disappeared, or they shot them saying they were trying to escape, like in Córdoba.[3] This was the worst worry we had.

My family was always very united. My husband always supported me. He always encouraged me to be with the Mothers and reminded me when it was time to go to a meeting. He had to help more in the house. Well, he helped with some things, not with the cooking or anything like that. When he died I had to take over the workshop, look after the family and find time to be with the Mothers. But being with the Mothers was always very important to me.

Dora de Bazze: Four months after my daughter and son-in-law were kidnapped their detention was legalized and they were transferred to Devoto.[4] On Mondays I went to Devoto to take food and clean clothes. Tuesday was the day when you had to take them money and I used to queue from three in the morning till three in the afternoon just to deposit money in the post office there. Visits were on Wednesdays. We were supposed to have twenty minutes with each prisoner but by the time they'd searched you there were only ten minutes left. You were strip-searched from head to toe every time, before and after each visit. They violated our human rights in a terrible way too. In Devoto they didn't let the women read magazines or books so they used to invent things to do, taking out threads from the sheets and using them to embroider. Once my daughter gave me something she had made and I tried to get it out and one of the *milicas* seized it and ripped it up and threw it on the floor.

After a month my son-in-law was transferred to the prison in Sierra Chica, five or six hundred kilometres from Buenos Aires. I managed to get a special authorization to see him because mothers-in-law couldn't visit, only the immediate family. So then I had to get the night train from Buenos Aires and at dawn I had to change and get the bus. It took two and a half days just to see him for half an hour and sometimes I arrived and they'd put him in the '*pozo*' [literally 'pit': punishment block], as they called it. They punished them for whatever stupid reason and then said, 'No visits today', so I had to go back again with all my bags. And the rest of the time I was fighting to find my son. A thousand things at once. I can describe it to you, but you have to live it to know what it's really like.

My husband used to help in the beginning. He used to support the Mothers and march with us. But then he did nothing. He never really understood our struggle. Now we don't speak to each other and when my daughter asks him why, he says it's because I only ever talk about human rights. She says that's because it's what I'm involved in. But now he believes I should be in the house all the time. I've always worked with him in the business but now he doesn't think I should do that any more either.

'Women are Stronger'
Hebe de Bonafini: You can't generalize about the attitude of the husbands. Some didn't want the women to leave the house unaccompanied because they were afraid they would be kidnapped too. Some men were very

supportive. My own husband used to look at me in amazement every Thursday and say, 'One more time? Don't you ever get tired of walking around that square?' Many women had to fight in secret from their husbands, especially in our society which is so *machista*. My mother tried to persuade me to stay at home as well. She believed my place was with the child I had, not the ones who were missing. She couldn't understand that we had to fight for all the children in Argentina. Of course we spent less time at home but it was still important to me that I should do the cooking and the housework myself, that I should still try to be the person I'd always been.

María del Rosario: The men had to change too. If we arrived late the men would be at home waiting, worried in case we'd been taken. Some men had to look after the house and children for the first time. I don't mean washing the clothes and ironing, we still had to do that, but the cooking and shopping. They changed a bit but this society is very *machista*. The man lives his life outside and the woman in the house. Most of the time we had to do both things, search for our children and look after the house.

Men helped with the logistical support. Some would watch us from the street corners to see if they took us prisoner, this kind of looking after us. But they didn't participate in the same way as us because they had to work. You have no idea of the weeks you spent at courts just to present a writ of habeas corpus. And because if the police insulted them, they would have hit back and they would have been taken. When *we* insulted them they thought, what can these old women do? They didn't understand how strong we were. But if a man insulted them, he disappeared – well, Mothers disappeared too. The kidnappings affected the men in a different way. Men think more before doing something. I think a mother doesn't think if her child is in danger. Many of the men stayed at home, believing they could do nothing. It seems that men have less resistance to all this. Women seem to be stronger.

Aída de Suárez: At this time it was very difficult for the men to participate. It was more dangerous for them because it was always the men they took first. Not that a father doesn't love his children as much but a woman is stronger. I think they're stronger for having suffered the pain of childbirth. This is the difference between mothers and fathers. If my husband had been alive it would have killed him to experience what happened. He used to say if one of us has to die he'd rather it was him because if he was left alone with the children he thought he wouldn't be able to manage. He couldn't manage when they were ill. If they had to have an injection he used to wait outside the room because he couldn't watch a doctor stick a needle in his child's arm. It upset him too much. He would have died of pain and anxiety if he'd had to experience this. I always knew I was strong. I'd spent many years living alone with the children and I'd always had to struggle.

Hebe de Bonafini: It wasn't less dangerous for women but perhaps a mother is prepared to take more risks. We had less fear. My husband was scared to death every time we went out. And women have more willpower. Men get tired quicker and give up. Men are perhaps more individualistic. When a woman gives birth to a child she gives life and at the same time, when they cut the cord, she gives freedom. We were fighting for life and for freedom. It was our insistence, our refusal to give up, which made us effective. Women, because we are stronger, and mothers, because we give life and we will defend life as many times as is necessary.

The Military Respond

After their success in stamping out all organized resistance of working-class and political organizations, the military dismissed as laughable the suggestion that a group of women could pose any threat to their position. In reality the sudden appearance of the Mothers in Plaza de Mayo had provoked serious difficulties in the seemingly impenetrable repressive apparatus of military rule. They had failed to anticipate that the trail of deceptions they had laid in government offices, police stations and military headquarters would be the setting for the first real challenge to their rule.

They were also surprised by the nature of the challenge. The military had acquired much of their moral authority by promoting themselves as the only ones capable of defending the values of Christianity and the family in the face of a threat from 'Marxist subversives'. They found themselves confronted by the very image which, in a vision they shared with the church, personified the stability and order of family life. They did not know how to react to the silent accusing presence of Mothers in the square and, in their underestimation of the strength and determination of the women, they fell victim to the misconceptions of their own *machismo*. They tried using force to break up the meetings, made arrests, issued threats, believing that this would be enough to frighten them off, but every week the Mothers came back in greater numbers. It was this temporary vacillation which gave the women the short breathing space they required to organize themselves.

Aída de Suárez: They started to call us *las locas* [the madwomen]. When the foreign embassies began to ask questions about the disappearances, because they didn't only take Argentines they took all nationalities, and the foreign journalists began to ask about us, they used to say 'Don't take any notice of those old women, they're all mad.' Of course they called us mad. How could the armed forces admit they were worried by a group of middle-aged women? And anyway we were mad. When everyone was terrorized we didn't stay at home crying – we went to the streets to confront them directly. We were mad but it was the only way to stay sane.

Marina de Curia: They didn't destroy us immediately because they thought we couldn't do anything and when they wanted to, it was too late. We were already organized. They thought these old women will be scared off by the arrests, that it would be enough. At first they tried to trick and deceive us, then to frighten us by taking us prisoner and then by threatening us with death. Once a man stopped my daughter in the street and told her he wanted to talk about me. He said, 'Tell your mother to stop bothering us. Tell her to stop seeing those old women or something serious will happen to her – we don't need to kill her or kidnap her.' At that time there were a lot of so-called 'car accidents'.

Another time I was giving out leaflets at the doors of the cathedral with the words of Pope Paul VI, something like 'If you want peace, defend life.' A young girl approached me and said, 'I've also got relatives who have disappeared.' She said she wanted to speak to me outside and stupidly I followed her. When we got outside I saw she was with three men and I thought, 'The police!' But I didn't want them to see I was afraid. I could see they were nervous and that in the street there were armoured cars, police on horses and men with dogs. 'I'm going no further.' They said, 'You have to come with us.' 'Why?' 'Because you're giving out leaflets.' 'Take them if that's what you want.' 'You still have to come with us.' At first I didn't resist because I think subconsciously I wanted to go with them. I wanted to see them face to face and tell them what I thought. But then of course I realized this was a bit romantic and that the last thing you should do is surrender yourself. Nobody knew I was there except one of my daughters who was standing at the door. One of them, who I later discovered was an ex-boxer, was holding my arm, but loosely because I'm just a little old woman, and I shouted, 'You're not going to detain me!' and I pulled away and ran inside the cathedral with the other Mothers.

I remember that night I didn't want to go home and I sent my daughters to stay with a friend and I went to my sister's house. Her husband didn't want me to sleep in their house because he thought it would endanger his family. I went to my sister-in-law's but she wasn't at home and in the end I knocked on the door of a Jewish friend of mine. I asked if I could stay because the police were looking for me. She let me in and said, 'We Jews understand what this means.' That's how she replied. She didn't ask for any explanation.

I knew I wasn't in any real danger that night. The military were just trying to frighten us. They'd never have given us a warning if they were really going to do something.

Dora de Bazze: I was detained many times, like a lot of the Mothers. Once they came and took eighty or a hundred women, herding us into a bus like sheep, pushing us and hitting us with their truncheons. In the police station we had to go in one at a time to speak to the chief. 'What were you doing in the square?' 'I'm looking for my son.' 'Sign here to say you won't go to the square on Thursdays again.' 'I'm not signing anything because I'm going to the square next Thursday. Put yourself in my place. If you lost a child, wouldn't you do the same?' 'You have to sign it anyway.' The next Thursday they took us again. It was like that. A psychological war. We were never afraid. On the contrary, we used to shout at them, 'Aren't you ashamed? Take off your uniforms you lousy vermin! Don't you realize the people don't want you military sons of bitches!'

I remember the first day we carried a banner. Nobody took banners to the square because it was very dangerous. One day I made a big one out of some material I had in the house and I painted on '*Dónde están los detenidos-desaparecidos?* [Where are the detained–disappeared people?] – *Madres de Plaza de Mayo*' and we put two broomsticks in the sides to hold it up. My daughter was terrified that day in case they took me. I rolled it up, wrapped it in brown paper as if it was something I'd just bought and took it on the underground. I had to be very careful because they watched all those places. I wasn't afraid at all. When I got to Plaza de Mayo I told the Mothers I had a banner to unroll. Everyone was happy – 'Let's open it!' There were a lot of *milicos* that day so I hid behind some other Mothers and opened it. There was a tourist bus passing and they were all looking, pointing their fingers at us. The *milicos* came and kicked us and one broke the stick and said, 'What are you going to do with it now?' I said, 'Stick it up your . . .' and we kicked them back. A journalist took a photo which came out in Holland, but it wasn't printed here. It was a tremendous thing. Thirty or forty Mothers shouting '*Dónde están nuestros hijos?*' and the *milicos* all lined up in front of us with truncheons and machine guns and behind them the tear gas trucks.

Secret Detention Centres

The Mothers had never questioned their belief that they would find their children. The dimensions of the horror were uncovered only gradually as some of the prisoners who were released from the secret camps came forward to tell of their experiences. The secret detention centres were the pivot of the Process of National Reorganization. Most were located within police and military premises under the direct jurisdiction of the armed and security forces and operated under orders from the highest military authorities, but their existence was consistently denied. On 22 December 1977 General Videla said, 'I categorically deny that there exist in Argentina any concentration camps or prisoners being held in military establishments beyond the time absolutely necessary for the investigation of a person captured in an operation before they are transferred to a penal establishment.'[5]

By refusing to acknowledge the existence of what was later established to be at least 340 illegal detention centres throughout the country they also denied the existence of their occupants, some 15,000, who are estimated to have passed through the camps in the first year of military rule.[6] Since these people officially did not exist they could be held without limit of time and with nothing to constrain the methods used against them.

Margarita de Oro: When I first met the Mothers we used to talk about how they were taken, when, what we could do to find them, where we could go.

This is what we talked about, never thinking that they'd been taken and would never return. I always believed they would come back. We all did. We all believed we would find them one day. We all thought that by going to the churches, the authorities, by going to the courts we would get them back in the end. We thought that there were so many prisoners they hadn't yet drawn up the proper lists. We heard rumours about camps but we didn't think it could be possible. I didn't know the word *desaparecido*. We always had the hope that tomorrow, or the day after, or in three weeks . . . the alternative was too terrible to think about.

María del Rosario: It's a very special state when a child is taken from you and you don't know what happened to that child. It's one thing to look after a sick child who you can give everything to. It's something you can understand, you can reason. It's sad but you can understand it. But this you can't understand. Where is he? Who's got him? Why did they take him? They didn't give us any explanation. We knew they were torturing and murdering people, we knew about the atrocities they were committing. We knew this because we got in contact with people who were freed from the camps and they told us. A few *desaparecidos* were released after two weeks or a month and when we heard about prisoners being freed we went to find them. Their families would try to hide them because prisoners were told not to speak. I had some neighbours and they took the father, a man of seventy, the son and a brother-in-law. The brother-in-law was thrown from a car, the father reappeared eight days later, his body covered in burns, but too frightened to go to the hospital and the son is a *desaparecido*. So he told me what he could remember and I told the other Mothers, but most of us couldn't find out anything about our own children. We used to go to the military headquarters taking food and clean clothes for them. How many mothers waited months leaving the light on at night in case they returned, how many mothers kept their child's favourite food ready, in case he came home, how many mothers continued buying them clothes for when they came back? It wasn't something you could understand. It was like a desperation that just grows and grows.

Dora de Bazze: If we heard that people were being detained in a place we used to go together to ask for our children. Once we went to Campo de Mayo because we were told they were holding prisoners there. We were so deluded that we believed they would say, yes, your child is here. I remember it very clearly because I was in the street waiting for a bus with two or three other Mothers and when the cars stopped at the traffic lights near the bus stop, I saw one which was exactly the same colour as my son's, the same model, everything. I said to one of the other Mothers, 'That's my son's car.' There were four men with huge machine guns inside and one of them must have heard what I said because he lifted the gun to the window and pointed it at me and put his hands over his mouth as if to say he would shoot me if I didn't shut up. The other Mothers stood there frozen.

When we got to the camp everything looked normal and the soldiers said, 'There's nothing here, we're not hiding anything. Come and have a look.' It didn't matter how much a mother knew her child was behind the door, you couldn't get inside. But I already knew about the camps from my daughter. She'd spent four months in Campo de Mayo and Vesubio. They released her saying they'd made a mistake but that we all have to suffer to make our country a better place. She's never told me very much but she said she saw young girls being raped and killed. She was always kept tied to her husband and they were tortured together. I knew exactly what they were capable of.

Elisa de Landin: My son disappeared after they had raided our house five times. It began in 1976 on 14 November after a bomb went off in the army communications centre in Campo de Mayo[7] and they came to my house searching for Martín. The last time they came was the night of 5 January when they took my husband and me to ESMA [the Navy Mechanics School]. They came at half past nine and waited for my husband to arrive. I was with my eighty-year-old mother. They left her alone, locked the door and gave the key to a neighbour. I didn't know this at the time. They blindfolded us and put us in different cars, my husband in one and me in another. I honestly didn't know what was going to happen to us.

It took about twenty-five minutes to arrive at this place. They took me up two floors in a lift and then up a spiral staircase made of wood and they made me take off my clothes and they laid me on a table or desk. I think it was on a door they'd put on a table because I could feel grooves and a desk doesn't have grooves like that. They tied my arms and legs to the corners, first with elastic and then with leather straps. I didn't know what they were going to do with me but afterwards I realized they'd already known exactly which of us they were going to torture. They'd put a black band made of elastic across my husband's eyes, but on me they'd used a piece of plaster which they'd taken from my home. They'd stuck it right across and under my eyes so that I wouldn't be able to see anything when I was lying down. They already knew it was me they were going to torture because otherwise they would have put plaster across his eyes.

They tied my husband to a post. I didn't see this but he told me afterwards. He said to them, 'Young man, this isn't the way to build a country', and they replied, 'We'll show you how a country is made.' But thank God they didn't touch him because he suffers from low blood pressure. In the pockets of his jacket he has a card which says 'Sufferer of low blood pressure. If I pass out do not give me medication.' So they must have seen this when they raided the house before and said to themselves, 'if we torture him he'll die'. So they tortured me.

They used the '*picana*' [see Glossary] which is terrible. Really I can't understand how someone can torture another human being like this. And they were laughing because it wasn't anything pleasant to see the naked body of a fifty-year-old woman, fat, moving like that, because the electricity makes you jump like a frog. And all the time they're asking, 'Where is

Martín?' They told me they were doing the same thing to my mother. I said, 'I'm going to end up in a bad way but you're going to end up worse because you're not going to be able to kiss your mother or your children.' They said, 'We haven't got mothers or children.' They were just savages.

There was a moment when I was about to swallow my tongue and they hit me across the stomach. One of my sons is a doctor and he tells me this is to stimulate the heart. I didn't lose consciousness. At least I don't think I did because I could hear them very clearly. But you are left stupid after the electricity. Your body is limp and useless. They told me they were going to throw me from the eighth floor and they pushed me forward. I wasn't afraid. I wasn't afraid because I said to myself, if this is it, if they kill me with the *picana* or throw me through the window, death is the same. Death is only once.

They took me to a cell. They said, 'Today you didn't talk but tomorrow you will', and this is terrible, this kind of torture, waiting for them to come back and take you again. Every time I heard the door open I was terrified.

I stood up and walked to the walls. It was one metre by one and a half and there was a stone bench. I was still blindfolded and my hands were still tied behind my back. I wanted to urinate and as I didn't know how long I was going to be in that place or if it was my last day, I strained and strained until I broke the straps and I urinated there, on the floor. There was a terrible smell. My husband says it seemed like they were toilets that had been converted into cells. He says that the walls were very high with small windows at the top.

I didn't know how much time had passed because you lose the notion of time. I didn't know if it was day or night. When I was being tortured I heard other people. I heard a man shouting 'Stop! Stop!' and I thought it was my husband. I heard police cars coming and going and aeroplanes taking off and another thing I heard was the noise of the pigeons.

There are palm trees in ESMA. I could hear a lot of people entering and leaving and names like '*conejo*' [rabbit], stupid names that didn't tell you anything.

The last time they came back I heard my husband's voice and I thought, 'Now they're going to kill us.' They didn't tell us they were going to free us. They took us and left us under a railway bridge. We'd been in that place for forty-eight hours.

When Martín found out, he wanted to see me and we met on a street corner. It was 20 January 1977. That was the last time I saw him. As he'd deserted from the army I didn't want to alert anyone to his disappearance so I didn't do anything to find him. And I was paralysed by fear. Then, yes, I was afraid. On 9 September of the same year my other son Horacio disappeared. They went into the factory and took the delegates, those who hadn't sold out, who fought for the workers. The factory owners handed them over. Then I lost all fear. It was enough. They tortured me for being the mother of Martín. What information could they get from me? So I thought, what won't they have done to our children to get information?

Hebe de Bonafini: In July 1977 a man I'd been at school with called me and said he had information about Jorge. I went to see him and he told me he had been detained by the police and thrown into a cell in the police headquarters where there were about fifty or sixty young people on the floor. One of them was my son. He had been badly beaten, tortured, left for days without food. This man said he was in such a bad state that at first he'd thought he was dead. In fact I found out later that he lived another year in different concentration camps. They talked and Jorge asked this man to let me know where he was. It was the police station I'd already been to, asking for information. I went back. I shouted everything at them. I told them that I knew my son had been there, that I knew what they'd done to him, what condition he was in, that they were murderers, until they threw me out and hit me in the street.

Many of us found out where they were held, how they were tortured, what instruments they used, the names of the torturers, where they lived. Slowly we reconstructed the events. Every day we heard new stories and every day the news got worse. We began to hear words like *capucha*, *submarino* [see Glossary], *picana* and we began to piece together the full extent of the horror.[8] All this changes you. It changes your values. It changes the way you think. We knew it was going to be hard but we knew we couldn't stop now that we were beginning to discover the truth.

Going Public

On Mother's Day, 5 October 1977, a half-page advertisement appeared in the national newspaper *La Prensa*. Entitled 'Mothers and Wives of the Disappeared — We are only asking for the Truth', it was a reference to a recent speech in which General Videla had said, 'Those who tell the truth will not suffer reprisals'. Addressed to the President of the Supreme Court, the Commanders of the Armed Forces, the Junta and the Church, it continued, 'The most cruel torture for a mother is uncertainty about the destiny of her children. We ask for a legal process to determine their innocence or guilt'. Beneath were listed the names and identity card numbers of 237 mothers. The newspaper had refused their request to print the names of their disappeared children. The Mothers had considerable difficulty finding a newspaper willing to publish their appeal at all. *La Prensa* had agreed only on condition the Mothers paid a rate considerably higher than that normally charged. In addition, the newspaper, which had always been careful to conform to the junta's censorship orders, took the precaution of including in the same edition an editorial attacking the evils of terrorism and subversion.

Some weeks later the Mothers, together with the other human rights groups, organized a petition to the junta. It demanded an immediate investigation into the disappearances, the immediate release of all those held in illegal detention, freedom for those detained without charges and immediate trial for all those with charges against them. It was accompanied by a list of 537 people known to have disappeared and 61 prisoners held under PEN. Between them the organizations had collected over 24,000 signatures.

Margarita de Oro: The organizations arranged to present the document at five o'clock at Congreso and they called everyone to the square to accompany them. The Liga instructed us to leave the telephone numbers of their lawyers with our families, so that if we hadn't returned home by eight o'clock they could ring these lawyers and find out where we were. At five o'clock we were all heading towards the square. The streets were full of plain-clothed security men trying to disperse us. I remember we were coming down one street in a column which stretched from pavement to pavement, one big mass of people, and the troops fired their rifles in the air and soldiers pushed some of us against the walls with their bayonets. The rest carried on marching, but they'd blocked the streets with tanks and tear-gas trucks, and there were rows of soldiers on their knees with their rifles aimed at us. They brought in the number 60 buses and herded us all inside like we were cattle and took us to the police station, about three hundred and fifty of us, including the French nun, Alicia Domon, who worked with Monsignor Novak. There were a lot of foreign journalists around and the police were giving them whisky to try and keep them out of the way. I'll never forget a fat woman there who asked if she could go to the toilet and this big police officer said no, so she said, 'I'll go here then', and she walked out to the patio and went there! They took us upstairs to the cells and began taking fingerprints and statements, all the time telling us that demonstrations were illegal and asking us why we were there. They all called each other Franco so we wouldn't know who they were. There were two from the security service who had mixed in with us but by then we could tell a policeman a mile off, it was as if they had a special smell. They had arrested us at about quarter past five and they released us at three in the morning. We were all apprehensive about walking out on to the streets because at that time in the morning anything could happen to you and no one would know anything about it, so we left in groups of three or four. But as we left, we saw that a few blocks away all our families were waiting for us with flasks of coffee, food and warm clothes. When we hadn't returned home by eight, they'd called the numbers we'd given them and the lawyers had told them where we were being detained. If it hadn't been for the Liga arranging the phone numbers I'm sure we'd all have disappeared.

The police had also arrested a number of foreign journalists, including employees of CBS, United Press and Associated News. In November, a BBC journalist was arrested while trying to interview the Mothers in Plaza de Mayo. The Military were becoming increasingly worried by the foreign interest being shown in the events in Argentina. Reports of torture and illegal detention had been circulating amongst European human rights organizations for some time, and these were corroborated by the findings of an Amnesty International mission to Argentina in 1976.[9] The regime dismissed these reports as the work of exiled subversives plotting to destabilize the government. Less easy to dismiss was the concern for human rights being shown by the new administration of the United States under President Carter. In August 1977, he had sent Patricia Derian to investigate the allegations of human rights abuses in Argentina. The military were taken by surprise by her tough and accusing approach, but their response was to repeat their denials and intensify the repression. Faced with the growing defiance of the Mothers of the Plaza de Mayo, and their reputation abroad under threat, the military no longer hesitated. Armed with the names and identity card numbers of those women involved with the Mothers, they were to inflict a severe blow to the movement.

Dora de Bazze: On that day and the days before, we had all been collecting money from our families and friends to pay for a new advertisement in the newspaper which was to be published on 10 December 1977, the International Day of Human Rights. I had managed to collect quite a bit of money which I was going to take to the Church of Santa Cruz where we had arranged to meet to put all the money and signatures together. By some twist of fate I was able to get to the square in time to see the Mother who was in charge of collecting it and she took it to the church, otherwise I would have been another *desaparecida*. They had already marked the Mothers they most wanted, the most active women. That day I was saved because I didn't go to the church.

María del Rosario: The Mothers were kidnapped on 8 December 1977 from Santa Cruz Church where the Irish fathers had given us a place to meet in an annexe in the gardens. We'd gone there to put together the last signatures and money we'd collected for our second advertisement. We left at about eight o'clock while a mass was going on inside, a special one because it was the Day of the Immaculate Conception. We left in twos and threes with one of the Mothers carrying the money we'd collected. She went on ahead with some others and I was about five metres behind with another Mother and behind us were another two. There were about five metres between each group of us. Suddenly two men appeared and took one of the Mothers in front. They dragged her to the side and when she began to shout other men appeared and took the Mother beside me. The one in front of us, Esther Careaga, was carrying the money and the one walking with me was María Ponce de Bianco. They threw me against the wall and told me not to move, saying it was a drugs raid. So I screamed to the other Mothers walking behind, 'They're taking us! They're taking us!' and they came towards us, thinking someone wanted to give us a lift in a car. Another man appeared, in shirtsleeves, and he pushed us away shouting 'Move on! Move on!' and we ran and hid in the church. The people were beginning to leave the mass so we mingled in with them, scared to death.

We never saw our friends again. Then I found out they'd already taken eleven more from inside. The next day we were waiting for Alicia Domon, the French nun who had been with us in the church. We were waiting for her in the doorway of the offices of *La Nación*, the newspaper which was going to publish our appeal. She didn't come and we realized she must have been taken that day. I didn't see her being taken. It was very dark and there was a terrible panic.

Two days later, on 10 December, the advertisement came out. We had arranged to meet that day in a church in Castelar, thirty-five kilometres from Buenos Aires, because one of the Mothers had had the body of her child returned and they were holding a mass in this church. When we arrived at the church we were told that Azucena had been kidnapped that morning. Later we found out they'd also taken Léonie Duquet, the other French nun who shared a house with Alicia, but who had no connection with us. Between 8 and 10 December they'd taken fourteen as well as the two nuns, including the three most militant Mothers.

All this was due to Astiz who had infiltrated us less than a month before, passing as the brother of a *desaparecido* and calling himself Gustavo Niño. He had come to the church that night to bring some money and had left a little before eight. We found out he was Astiz many months later. Until then we had really believed that he was the brother of a *desaparecido* and that he'd also been kidnapped that night.

When we returned to Plaza de Mayo the next Thursday there were very few of us and we were spread out in cafés along Avenida de Mayo. I was sitting at a table on the pavement and this Astiz appeared and we told him not to stay with us because we were afraid that he would be taken. After that we never saw him again. About six months later we got information from France, from one of the women who'd been in the church that night and had gone into exile in Paris, who'd recognized Astiz passing as Eduardo Escudero, working amongst the resistance in Paris. They discovered his real identity, that he was Lieutenant Alfredo Astiz and that he was infiltrating the exiled families in France. Later we found out he was working in the embassy in South Africa and we tried to take him to court but he'd vanished, until he appeared in charge of South Georgia when the English arrived. We thought then he'd be tried but the English let him come back to Argentina and he continued his military career as if nothing had happened.

Aída de Suárez: I remember Astiz well. He was a young man, well-dressed, very polite. We really believed he was the brother of a *desaparecido* and we felt very maternal and protective towards him. Azucena was especially attached to him. We used to surround him when the police attacked us in the square, we made a circle of Mothers to protect him. We used to say to him, 'Son, don't come. They'll kidnap you like they kidnapped your brother.'

Azucena was a truly admirable person. She had a kind of inner strength which you couldn't help but be affected by. She was always full of ideas. She was a great woman, a great fighter. We owe a lot to her, to her determination and courage. They thought that by kidnapping her, by kidnapping the fourteen Mothers, they would destroy our movement. They didn't realize this would only strengthen our determination. We said, no, they're not going to destroy us, we will continue, stronger than ever. They thought we would be too afraid to go back to the square. It was difficult to go back, the kidnapping of Azucena was a terrible blow, but we went back.

The women were no longer *locas*. Their defence of the lives of their children had become a collective assertion of the right to life which challenged the very basis of the military's system of repression. The junta recognized they were facing the first serious threat to military rule and the Mothers found themselves characterized in the same terms which were being used to depict their children. General Ramón Camps, commander of the police of Buenos Aires province, said,

Don't forget that these ladies are continuing the subversive activities begun by their children. The position they take only goes to emphasize that they are as subversive as their children. If you believe organizations like Las Madres de Plaza de Mayo, then you must be one of them.[10]

Notes

1. Munck, Ronaldo, 1984, Chapter 10.
2. Walsh, Rodolfo, 'Open Letter from Rodolfo Walsh to the Military Junta, 24th March 1977'. Walsh, one of Argentina's best known investigative journalists, disappeared the day after the letter was written.
3. Summary executions of political prisoners took place in Córdoba Penitentiary on various occasions, justified under the Law of Escape. See Amnesty International, 1977.
4. Amnesty International estimated that there were 560 political prisoners in Devoto prison at the time of their mission to Argentina in November 1976, and 600 in Sierra Chica. See ibid.
5. *Gente*, 22 December 1977.
6. The exact number of people who disappeared in Argentina will never be known. The National Commission on Disappeared People, created in 1983 by the new constitutional government, dealt with 8,960 cases of disappearances, while accepting that this was not a final figure. Other human rights organizations use estimates ranging from 15,000 to 20,000. The Mothers' figure of 30,000 is based on the premise that for every person registered as disappeared, another two went unreported owing to the unwillingness of families to present the evidence, fear and the absence of witnesses, particularly in the cases of the large number of disappeared foreigners.
7. A bomb was planted in the Campo de Mayo garrison on 2 October 1976 timed to coincide with a visit by General Videla who missed assassination by minutes.
8. For accounts of life in the camps, see Timerman, Jacobo, 1982; Partnoy, Alicia, 1988; National Commission on Disappeared People, 1986; and Amnesty International, 1980.
9. See Amnesty International 1977.
10. Taken from the film documentary, *Las Madres, the Mothers of Plaza de Mayo*, by Susana Muñoz and Lourdes Portillo.

4. International Solidarity

If it hadn't been for international support we wouldn't be here talking to you today.

Juanita de Pargament

The Argentine junta could confidently rely on the support of those Latin American regimes which were pursuing objectives similar to their own. Securing the co-operation of other foreign governments, however, was a more delicate matter. The regime's attempts to conceal the exact nature of its system of repression were calculated to avoid the kind of international outrage which had followed General Pinochet's bloody coup in 1973 and which had provoked some nations, including Britain and the Soviet Union, to cut off aid and arms supplies. Most foreign governments responded to the statements issued by Argentine embassies throughout the world promising that the new regime would demonstrate full respect for the law and the nation's international obligations by swiftly recognizing the new regime. Most were unwilling to condemn the regime on the basis of the reports being compiled by national and international human rights organizations, although several expressed their concern about particular cases.

The murders of priests and nuns provoked statements of protest from several foreign governments and from the Pope himself, and international Jewish organizations and the Israeli government registered their unease about the situation of Jews in Argentina. Some governments were prepared to take up individual cases of nationals who had disappeared in Argentina. The French President, Giscard D'Estaing, intervened on behalf of the two nuns kidnapped in 1977 and also in that year the Swedish ambassador approached General Videla about the case of Dagmar Hagelin, an eighteen-year-old Swedish girl who had been shot and kidnapped in a Buenos Aires street. Neither government was successful in its attempts to discover the whereabouts of the victims.[1]

In some cases, however, pressure from governments or their embassies did save individual lives. The British Foreign Office, for example, intervened on behalf of a British woman who was subsequently transferred into legal detention and President Carter raised the cases of Jacobo Timerman, the celebrated publisher, and Alfredo Bravo, the secretary-general of the teaching union and co-president of the Permanent Assembly for Human Rights, whose detentions were also legalized.[2] Ultimately the effects of such approaches were limited. To treat events in Argentina on the basis of individual cases of human rights abuse only permitted the military to divert attention away from the organized and systematic nature of the repression and to respond in terms of isolated 'errors' or 'excesses'.[3]

It was President Carter's human rights initiative which posed the greatest external threat to the junta's political and economic project. Carter had made the granting of US economic aid and military assistance conditional on the human rights performance of the recipient nations. On the basis of the evidence presented after Patricia Derian's visit in 1977 the US government had already blocked loans and military aid to Argentina and Carter was pressing Videla to accept a fact-finding mission from the Human Rights Commission of the Organization of American States. To counter the accusations the junta employed Marstellar Inc., a top US public relations company, to improve its image abroad and launched a press campaign within the United States with the objective of promoting Argentina as a secure haven for foreign investment. Their economic project depended on the willingness of foreign capitalists to invest in Argentina and the United States was the country's biggest source of foreign funds.[4]

The World Cup

1978 provided the regime with a unique opportunity to turn the tide of international opinion in its favour. Some years earlier the Peronist government had taken the overwhelmingly popular decision to host the World Cup in Argentina. Despite the spiralling costs, the junta agreed to assume responsibility for the event, keen to exploit its political potential. While the foreign television cameras were focused on Argentina, the junta would put into operation all the propaganda machinery at its disposal to create a picture of peace and stability intended to disarm its foreign critics and silence internal dissent. The 'Boycott the World Cup in Argentina' campaign organized by international human rights groups in response to the kidnapping of the two French nuns was used as evidence of a foreign conspiracy against Argentina, orchestrated by exiled subversives. In the words of General Lacoste, 'Why do the Europeans continue to refuse to come to a cultured and civilized country like ours? What have they got against Argentines?'[5] Appealing to patriotic sentiments, the military called on the people to mobilize in defence of the nation's honour and to present to the world its 'true image'. Only the presence of the Mothers in Plaza de Mayo suggested another image of Argentina.

> The clock on the cathedral which dominates Plaza de Mayo shows three o'clock on Thursday 8 June . . . little by little the centre of the square comes alive. There are journalists, but above all women: many women who are talking in small groups . . . The clock strikes 3.30. In a few seconds, between

three and four hundred women take out their white headscarves and place them on their heads in a distinctive way. A silent procession now begins towards the end of the square where Government House is situated.[6]

While reports like these began to appear in newspapers all over the world, the national press confined themselves to coverage of the football. In the imagined Argentina there was no place for the Mothers.

Renée Epelbaum: Shortly before the World Cup some of us Mothers were walking down Florida Street after our usual demonstration in Plaza de Mayo. Suddenly I was surrounded by a group of plain-clothed security men. They dragged me over to one side and tried to get me into a patrol car. I knew it meant that I was going to disappear and if I disappeared, who was going to fight for my children? Because I'm a widow, I'm the only one of my family to survive. These men grabbed my arms and legs. Suddenly I heard the word 'image'. They let me go. A uniformed police officer had given the order to let me go because by then several foreigners had gathered around us. They were tourists here for the World Cup.[7]

Aída de Suárez: Their objective was to create so much terror that nobody would protest, but we continued with our march in the square. Once we were joined by some of the people who had come with the Dutch football team. Right in the middle of the World Cup they brought a huge bunch of carnations to the square and gave two to each of the Mothers. They dared to show their solidarity and defy the authorities by coming to the square.

People said we were unpatriotic because we were giving the country a 'bad image'. But we were only telling the truth about what was happening. What about the image I would give as a mother sitting in my home with no right to go out and look for my children? While the murderers were killing Argentines and throwing them into the sea? I have a relative who, unfortunately, is in the navy. He told me that while the Argentine team was playing Peru in the World Cup they drugged two hundred youngsters, loaded them into an aeroplane, flew the plane to some place in the south and emptied them into the sea.[8] Afterwards they killed the pilot to silence him. He told me this. I asked him how he could be a part of this horror and he said he had three children, he couldn't do any other work, he needed the money – but I'm not trying to justify him. For me this person is no longer a cousin of mine. He is an accomplice of the military assassins.

Elisa de Landin: The people were happy, enjoying the football, and I was in tears, thinking what indifferent people we Argentines are. Young people are being taken away and they are celebrating as if it were a party.

The grim reality behind the celebration was a sharp increase in the number of kidnappings carried out by the security forces. The clean-up campaign in preparation for the event had left another 367 disappeared, with at least 46 people taken during the competition itself.[9]

Elsa de Becerra: During the euphoria of the World Cup, while they were preparing the stadiums for the visiting teams, I received the news that armed men had gone to the house of Elsita, my eldest daughter, in Buenos Aires, broken down the door and taken her away in her nightdress. I've seen the testimonies of people who saw her in El Banco [literally, the Bank], a camp which many, many people passed through. I know how they tortured her. I know that they knocked out her top teeth. I know that they raped her. I know in what kind of conditions she was kept. I have information about her until October 1978 and after that, I know nothing.

The junta could not have wished for a better result in the World Cup. The press photographs showed the generals surrounded by rejoicing crowds the day after the Argentine team won the final against Holland. They proved less successful, however, at controlling the image of Argentina which was being transmitted to the rest of the world. Despite the heavy restrictions imposed on the movements of foreign journalists on the pretext of security considerations, and to the fury of the military, many had devoted their attentions to the events in Plaza de Mayo. Dutch television had even sent out pictures of the Mothers in place of coverage of the official inauguration ceremony of the event. The women had discovered that outside Argentina there were people who were prepared to listen.

Building Bridges

Hebe de Bonafini: Soon after the World Cup an international conference on cancer was held in Buenos Aires. We went to see the doctors, in the same way as we went to see all foreign people of any influence who came to Argentina. We saw Cyrus Vance when he came and we managed to get a message written on a tiny piece of paper to the King of Spain when he was here. These doctors listened to us and the following Thursday some came to join us in the square. That day we couldn't get into the square because it was full of police but we gathered at the corner. Before this, at most of the marches we had walked in silence. One of the doctors who came, a woman, began to shout over and over again, '*Con vida los llevaron, con vida los queremos*' [They took them alive, we want them back alive]. They couldn't touch the foreigners because they were wearing their official cards from the conference. For us those words said everything and it became our battle-cry.

The Mothers had recognized the value of building their own bridges to the outside world from an early stage.

Letters
Dora de Bazze: We'd always gone to foreign embassies asking for help, because there are *desaparecidos* from twenty-six countries and we thought they might be able to do something. Then we realized that abroad there were

people fighting for human rights, so we got the addresses of people like Willy Brandt and politicians in the United States. At that time I had a lot of faith in Carter, after Patricia Derian came here, and I said to my daughter as a joke, 'The day Carter comes to power they'll free you.' And exactly the day Carter came to power they released my daughter. So we began to have hopes that these people abroad could do something and we began writing to them. We used to spend whole nights drinking coffee and typing letters. Those of us who knew another language would write in that language and those Mothers who had typewriters would type them up. If we had any foreign connections we would write to the government and groups in that country. My son is quarter Chilean, Arab, Italian and German, so I wrote to people in all these countries. I've still got the reply I received from Willy Brandt. He was very sympathetic. He wrote letters to the military expressing concern about what was happening in Argentina. But it became very difficult to send letters abroad. You couldn't send them by post because they opened them in the post office, so we had to find friends inside the embassies who would send them by diplomatic post or with people who were leaving the country.

Marina de Curia: Some other relatives of *desaparecidos* gave me a list of international human rights organizations. There was the Red Cross, Amnesty, a French commission, organizations I never knew existed. This person had moved heaven and earth contacting all these organizations and after three months his daughter's detention was legalized. We wrote to all of them. We never knew if they arrived or not. We tried to find people who were leaving the country to take them and we smuggled them out through Bolivia when it was under civilian rule. People were afraid to help us. They were afraid they would be found with the letters.

Hebe de Bonafini: To stop the information being censored we had to write in code. Some of the Mothers who helped us lived abroad and we maintained contact with them, although their replies used to arrive in an envelope with different handwriting, with an Argentine postmark and with the letter torn into little pieces. It was us who were in a dangerous situation and abroad they became desperate if a lot of time passed without a reply from us. I wrote to María Eugenia García in Spain,

'*3.150 palomas*
surcaron el blanco cielo,
mientras que 120 azules
jugaban a ser muy buenos.
Cuando caía la tarde
casi se lleven lo ajeno

pero no pasó de un susto
que no impidió nuestro vuelo.'

'3,150 doves
cut through the white sky,
while 120 blue ones
played at being very good.
When evening fell
they almost took away what
        wasn't theirs,
but it was no more than a fright
which didn't interrupt our flight.'

Signed *Las Palomas* [The Doves]

Our coded poems circulated among the exiles and militants. I found this one to María Eugenia many years later, framed and hung on the wall of a living room in someone's house.[10]

Visits Abroad

María del Rosario: In 1978 we still believed in the institutions and the Organization of American States supposedly had this Human Rights Commission which was supposedly there to defend the people. We decided we had to go to the United States, to their office in New York, to ask them to do something about what was happening in Argentina. At that time it was just a month since John Paul II had become Pope, so we decided to go to see him too, believing that when he heard our stories he would have to do something. It was our first desperate attempt to find a solution to our problems abroad.

It wasn't easy to get our passports, we spent a month going backwards and forwards before they let us have them, and we were very frightened about coming back because we knew they would find out what we were doing abroad. But fortunately nothing happened, they searched everything but we got out of the airport without too many problems. We'd been very careful to see as many people as possible to cover ourselves, people in the State Department, the President of Italy, so that if something happened there would be repercussions and they would think twice before taking us.

We got all the interviews we wanted. They already knew about us – it was over a year after we'd started meeting in Plaza de Mayo – but the difficult thing was to try and make them do something about it. Afterwards we realized that these organizations work for the benefit of each other, not for the people.

Hebe de Bonafini: We went to the United States and Rome first because we had always gone to the powerful for help, to the church, the military, the judges and we knew that the United States State Department had something to do with the disappearances, Carter and all that story, so we knew we had to ask them to intervene. We knew it was a country with a lot of power, so we decided to go and speak to the people there. Just like that! As if it were easy, totally unconscious of any difficulty. And to Rome to see the Pope! As if we were just going round the corner. We got our passports, packed our bags and left.

Just imagine. None of us had ever been abroad before, we'd never spoken to people in such positions of power and we didn't speak English. We were met at the airport by a young Argentine, a friend of a friend of a friend who asked us where we wanted to go. 'The State Department,' we said. He stopped the car and stared at us as if we were completely mad. But he took us there and they saw us. There was a department for Latin America – you know that in the United States and other powerful countries they have everything organized – and they were interested in talking to us. We told them that we were mothers from Argentina, that our children had disappeared and that we wanted them to help us. The first thing he asked was who'd paid for our journey. This was what the State Department of the USA was interested in, who had paid for our trip. We had very little money. We went with what we'd put together between us. We each gave a little and we had a collection among our families and friends and the rest of the money we'd had to borrow from the bank. On the plane I'd put everything we didn't eat into a little bag, the cheese, the cakes, the biscuits, so I picked up this bag, threw it on to his desk and said, 'You can tell us how many days we can stay here. This is all we have.' So this man from the State Department was a bit scared by this.

Of course they already knew everything that was going on in Argentina. They were very much aware of the situation. We told them we wanted their government to intervene directly to stop the kidnappings. Well, you always leave with some illusions after meetings with the powerful. They are very clever, they're never going to tell you they can't do anything.

We spent a few days in the United States. We spoke to Edward Kennedy, congressmen and journalists and visited other human rights organizations and we also went to speak at the United Nations. We didn't have anything prepared. I've never used a prepared speech. I've always considered that if you talk to people, explain exactly what's happened, you can work things out. So the first times I spoke abroad what I felt I had to do was explain what had happened to me, what had happened to us, how we felt. I've never worried too much when I'm criticized that my language isn't how it should be, that sometimes our language is too simple, that we don't talk about imperialism. I reply that we will continue speaking as we know how and as we feel. The first time I spoke in the United Nations we didn't have anything written down and we saw all the organizations with everything ready, with files and papers and we had nothing. Someone said that they would represent us if we wanted and we said, 'No, we're just going to speak.' I wasn't afraid because, as I said before, I believe that everyone is equal. There are no categories, however much they want to make them.

And we don't have to invent anything. We just tell the truth. When you are telling the truth you can say it a thousand times in different ways, but it's always the truth. It's the truth about what happened to us, how we felt, why we went out to the streets, what we were looking for, what we were doing. What do I need to prepare if I'm here all day? Those who aren't fighting something all day have to write things down. We spend all day with our heads buried in this and we've never stopped. I've never stopped coming here, reading everything that comes, answering letters, so we are very well informed. So what are we going to study? How they took my children away? How they hit us in the square? What I should say to a murderer? What I should say to someone who I want to help us? I've never worked out what I'm going to say beforehand, which I think is the best way, even though many people might consider it's too direct. I say what I think. When we agree I tell them, when we don't I tell them.

In this way we changed the language for a lot of people, because when you go to a meeting of the bishops and say everything you think, even though it might be very direct and very terrible, they don't take it very well. We always used to go to San Miguel where the bishops meet and stay there for the whole day until the bishops saw us. One day we went with another woman whose son was a prisoner. Two Mothers went in and she came in with us. She began to ask the bishop for forgiveness for occupying San Miguel and I said, 'She is speaking for herself. We, the Mothers aren't apologizing. We'll come back as many times as is necessary. We're not asking forgiveness for anything.' I don't regret what I said. It was very hard at the time, but it was the truth. This is what built up the strength of the Mothers, to say what we thought and not to worry that the other one is a mother whose son is a prisoner and that she wanted to be in with the bishops. We don't have to be on good terms with the bishops. The only people we have to be concerned about is our children.

We had no money left to go to Rome, but we managed to raise enough for the air ticket in the United States. As soon as we got there we began writing letters asking for meetings, to the Pope, to Pertini, to the head of the Jesuit community, to members of parliament, in a very cheeky way. We were staying in a disused flat that belonged to a friend of ours, sleeping on the floor, and another friend gave us access to his telephone. The flat was outside the city and one day, after we'd been to the supermarket to buy food, I called this friend and he told us a meeting had been arranged with President Pertini and we had to go immediately to the Quirinal Palace. The other Mothers said, 'Throw away the bag,' and I said, 'No, why do we have to throw away our food, he eats too doesn't he?' We got to the Quirinal and there was a guard of honour lined up in formation at the entrance and we whispered to each other. 'Let's go over to the side, out of the way' – and it was for us! The guard of honour was for the Mothers! And me with my plastic bag full of shopping in the middle! This was our first interview with Pertini and it was very powerful. He gave us a lot of encouragement. He was a very brave man, a man who had spent fourteen years in a concentration camp before becoming president, a man who understood what fascism meant.

We got interviews with a lot of influential people. We went to see Susanna Agnelli [a member of the family which owns Fiat], don't ask me why, but anyone we heard about we went to see, so that people would take notice of us.

Then going back – at that time, in 1978, women had left Chile and Pinochet hadn't let them back in the country and we said to each other what happens if we get home and Videla sends us away too? But in the end there were no problems. They searched everything but they couldn't touch us because too many people knew about us. We'd met too many people. We didn't see the Pope. The Pope wouldn't see us.

María del Rosario: We were only able to see the Pope in a public audience which we obtained through an Argentine bishop in the Vatican. We went to see this bishop in Rome and he gave us the invitation. The place was like a big theatre with seats down the sides. There were three of us Mothers. Two had positioned themselves at the front and I was in the middle section. The Pope walks along the middle, moving from side to side receiving people, holding out his hands to them and receiving their kisses and little things they offer him. Everyone gave him a cross or a religious card, things like that. In my hand I had a photograph of Azucena. As I raised my hands to give it to him he closed his fingers and he wouldn't take the photo of Azucena. He didn't want me to give it to him. Other groups of Mothers saw the Pope another three times. They went to see him in Brazil where he spoke for two minutes with the Mothers, then in Mexico and then again in Rome.

Laura de Rivelli: About twenty of us went to Brazil to try to see the Pope. I remember we had to take the coach from a local church and when we all arrived they issued us with tickets, like anyone else, but when they discovered we were *Madres de Plaza de Mayo* they told us they'd had to cancel a coach and that they wouldn't be able to take us. But in the end we got there. We'd made a huge banner explaining who we were and what we wanted, about thirty-five metres long and about the same height as myself, and we took this with us.

We didn't know anyone in Brazil. As soon as we got there we went to find a hotel and two or three Mothers went to the parliament building in the centre of the city where they met a journalist from an important Brazilian newspaper. One of the Mothers told him she knew someone from that newspaper and he asked them who they were. When they said that they were *Madres de Plaza de Mayo* he immediately drove to our hotel, which was about twenty kilometres from the centre, to collect the rest of us. He was very interested in talking to us. In fact so many people wanted to interview us that we had to stay on in Brazil another few days.

When we got to the street where the Pope was going to pass by we looked for a big place where we could put the banner. One of us spotted some windows in a building which was just opposite the balcony where the Pope was going to speak. We went to have a word with the doorman and he said it was all right to hang it from the windows. It was such an enormous banner that it covered all the front and a bit of it went round the corner. It was very impressive. You could see it from everywhere. Obviously people didn't have a clue what it said, because in Brazil they speak Portuguese and the words were in Spanish, but some began explaining what it said and everyone was talking about it. In the end the police came and pulled it down but by then everyone had seen it.

We managed to speak to the Pope. It was very difficult getting the meeting. It was the archbishop who finally arranged it. At first he was told that the Pope would speak to only one of us and we said no and I remember the archbishop was arguing with them, banging the desk and saying '*Todas, todas!* [All of them] and in the end he did see us all. He spoke to us in a private place. He didn't want any journalists present and he didn't want anyone to take photographs. He blessed us all and he seemed very concerned about what we were saying. He told us to have faith and he said he already knew that some of our children were going to come back. He said 'some of them'. And we asked ourselves, how could he know that? The sad truth was that not one returned.

María del Rosario: The church never gave us a reply. Because of this, after so many years, we've arrived at the conclusion that these organizations, these great powers, aren't there to serve the people. They're there for the benefit of each other, their politics, their businesses, their privileges, not for the benefit of the people.

Foreign Indifference

Free Enterprise

From the beginning Carter's human rights programme was undermined by fundamental contradictions in US foreign policy. In the first place, the threatened use of economic sanctions to induce governments to improve their human rights record was attacked by domestic business groups as government interference in the free movement of trade and contrary to the precepts of free enterprise capitalism. Moreover, these were precisely the principles embodied in the Argentine regime's economic programme, which had been welcomed not only by business, but also by the IMF, the World Bank and other financial and trading institutions in which US interests predominated. Business groups argued that any attempt to damage the economic relationship with Argentina was also against the public interest and the vast multinational companies began an intense campaign against the inclusion of such clauses in international agreements.

It was not only in the United States that business was eager to profit from Argentine repression. The opening of the Argentine market to foreign goods and cheap sterling had led to a doubling in value of Argentine imports of British goods between 1976 and 1978. British banks were lending large sums to the junta and the Board of Trade was taking an increasingly pro-Argentine stance.[11] The Soviet Union was also strengthening its trading links with Argentina. Soon after the junta took power it promised to buy Argentina's grain surplus for the next ten years in an agreement which offered the junta much-needed foreign currency and which became increasingly important to the Soviet Union after US grain exports were cut following the Soviet invasion of Afghanistan.

'National Security'

In the second place, the restrictions on military aid were seen as conflicting with long-established US policy in Latin America, the guiding principle of which was national security. Since the Cuban Revolution in 1959 this had been dominated by a concern to destroy revolutionary movements elsewhere in

Latin America and to retain the area within the US sphere of influence. Kennedy's Alliance for Progress, ostensibly an attempt to combat the kind of poverty and underdevelopment which bred unrest, had encouraged the military to take a larger role in government affairs. Their chief function, however, according to the doctrine of national security, was to safeguard internal security and wage war against the 'subversive elements' within their borders. The US promoted this doctrine in Latin America and provided training to friendly Latin American armed forces in several of its army schools within the United States and in the US Army School for the Americas in Panama. As General Camps explained:

> France and the United States were the great proponents of the anti-subversive doctrine. They organised centres, particularly the United States, to teach the anti-subversive principles. They sent advisors, instructors. They sent out an extraordinary quantity of literature.[12]

Compared with other Latin American nations, a relatively low proportion of Argentine officers were trained in US methods of counter-insurgency, which included courses on the theory and practice of torture, but it was to be a doctrine which the Argentine armed forces found particularly relevant to the internal conditions of Argentina. Their fiercely anti-communist and pro-Western stance coincided with the proclaimed security interests of the United States whose concern to retain an important Latin American ally was to override any human rights considerations. The US feared that isolating Argentina would drive the junta into the hands of the Soviet Union. At the August 1977 session of the UN Sub-Commission on the Prevention of Discrimination and the Protection of Minorities the USSR had already voted against any discussion of Argentine human rights violations. Moreover, in an unlikely political alliance with the military government, consistent with their closer economic links, the Soviet Union had instructed the Argentine Communist Party to show 'critical support' for the junta. In return the junta allowed the Communist Party to exist more or less openly.[13]

Carter's initiative was effectively neutralized when in 1979 the two nations engaged in joint military exercises and supplies of weapons found their way to Argentina. The military relationship, like the economic one, suffered no more than a brief setback during the Carter presidency.[14] It was against this background that the Inter-American Commission on Human Rights of the Organization of American States finally arrived in Argentina in September 1979.

Inter-American Commission on Human Rights

Elsa de Becerra: The military tried to sabotage the visit. First they tried to introduce the *Ley de Olvido* [literally, Law of Forgetting]. This meant that after someone had been missing for a certain length of time they could be declared legally dead. By declaring them dead the family could then get a pension. They wanted to stop the word 'disappeared' being used. This was their way of burying the issue. Perhaps they thought they could buy our silence. Almost no one accepted it, least of all the Mothers. The Mothers will never sign our children's death certificates.

The Mothers from Mendoza went together to Buenos Aires to give our evidence to the Commission. The city was covered in posters in the colours of the Argentine flag which said, '*Los Argentinos somos Derechos y Humanos*'.* The visit coincided with the Junior World Cup which was being held in Japan. As we waited in line along the avenue crowds of young people poured into the streets shouting at us and insulting us, waving their flags. On one side were queues and queues of people waiting to see the Commission and on the other side this crowd of drunks celebrating. It was like the meeting of two different worlds. It had all been planned in advance. A sports presenter had called over the radio for everyone to gather in Plaza de Mayo to show the Commission the 'true face' of Argentina. They came in their companies' vehicles. We knew they had been sent to provoke us. I hope they're all wondering now how they could have done it. But other people opened their eyes. They could see that we weren't subversive, all those thousands of families, waiting day and night, sleeping there. It made them think.

Dora de Bazze: While I was waiting in line to see the Commission, believing, like all the Mothers, that they were going to do something, I spoke to a young man in the queue. He said he'd been detained in a concentration camp and had brought a list of the names of other people he'd seen there. On this list was my son's name. We already knew that my son was in a concentration camp because some time before we'd received an anonymous call saying that he was alive but they never told us where. This man said he'd been freed from the camp because he told them he was a member of the Communist Party. Many people were saved by this. He said he used to give out the food and that one of the boys in there was called Hugo Bazze. He said the day he was freed they transferred the whole group out of the camp. There were many so-called 'transfers'. For instance, Transfer 1 might mean they were going to be killed, Transfer 2, that they were going to be taken to another camp, and so on. They had their own codes.

So my daughter went to talk to him. She wanted to go because she'd already been in a camp and she thought the boy would speak more openly to her than to me. She talked to him for a long time but I don't think she ever told me the truth about what he said. I don't know if he told her Hugo was dead, she never told me. But she said that the boy had been with him and that he had been transferred that day. That means my son had been alive in that camp for four months. I always used to say, if they're going to kill him I hope they do it quickly, so he wouldn't have to suffer, and then I found out this, that he'd been held in a concentration camp for at least four months.

---

* This is a play on words: 'We Argentines are right (*derechos*) and human (*humanos*). The Spanish for human rights is '*Derechos Humanos*'.

Graciela de Jeger: When the Commission visited Tucumán people came not only from this province but from all the surrounding provinces to give their testimonies. They were here for three days. There was a long queue of people waiting even though we were being photographed by men standing on the roofs of surrounding buildings and even though they'd put infiltrators in the queue. It was there I came face to face with the dreadful reality of what had happened. In front of me was a woman who'd come from the sugar region in San José, an area which suffered terrible persecution. She said to me, 'I don't know what to do because there's one family from my area where they took everyone and there's nobody left to report the kidnappings.'

People had expectations of the Commission. At that time the human rights groups had four hundred reports of disappearances and the Commission received over a thousand. People came who had never reported a disappearance before, people who didn't believe in the human rights organizations or who hadn't bothered, thought that a Commission from the Organization of American States could do something. They were saying things like, 'After this they'll have to give us an answer.' We felt hopeful because for once someone was listening to us.

Marina de Curia: I didn't have too many expectations of the visit. They'd given more than a year's warning to the government. Instead of coming immediately they waited a year and then they delayed it another six months. Of course, this gave the military time to put their house in order, to destroy all the evidence of the camps. They sent telexes to all the military units with precise instructions on how to reply to the investigators. They raided the offices of human rights groups and confiscated the documentation they had prepared for the visit. They shot prisoners, they transferred them. In the prisons in Córdoba they shot a lot of people before the OAS came, including official prisoners. I regret not keeping an article which was published in the newspaper which said the United States government had asked for information from its embassy in Buenos Aires about reports that they were shooting people in Argentine prisons. Also, I already knew that the OAS had been to Chile and nothing had changed. But in your heart you always have some hopes.

Elsa de Becerra: They had time to clean up the prisons and get rid of the evidence and they tried to stop prisoners seeing them. The Commission had made the military promise there would be no reprisals taken against people who asked to see them, but Jorge had asked for an interview with them and when I saw him a few days before they were due to visit his prison he told me he'd been threatened. In the end it did nothing except make them realize that abroad they were becoming discredited, that they were beginning to see what was happening. But it didn't change anything. By 1979 there were fewer disappearances and some prisoners began to be freed. They didn't believe that after so much torture and all the horror the prisoners had suffered they would testify. Perhaps they thought this would be enough to stop the protests. The military never thought that the families, and above all the Mothers, would have the courage to go on.

On the eve of the Commission's departure, the junta, anxious for a favourable report, freed the publisher Jacobo Timerman and expelled him from the country. It was not enough. The preliminary findings of the investigation, released before the members of the Commission left Argentina, spoke of grave violations of human rights and widespread use of illegal detention and torture and placed responsibility on the actions or negligence of the public authorities. Most damaging for the military was the citing by name of several of the officers directly implicated in illegal activities. Many of these belonged to the hard-line, nationalist sector of the army who had strongly opposed the junta's decision to allow the visit, seeing it as a surrender to the interests of foreign governments.[15]

Within days of the release of Timerman, General Menéndez, commander of the powerful Third Army Corps, staged an abortive rebellion against the military leadership. This was followed by a series of statements defending the methods used by the armed and security forces in the 'war against subversion'. General Riveros, who had been expressly mentioned in the Commission's preliminary findings, made it clear in a speech published in the wake of the visit that he was not prepared to act as a scapegoat for the junta: 'We fought this war with the doctrine in our hands and written orders from our superiors.' To stem the growing discontent and to reassure those officers who felt they were being abandoned by their superiors, the military leaders were forced to clarify their stand on the issue of the *desaparecidos*. General Videla led a chorus of speeches defending the regime's actions: 'The war against terrorism has been an authentic war, with its inevitable and sad consequences of deaths, prisoners and missing people . . . necessary so that 25 million Argentines can work in peace and liberty.'[17] It was a position endorsed by both President Viola and General Galtieri, the new chief of the army and one of those named by the Commission for his role in human rights abuses.

Outside the armed forces the domestic repercussions of the visit were limited. The final report of the Commission, though widely circulated in military and diplomatic circles, was to remain unpublished in the Argentine press.[18] The rule of the junta, assisted by changing international circumstances, suffered few serious setbacks.

By the time the report was presented at the General Assembly of the OAS, Ronald Reagan had been elected President of the United States and this had signalled a change in US relations with Argentina. The Argentine military's open support for anti-communist forces in Central America, which had included provision of weapons for Somoza in Nicaragua and training of death squads in El Salvador, Honduras and Guatemala, made them a useful ally in Reagan's design for Central America. The United States rejected an outright condemnation of the Argentine government at the General Assembly.[19]

In Britain too, the new Conservative government warmed to the regime. Within a month of taking power they had restored full diplomatic relations and an ambassador was sent to Buenos Aires for the first time since February 1976.

when a British research and communications ship was fired at by an Argentine destroyer in the South Atlantic. This was followed by a series of diplomatic exchanges designed to improve Anglo–Argentine relations.

Solidarity Groups

The Mothers were disappointed, though not surprised, by the failure of foreign governments to take a strong line against the regime. They had succeeded, however, in drawing international attention to what was happening in Argentina and in making it more difficult for the junta to continue acting with impunity. The women in the white headscarves had come to represent to the world the image of resistance to the military regime, and their courage and determination inspired the organization of foreign groups in support of their struggle. International solidarity offered them both the resources they required to continue their struggle and a measure of protection for their own personal position.

María del Rosario: After the World Cup, when the journalists from all over the world went back with reports about what was happening in Plaza de Mayo, people abroad began to take more notice of us. A Dutch reporter who was interested in what we were doing stayed on a month and when he returned to Holland he wrote a big article on us in the newspapers and in 1978 our first support group was established by the women of SAAM, which in Dutch stands for 'Solidarity with the *Madres de Plaza de Mayo*'. The wife of the ex-Prime Minister, writers, journalists and artists all joined and there was a singer who recorded a song about us to raise money. This was our first financial help. In France people began demonstrating outside the Argentine embassy in support of our struggle. After that solidarity groups were set up all over Europe and in Canada, organizing events, raising money. Financially, we've managed only because of foreign support.

Some of this support was being organized by Argentine exile communities. People had begun leaving the country in large numbers with the growth of the Triple A and this movement had accelerated after the coup. About two million left Argentina during the *proceso*, a quarter of a million in the months immediately after the coup.[20] Those with dual nationality were able to escape to Madrid, Rome, Paris and Mexico City. The UN High Commission for Refugees had appealed urgently as early as June 1976 for Western European countries to save the lives of Argentine refugees, but the response was only lukewarm. Seven months after the appeal, for example, only thirteen had been allowed to settle in Britain.[21]

Rita de Krichmar: I went to live in Mexico in 1979. After the disappearance of Irene and my son-in-law I sank into a depression. I saw a psychologist but I didn't agree with the way he was treating me. He said they'd probably gone to Australia but how would she have left her baby and how could you explain the child appearing in the middle of the night?

I began to build up my own defences by occupying myself with those left. I wanted Nora, my other daughter, to leave the country. I knew that she was in danger too and, as we have friends in Mexico, I wanted her to go there. Nora made me promise that I would send her the baby so that she could bring her up in Mexico. She was eighteen then. She went with her husband, they found a flat and I used to receive postcards saying that they were waiting for Marina. Because we weren't able to get her parents' permission for Marina to leave the country, and because we wouldn't register them as dead, we had to get authorization from the juvenile courts. We'd never say they were dead. In 1977 we went to Mexico with Marina. I'd looked after her for almost a year and it had helped me recover my strength and Nora was pregnant, so I spoke to her. I thought she would let me take Marina back with me, but she said no. I returned to Argentina alone and continued with the search for information about Irene.

We did a lot of things privately. I hadn't yet connected with the Mothers. We didn't recognize the whole problem, that it had happened all over the country to many families. And I was afraid. I didn't want to bring attention to myself in case they refused to give us passports. The children were all we had left and I wanted them to be safe. In the end I went to Mexico to be with Nora and the children. I felt my whole world was there. Afterwards I realized my position was egotistical and I changed my way of thinking. At first the only thing which concerned me was to find my own, and then when I went to the square I saw all the women suffering like me, all these women who'd also lost children, children who were just as excellent as mine.

In Mexico I joined a group of families of *desaparecidos*, not mothers alone, but we were aware of what the Mothers were doing here and and we did what we could. We tried to meet on Thursdays outside the embassy but it was difficult to organize because Mexico City is so big and the distances were so great. We used to organize events and sign petitions. When there was a demonstration here, we organized one in Mexico. We marched in front of the embassy in Mexico together with the other exiles.

Hebe de Bonafini: Afterwards people got to know of us and began to invite us to their countries, so we travelled everywhere. We went to many neighbouring countries and realized that there was oppression all over Latin America. We made connections with women in Uruguay, El Salvador, Chile and all those countries where there are *desaparecidos*. We walked into Paraguay where we said so many things against Stroessner [military dictator of Paraguay from 1954 to 1989], that he was a dictator, that he trampled on the people, that they tried to arrest us. We found that we were following the same path as the people of many other Latin American countries who are fighting for justice and freedom. And we've made a lot of trips to other parts of the world. We never went to the USA again. We decided not to go there while they still have their feet in Nicaragua. We went to Holland, Norway,

Denmark, Sweden, Switzerland, Spain, France, Italy, Germany, everywhere. We found support for our struggle amongst ordinary people in many countries. They raised the money that helped us continue our struggle. This is why I believe that foreign solidarity is so important for our Latin American countries.

Notes

1. A week after the disappearance of Sister Alicia Domon and Sister Léonie Duquet the French news agency, AFP, received a note purporting to come from Sister Alicia, together with a photograph showing them standing in front of a Montonero poster. The note said that she had been kidnapped by guerrillas and outlined a list of demands in return for her release. It was clearly a forgery. A survivor of ESMA later testified that Sister Alicia had been forced at gunpoint to write the note. Both nuns were seen in ESMA together with families of *desaparecidos* who had been taken from the Church of Santa Cruz, and both were tortured until they were finally 'transferred'. See National Commission on Disappeared People, 1986. Dagmar Hagelin was held up by armed men who were occupying the house of a friend she had gone to visit in a clear case of mistaken identity. She ran away and was shot in the street by a man later identified as Lieutenant Astiz. Her father campaigned tirelessly for her release. In 1978 he received information that she had recovered from her injuries and witnesses later testified that she had been held in the extermination camp, Villa Joyosa.

2. Jacobo Timerman's newspaper, *La Opinión*, occasionally published articles on the human rights situation in Argentina. The newspaper was closed down in April 1977 and on 15 April Timerman was kidnapped and held in a secret detention centre. His experiences are described in his book, *Prisoner Without a Name, Cell Without a Number*, which clearly demonstrates the strong current of anti-Semitism within the armed forces. He later passed into legal detention followed by a period of house arrest. He was finally expelled from the country and deprived of his citizenship during the visit to Argentina of the OAS Commission for Human Rights. Alfredo Bravo was kidnapped on 8 September 1977 from the school where he was a teacher. After being tortured in a secret camp his detention was legalized and he was released under 'supervised freedom' on 16 June 1978. A note presented by the Argentine government to the Inter-American Commission for Human Rights on 21 December declared, 'The Argentine Government denies that actions relating to Señor Alfredo Bravo constitute a violation of Human Rights: they are based on legal procedures'. See National Commission on Disappeared People, 1986.

3. It remains undeniable that the actions of several foreign embassies in Argentina did save lives and did provide assistance to families of disappeared people. Those most frequently mentioned by the Mothers included the US embassy under 'Tex' Harris, and the Swedish, Dutch, Mexican and Israeli embassies.

4. The US had begun to replace Britain as the biggest foreign investor in Argentina during the First World War. By the 1980s Britain was supplying only 8% of the total direct private investment. See Dabat, Alejandro and Lorenzano, Luís, Chapter 1.

5. Quoted in *Madres de Plaza de Mayo*, No. 7, June 1985.

6. Quoted in Tiffenberg Goldferb, Ernesto David, 1984, Chapter 3:2.

7. Quoted in the film documentary, *Las Madres, The Mothers of Plaza de Mayo*, by Susana Muñoz and Lourdes Portillo.

8. The navy and air force's preferred method of disposing of bodies was throwing them into the sea, rivers or lakes. The army favoured secret burials.

9. *Madres de Plaza de Mayo*, No. 7, June 1985.

10. De Bonafini, Hebe, 1985.

11. For a review of British foreign policy towards Argentina see Simpson, John and Bennett, Jana, 1985, Chapter 19.

12. National Commission on Disappeared People, 1986, Chapter v.

13. Only four members of the Argentine Communist Party are registered as disappeared during the entire period of military rule. See Simpson, John and Bennett, Jana, 1985, pp. 279–80.

14. See Shoultz, Lars, 1981, Vogelgesang, Sandy, 1980 and Hoffman, Stanley, 1981, for analyses of Carter's human rights initiative. European countries, including Britain, also played an important role in supplying the Argentine military with sophisticated weaponry.

15. Some political commentators have detected the existence of different wings within the armed forces. The nationalist wing is associated with the 'hard' or 'fascist' elements, particularly in the army, as opposed to what has been called the 'moderate' wing. In some versions of this analysis Videla is seen as 'moderate'. This kind of analysis lay behind the positions taken towards the military government by some political parties, e.g. the Communist Party. It was also only a short step from here to talking about levels of responsibility, see 'Prosecutions', Chapter 8.

16. Quoted in *Madres de Plaza de Mayo*, No. 3, February 1985.

17. From an interview for a Spanish newspaper, quoted in Bousquet, Jean-Pierre, 1980, Chapter xv.

18. Organization of American States, 1980.

19. For an account of US military links with Argentina during the Carter and Reagan years see Verbitsky, Horacio, 1985.

20. Simpson, John and Bennett, Jana, 1985, Chapter 8.

21. Ibid., Chapter 19.

5. The Association

It was a hard time for us, but we weren't broken. They thought there was only one Azucena, but there wasn't just one. There were hundreds of us.

Aída de Suárez

Plaza Mayor
With our wounds exposed to the sun, Plaza de Mayo,
we show you these Argentine mothers,
we don't understand why there is so much injustice,
or what crimes we are suffering for.
Can it be that the men of this earth
have lost their souls and their reason?
Maybe we are punished for being women
who bore the worthy children of the future,
        who honour humanity.
For yesterday's children,
        those of today, those of tomorrow,
historical witnesses to the nation,
in silence, like beaten dogs,
we walk across your paving stones
to say to the men who hurt us,
we are mothers, Argentine women,
why are we being punished?
In the name of the children of the children of the future,
we ask you,
in the name of history, we demand
Justice and Peace,
that is what we want,
think of God,
He is the final judge.

María del Rosario
August 1977

The Closure of Plaza de Mayo

Inside Argentina the silence around the Mothers was still complete. The junta's control over all channels of information meant the public knew nothing of their trips abroad. The majority knew nothing of the Mothers. The military, however, were not short of information and 1978 and 1979 proved to be the years of greatest repression of the movement. Conscious that an all-out attack on the women would now provoke an international reaction, the junta moved in police and security forces to occupy the territory which had become the focal point of the Mothers' struggle. Throughout 1979 the Mothers had kept up their weekly demonstrations in Plaza de Mayo but their numbers were falling as the harassment and the arrests increased. At the end of 1978, three weeks after 2,500 people from all the human rights organizations had congregated in the square to present another petition to the junta, the square was sealed off with metal barriers and a cordon of armed police.[1]

> **Carmen de Guede**: I remember one time when we went to the square and the police had blocked it off with metal barriers and men with rifles and grenades were trying to push us back. We ran to the steps of the cathedral, thinking if we got inside we would be safe, that they wouldn't be able to get us in there. But the priests locked the doors. They wouldn't let us in. We stood on the steps with our banner *'Queremos a nuestros hijos'* [We want our children]. We tried to get back into the square and the police chased us out. Everywhere we went they came after us with guns and truncheons to break us up. We wanted to get inside but every time we tried to get through they forced us back. We began to sing the national anthem and I don't know why but when they hear the national anthem, the police and the army have to lower their weapons. When we finished we began to sing it again and again so they couldn't raise their guns. When we tried to get out they ran through the streets after us and surrounded us and emptied the buses and put the Mothers inside. I was with the two little ones, standing in a doorway of a bank, and the people inside let me in with my children so the police wouldn't take us.

During 1979 the women could manage only token gestures of defiance. In surprise 'lightning strikes', they gathered on the edges of the square and ran across to break through the barricades before the police turned them back. Without Plaza de Mayo the Mothers faced the very real possibility that their movement would disintegrate and that everything they had achieved in the last two years would be lost. A long time had passed since their first improvised meetings in the square. Their perception of the society they lived in and of their place in that society had changed. Their search for their children was becoming a permanent struggle against injustice.

> **Hebe de Bonafini**: I experienced a terrible, a very brutal change. In the beginning we didn't realize that we weren't going to find them. In the

beginning you search and everywhere you go you really think you'll find them. And later, you realize you won't. It was when someone told me, 'Your son is in a concentration camp,' that I realized I wasn't going to find him, that it wasn't going to be easy. It was like someone had hit me, shaken me up. And then in December they took Azucena and my other son and you feel as if they're tearing you apart, that they're taking everything away from you. Then you realize you need to understand what's happened to be able to fight.

I began to read everything I could find so that I could understand what they were doing, everything, how they were torturing them, where. It was the only way to get the strength to fight them. And then you realize that it's not just your own sons that matter, but all the *desaparecidos*. All these were stages, sudden shocks. In a few years a world had opened up before me that I'd never seen before, that no one had ever shown me, a world that I'd never believed was also my own. My life had been the life of a housewife – washing, ironing, cooking and bringing up my children, just like you're always taught to do, believing that everything else was nothing to do with me. Then I realized that that wasn't everything, that I had another world too. You realize you're in a world where you have to do a lot of things.

We had developed into an organization without knowing it. We didn't know what an organization should be like, we just thought if we had something more formal it would give us better protection and it would encourage more women to join us. When it was suggested that I should be the president, I didn't need to think twice.

The Association is Formed

On 22 August 1979 the Mothers registered themselves legally under the name they were given by the people who saw them in Plaza de Mayo,

> The Mothers, as signatories, have resolved to constitute the *Asociación Civil Madres de Plaza de Mayo*. The decision to establish the Association is a consequence of the meetings which we have held for more than two years in the Plaza de Mayo in the Federal Capital and in other places in this city and in the interior of the country. These meetings began spontaneously as the result of the actions which hundreds and then thousands of Argentine mothers carried out in Government House in Buenos Aires in an attempt to discover the whereabouts of our children, detained by representatives of the Armed and Security Forces from 1976 and whose destiny is unknown to us. We are mothers of *detenidos–desaparecidos* and we represent many thousands of Argentine women in the same situation.
>
> Nobody has called us together, driven us on or manipulates us. We are against violence and any kind of terrorism, whether from individuals or the state. We believe in peace, brotherhood and justice. We desire the implementation of a democratic system in Argentina which respects the

fundamental rights of people. Believers or not we adhere to the principles of Judeo–Christian morality. We reject injustice, oppression, torture, murder, kidnappings, detentions without trial, detentions followed by disappearance, religious, racial, ideological and political persecution. We do not claim to be the judges of our detained and disappeared children. We only want to be told where they are, what they are accused of and that they be judged through a proper legal process with the legitimate right of defence if it is considered that they have committed a crime . . . Our first objective is to obtain a reply from the country's civilian, military and judicial authorities. Where are our children? What have they done with them? . . . And finally we want to work to construct an Argentina where there is justice, where nobody can be detained and disappear as has happened to our children, where the law is respected and where it is possible to live in liberty, tolerance and respect.[2]

María del Rosario: We set up the committee because by this time we already had a lot of commitments. We had to sign documents, give telephone numbers and addresses where we could be contacted and we had to make ourselves responsible for what we said. We'd never been an anonymous, clandestine organization. We'd always operated in the light of day.

I became secretary because from the beginning it was me who carried around all our papers and wrote a lot of the letters. I'd turned into the secretary without realizing it. It wasn't because I was experienced – I work as a dressmaker and I'd never liked writing or anything like that – it was the desperation. At night when I couldn't cry any more, when there were no more tears left, I sat down and wrote. I even wrote poems, very infantile ones at first, calling on God to help us. The first poem that circulated in Plaza de Mayo was one that I wrote, called 'Plaza Mayor'. After that a lot of the Mothers began to write. It seemed to give us some relief, to calm our anxieties. We wrote so many that when we got our office we published our first book of poetry. We couldn't use a commercial publisher so we got them printed privately and sold them among ourselves.[3] In 1979 we also began producing our own bulletins, written by hand and photocopied and distributed by us. We thought, if the papers are ignoring us, why not make our own?

Juanita de Pargament: I became the treasurer because everyone said I knew how to count the money. When we used to collect money amongst ourselves in the square it was me who carried it around in a little bag, counted it and tried to make it last as long as possible. As a legally constituted association we had to keep proper books and account for what we were spending.

Soon after we formed the committee the Dutch women of SAAM offered to send us a donation to rent or buy offices. Until then we had no permanent meeting place and nowhere to direct people to. With a cheque for $25,000 from the women in Holland we set about looking for an office. In the end we had to buy because no one was prepared to rent to the *Madres de Plaza de*

Mayo. The *Madres* were still the mothers of subversives and they were afraid to rent to us. Our first office was small and it didn't have any furniture. We'd forgotten about the furniture, but everybody brought something, and we managed to get desks, tables and chairs. We called it the Mothers' House. The military never came there. They didn't want to risk the reaction it would cause abroad.

Provincial Groups

The creation of a formal organizational structure also made it easier to co-ordinate a national response to a plan of repression which had been applied systematically across the country. Families drawn into the nightmare sequence of kidnapping, disappearance and torture had all followed a similar path in the search for their children. Many, especially the women, had persisted with the seemingly hopeless quest for information which inevitably led them to the authorities in Buenos Aires. As they began to discover the truth behind the trail of deceptions and lies laid by the military authorities their fear was replaced by a determination to fight. Some had joined the Mothers in Plaza de Mayo and returned to their provinces strengthened by their example. Mothers of *desaparecidos* throughout the country had begun to combine their efforts with the women in Buenos Aires and some had taken the name of *Madres de Plaza de Mayo* as their own.

Mendoza
One of the first groups to form a provincial branch were the Mothers in Mendoza, a city 1000 kilometres to the west of Buenos Aires.

Elsa de Becerra: I met other people, mainly women, in all the places I went to, in that terrible vicious circle which was like another form of torture. The federal courts – nothing, military barracks – nothing, police – nothing. Nobody knew anything. And then they began to tell us that maybe our children had run away from us or that we didn't know what our children were really doing, that they had been planting bombs, and they began to threaten us, saying if we didn't keep quiet the same would happen to us as had happened to them. Especially when they saw that we were meeting each other, mainly in the headquarters of the Eighth Brigade where we all went for information. It was the military themselves that brought us together. They organized us in the beginning.

We began to talk to each other, in spite of our fear and the fact that some of us, then, were still a little ashamed to say that our children had been taken. We began to realize there were four, five, six, seven of us, more, because yesterday there were people who aren't here today. We took addresses and phone numbers and we began to consider joining together to do something. In 1976 people from the *Liga* were already meeting. At first we met in private houses as *Familiares* [Families of *Desaparecidos* and

Political Prisoners], husbands, wives, mothers, everyone and later we found a priest, Father Pablo, who gave us a place to meet in his chapel on the outskirts of the city. He was the only one who ever gave a mass for our children. Later when they started telling us we had to ask the Ministry of the Interior for information, we began writing letters and when they didn't reply we went there, to Buenos Aires. Lots of women from different provinces converged on the Ministry and that's where we met the Mothers. I even met women from Mendoza who I'd never seen before . . .

Margarita de Oro: I didn't know anything about the groups meeting here. My son was kidnapped in Buenos Aires and I had to go there to look for him. I did everything in Buenos Aires. It was there that I met Elsa and some of the other people from Mendoza who were looking for *desaparecidos*.

Elsa de Becerra: We went to all the human rights organizations, to the League, the Permanent Assembly, the Ecumenical Movement,[4] but as they were people who weren't personally affected, no matter what good intentions they had, they were more philosophical. It didn't mean the same to them as it did to us. We realized we had to do something more rapidly and together. When I heard about the Mothers I went to Plaza de Mayo and it was there that I found the strength to fight. At first I was with the Families of *Desaparecidos* of Mendoza and we supported the activities of the *Madres de Plaza de Mayo*. We were already working with them in 1977, when the first advertisements came out.

María de Domínguez: When I found out that my son and his wife had been taken I went everywhere searching for them. I went to Buenos Aires for the first time, looking for information. At that time there were already groups of families of *desaparecidos* meeting in Mendoza and when they found out about another disappearance, they went to see the family. They came to me and I began to work with them. We used to go to Buenos Aires for the big events organized by the Mothers there.

At first we knew nothing about the torture camps. I had some idea about what was happening in ESMA, in Buenos Aires. Then we realized it was happening here. At first the people who had been through the camps would say nothing because of the terror. The police headquarters was functioning as a clandestine centre where people were tortured and in the official prison itself there was a section where young people were secretly detained, especially the young pregnant women. In the south of the province there was another big camp. We knew about them but we couldn't do anything. We compiled files on every disappearance in Mendoza. It didn't matter what proof you had, they denied everything. It was like banging your head against a wall, like fighting against a completely invisible enemy. We used to write letters together to the courts, to the military and to the police. We asked for meetings. They always said they knew nothing.

Elsa de Becerra: In 1979, after the Mothers in Buenos Aires formed the Association, we broke away from the Families and met directly as *Madres de Plaza de Mayo de Mendoza*. By then we had a very clear idea of what the struggle was about, that it wasn't just for one child, but for all the *desaparecidos*. We began to march every Thursday in the main square here in Mendoza with our white headscarves. We don't have a Plaza de Mayo so we met in Plaza San Martín at midday, the time when the most people are around. When we could we went to Buenos Aires. Plaza de Mayo is the centre of our struggle. For us it's like a meeting place with our disappeared children.

In the beginning there were about fifty of us. We went to the unions because many workers, rank and file workers, disappeared. We knocked on the doors of the CGT in Mendoza and they turned us away. We took a list of the unionists who had disappeared and told them they had to do something. They didn't. They didn't want to be implicated. We drew up petitions. We made leaflets and took them to the factories and gave them out in the square to try to make people understand what was happening. We went with posters and placards explaining who we were and what we wanted. When famous people came here we tried to see them. When the church congress met here we went with our lists of *desaparecidos* and all our files were stolen and the police assaulted us. We received telephone threats all the time but they never touched us in the square. It wasn't like in Plaza de Mayo where the police moved in to detain everybody. They always watched us and photographed us, but that was all. I suppose it was because there were very few of us. Mendoza is a very conservative society. It's the only province in the country which elected Conservative candidates in the elections in 1983. But youth groups approached us and when we organized a big demonstration, despite the military, people came to join us. Some of the militants of political parties, who didn't dare express their resistance, marched behind us. It was us who organized the resistance.

La Plata

In La Plata, the capital of the province of Buenos Aires, 60 kilometres southeast of the federal capital, women had also begun to join forces with the Mothers of Plaza de Mayo.

Valprida de Torres: The disappearances began after the coup in 1976. Before this they took people at night and killed them. The situation in La Plata was very bad. Every day cars with rifles at the window patrolled the streets and army trucks stopped buses, took people out one at a time and asked for identity documents. Every day they closed off streets and searched the houses one by one. We had to live from morning to night with the police, the army and the security services on the streets.

Laura de Rivelli: This is a city with a lot of *desaparecidos*. It's a university city and people come from all over the country to study here. Many foreigners as well: Bolivians, Paraguayans, Chileans, Uruguayans have all disappeared from here. We've got a big university which caters for all specializations. One of the first things they did was to close down the student refectory where you could eat very cheaply. This was something bad for them.

Valprida de Torres: Even before the coup all students entering the university had to be searched. After the coup they began to disappear. Some of the university teachers themselves informed on them.

Laura de Rivelli: And there were many teachers who were themselves kidnapped and then disappeared.

Valprida de Torres: There was an organization called *Centro Nacionalista Universitario* [University Nationalist Centre], a fascist organization which denounced student leaders who were then kidnapped. They were a group of young people who dedicated themselves to denouncing their fellow students.

Laura de Rivelli: I don't think there is a square or a street in this city where there hasn't been a disappearance. They say there are 1,500 in the city alone, some taken individually, some in groups. *La Noche de los Lápices* was one case but not the only one. Many secondary school students were taken. And not only students but also workers, unionists, professionals.

Josefa de Neim-Melo: They took everyone. My son disappeared while he was doing military service in Bahía Blanca. In this city people could see exactly what was happening but they were afraid to speak out. There are families here who didn't report a disappearance for two, three years because they were afraid of what might happen to their other children, and other people, who weren't directly affected, who reacted with indifference.

Laura de Rivelli: Most of the people who live here work in public administration. La Plata is the capital of the province of Buenos Aires so all the government offices are here and people depend on the government for work. They felt they had to be very careful. There are many things which work against people expressing themselves freely in this city. Almost none of us knew each other before. We met in the courts and the government offices and in Buenos Aires. It was something spontaneous. It happened first in Buenos Aires because that's where we all went for information. When we saw what the women were doing there, we came back knowing that we couldn't sit at home and do nothing. We didn't have the money to go to Plaza de Mayo every Thursday so to stop our group disintegrating we began to organize Mothers here. In the beginning there were only four or five of us. We decided to meet in the Plaza San Martín every Wednesday at half past three. We chose Wednesday so that those who could, would be able to go to Plaza de Mayo on Thursdays. We met here in the square with our headscarves every Wednesday, at first just to talk. We sat on the benches making plans or we met in people's houses or went to churches.

Valprida de Torres: While we were praying the priest would walk up and down the aisle to see that we weren't passing messages. Once when we went to a church to ask for a mass and they found out we were *Madres de Plaza de Mayo*, they told us to leave. They threw us out just as if we were criminals.

Josefa de Neim-Melo: When they took my son the first place I went was to the church. I saw Mgr Plaza [Archbishop of La Plata] who said, 'Señora, if your son had nothing to do with subversion then he'll probably come back a little beaten up, but he'll come back. But if he's a subversive, he'll disappear.' Mgr Plaza told me this. The church knew very well what was going on. There's one testimony of a man who saw Mgr Plaza inside a concentration camp.

Laura de Rivelli: They didn't arrest us here, or even touch us. It wasn't like in Plaza de Mayo. The only time they ever really showed they were bothered by us was when they had organized the celebration to commemorate the centenary of the city. They had painted every single building, made everything look pretty for the arrival of the President. We suddenly appeared with our banners and placards, a lot of us, because Mothers had come from Buenos Aires as well, and they tried to remove us, but they didn't arrest us. I was arrested many times in Plaza de Mayo, but I was never afraid. The pain of losing one of your family was so great, and then, when you found out that many, many more had disappeared, not just your own, the struggle became something different.

Josefa de Neim-Melo: When a mother loses a child that pain is stronger than fear or terror.

Laura de Rivelli: If a mother loses a child she would risk anything. That's why it was the women who were fighting. Some of our husbands supported us and some didn't. Every case was different. But if you're asking if the men learnt to wash the plates as we learnt politics, the answer is no. We still had to do the washing and ironing as always. It's possible to do both. If you believe in something strongly enough you find a way.

Tucumán

It was the northern province of Tucumán which had been the first victim of the military's 'war against subversion'. In the provincial capital, San Miguel de Tucumán, 1,100 kilometres north-west of Buenos Aires, there were also women who had become aware of the struggle of the Mothers of Plaza de Mayo.

Rita de Ponce: Amongst the group of mothers who had formed in 1975 to defend the political prisoners began to appear the mothers and families of the first *desaparecidos*. At that time we couldn't believe in such a dreadful thing as disappearance. We didn't think it was possible. We believed that it was because there were so many prisoners and they hadn't made up the proper lists yet or that they weren't willing to give out the information. We thought it was just a matter of time. We began to hear rumours that in a school in Famaillá there were prisoners, but they were just rumours.

Then one day, when my son was taken prisoner in 1975, I went into the police station to try to take him some food and with all the anxiety of a mother who wants to see her child, I began to walk down the corridors searching for him. Someone said, 'Where are you going?' and I said that a police officer had sent me. I carried on walking and I could see there were rooms with lots of people lying on the floor and there was an old woman, her feet all swollen and held up against the wall by something I couldn't see, because I was looking through a half-open door. Then one of them appeared and asked me what I was doing. He was very angry. I said I was sorry, I'd lost my way and that this wasn't the place they'd sent me to. But I'd already seen it all. It was a terrible shock. Later we found out there were thirty-three of these clandestine detention centres, concentration camps, in Tucumán, including the first in the country and Arsenales, the extermination camp [see Glossary].

Marina de Curia: Someone who'd come from the capital came to us and said, 'Do you know that in Buenos Aires there is a group of mothers who march around the Plaza de Mayo every Thursday and do you know what they do? They present habeas corpus writs all together and they take them all to the court on the same day.' I'd already heard something about the Mothers even though there was never anything in the newspapers. She took out from her bag a copy of the document the *Madres de Plaza de Mayo* were using in Buenos Aires – because as you couldn't find a lawyer to do it, you had to draw up the papers yourself. When we heard that they were presenting hundreds of habeas corpus writs on the same day to shock the judges we decided to do the same. We made copies of the document and went to find other mothers of *desaparecidos*. We presented sixty in one day. They began to get worried then because they realized that we were in contact with each other, that we were beginning to organize. Then someone came from Buenos Aires, a person from *Familiares*, to organize us and we began to work with them. Before that we used to meet in the gardens of a church where we would pray and talk, more of us every time, and after we joined the *Familiares* the priest came out and invited us inside and gave us a room to meet.

Graciela de Jeger: The bishop had authorized it. It was an attempt to contain us, to keep us off the streets and under their control. They preached resignation and never paid any attention to our petitions.

Marina de Curia: There was one priest who was responsible for attending to the families of the disappeared and we took him a list of nearly two hundred cases, which was what we had collected then. He always gave excuses, he had no time, next week, someone was away, tomorrow.

Then one day he called us to say he had official information. This categorized the disappeared into three groups; *desaparecidos* without a record (we asked him what this meant but he didn't answer), *desaparecidos*, and prisoners held under PEN. So we went to the church to see him and there was my son on the list – '*desaparecido* without a record', my daughter – 'PEN', Nellie's son – '*desaparecido*'. So we thought the *desaparecidos* are dead, the ones without records they're going to free and PEN, legal prisoners. He said the information had been given to him by a government official – he didn't say who. Immediately I went to see a judge. He said he couldn't do anything without the number of the case. I went back to the priest and I made a mistake because I asked to speak to him alone. I said that I'd told a judge what he'd told me and that the judge needed more information and I asked the priest to speak to him. He shouted, 'No! I won't speak to anyone! And if you tell this to anyone else I'm going to say it's not true.' This is our church.

When I got hold of a list of human rights organizations abroad, like the Red Cross, Amnesty, the OAS, I took the list to a meeting of Families, believing it was a great discovery, and the Father saw the list and said, 'If you write to one of those organizations you won't meet here again.' They didn't want us to go out on the streets or to contact human rights organizations abroad so we thought, 'This organization is designed to stop us.' We spent a year with them fighting from inside before we decided to separate and establish a group of Mothers.

Graciela de Jeger: *Familiares* were being manipulated by the Communist Party to put the brakes on the fight and the CP had this policy of 'critical support' for Videla, that he was a 'patriotic general', that he was from the centre and if you didn't support him the 'right wing' of the military would take power.

Marina de Curia: I said to them, 'You're telling this to me, a mother with two children disappeared?' And in the few masses we got for the *desaparecidos* they didn't want their children named, they said everyone should pray for their own children. Some wouldn't recognize that their children had been political militants. It was the struggle of the *Madres de Plaza de Mayo* that made us accept our children as they were and be proud of them. We were disheartened by the other groups and we were impressed by the clear and courageous actions of the Mothers in Buenos Aires. Their ideas coincided with ours. We joined the Mothers because they were the only genuine fighting group.

Graciela de Jeger: I'd been to *Familiares* four or five times but at this time I was working so I couldn't do much. Anyway they were very passive. At that time I didn't know anything about the *Madres de Plaza de Mayo*. In December 1977 I went to the Ministry of the Interior – you had to go every two months otherwise they closed the case – and I remember I was standing in the queue, looking at all those men, thinking, what can I say to them when they know perfectly well what's happening? I was too scared to stay in a hotel but through some friends I got access to an office. I used to go in at seven in the evening and I had to be out by seven in the morning and the rest of the day I spent wandering around the streets. Or in the National Library. I've never read so much. I went to *Familiares* who were working from an office given to them by the *Liga*, the oldest human rights organization in the country. The *Liga* had always existed and helped with legal advice and assisted the political prisoners, but this phenomenon of organizations composed of people directly affected by the repression was something new. I gave my details to *Familiares* and when I left I saw a big notice which said '*Familiares* advise you not to go to Plaza de Mayo because you will be detained by the police.' Well, I went anyway and marched with the *Madres de Plaza de Mayo*, but there were very few women there. Later I discovered it was the first Thursday after they'd taken Azucena. I returned to Tucumán and didn't keep in contact with them.

In 1978 I became ill and was under treatment. It was basically depression, but the therapy was very inadequate because this was a completely new thing and they didn't know how to deal with it. They tried to help you with the period of mourning, but we were talking about *desaparecidos*, not dead people. It was my son who told me that some of the women had broken away from *Familiares* because they wanted to go out to the streets and that was when I joined them.

Marina de Curia: As Mothers we were alone. We didn't have the apparatus and the money of a political party. *Familiares* used to pay for the space in the church. We didn't know this at the time. In contrast we never gave our Father a penny because we didn't have it. He disobeyed the orders of his bishop and gave us a room to meet. When the bishop told him to stop, instead of telling us to leave, he used to go out early on Thursdays leaving the door of his house open and we used to meet in his dining room. He never refused us a place to meet. But the church in general threw us out when we asked for a mass for the *desaparecidos*.

Graciela de Jeger: So we took them by surprise. First we went to a mass in the cathedral and when we got inside we put on our white headscarves and prayed in loud voices for the *desaparecidos*. The next Sunday we went back and they'd brought a choir to sing loudly to drown our voices. So we decided to go to different churches to surprise them, one week one church, the next week another one.

Marina de Curia: It was very dangerous. We were always being threatened and intimidated. The military never really tried to hide what they were doing here. I think Tucumán was the only place in the country where the torturers never even tried to hide their identity.

Neuquén
The provincial capital of Neuquén is 1,000 kilometres south-west of Buenos Aires.

Josefa de Mujica: In Neuquén there were never armed confrontations, bombs or anything like that. What they called *enfrentamientos* were clear cases of kidnappings. After the coup they closed the university and from June to July 1976 forty-eight people were kidnapped. Every case was the same. They broke into houses, searched through books and papers, destroyed everything and took away the young people.

In my case I was alone in the house with the new baby and my other granddaughter. My daughter Susana had gone to the hospital for a check-up because she still had the stitches from the Caesarean. Five armed men broke into the house and searched through everything. They didn't leave anything untouched. They split open the mattresses and even poked a stick up the chimney. They guarded the exits and wouldn't let me use the phone. I wanted to get hold of Susana to warn her not to come home. When I tried to shout for help they hit me. I couldn't do anything because I was worried they would harm the children. When Susana's husband arrived they took him and then, when Susana came, they took her. She hugged the children and they pulled the baby from her arms and took her away.

I started early the next morning going everywhere to report what had happened but they always said they had no information on the incident. Of course the neighbours were afraid to speak. Everyone lived in isolation, inside their houses, trying not to communicate with anyone, afraid that if they said anything they would be taken too. Others preferred to ignore what was going on. It's impossible for people not to know when more than forty are taken from their homes in a month in a small place like Neuquén.

I saw one lawyer who was an adviser in the prison and he went to see if Susana was there, but she wasn't. They had already been taken out of the province. They denied that there were camps here, but there were. Places where they held them until they were transferred elsewhere. Susana's husband appeared after two weeks. He'd been blindfolded the whole time and they'd taken him first to a place he thought was a shed because of the way the voices echoed and then by aeroplane to Bahía Blanca. All the torture and executions took place in Bahía, at the headquarters of the Fifth Army Corps.

Neuquén was one of the few places in the country where the church supported us. The Mothers didn't exist in Neuquén then. There were just groups of families of people who had been kidnapped. We didn't call them *desaparecidos* because we didn't know. Our bishop, Jaime Nevares, was a great man. When Videla came to the city Nevares refused to meet him. He was always being watched and threatened and of course he was isolated. The church didn't support him. He went to the army and to the courts but it didn't do any good because the military controlled everything. It was their 'justice'. But anyway the lawyers behaved very well. Perhaps because it's a small place things operated in a different way. In a small place everyone knows everyone. The lawyer, the doctor, the priest are people you see every day. But it was still useless because everything had been prepared throughout the country from the moment they moved into Tucumán.

I stayed in Neuquén until the baby had recovered. I had to leave Susana's house and go to stay with friends because the telephone rang every day with people threatening me, saying that if I didn't take the children and leave the city they would blow up the house. I didn't want to leave because I thought Susana might appear at any time, but with the threats, and the children, and my worries about my other daughter who was teaching in an Indian community in the south of the province . . . This was a problem all the families had, how to protect the other children and yet fight for the one who wasn't there.

After two months I went to Buenos Aires. I went to all the human rights organizations. I already knew about them. And then I met the *Madres de Plaza de Mayo*. The fact that we were together helped us a lot, because everyone else had rejected us. I took information about the Mothers back to Neuquén, because no one knew anything about them there. I used to come and go between Buenos Aires and Neuquén taking information about what they were doing. We began to form our own group of Mothers in about 1979. There were very few of us. We collected all the information we could get on the kidnappings and the camps, we wrote letters together. We didn't march because there were very few of us but we went to Buenos Aires for the big campaigns. We organized meetings and demonstrations in Neuquén as well, to let people know we existed. We began to get a lot of support. Even if people didn't work with us directly, they came to see us, they joined us on the demonstrations. It's one of the places where we've had the greatest popular support.

The Grandmothers

Amongst the women who congregated in Plaza de Mayo were Mothers who were searching not only for their sons and daughters, but also for their grandchildren. Babies and young children were not exempt from the actions of the security forces but rather their abduction formed part of a deliberate strategy to stop the spread of 'subversive ideas' to future generations. General Ramón Camps elaborated on this strategy in an interview in 1983:

It wasn't people that disappeared, but subversives. Personally I never killed a child; what I did was to hand over some of them to charitable organizations so that they could be given new parents. Subversive parents educate their children for subversion. This has to be stopped.[5]

When children were present at the time of a raid by security forces they were sometimes taken to a neighbour or a member of the family or they were left abandoned. The rest simply disappeared with their parents. Prisoners released from the detention centres testified to the presence of young children inside the camps. Some of these children were forced to witness the torture of their parents and others were themselves tortured. The evidence also suggested that pregnant women were being held until the moment of the birth of their babies.

The grandmothers believed that there was a very real possibility that their grandchildren were still alive and in the hands of members of the armed forces. These women had begun to join together around the very distinct task of finding their grandchildren.

Marta de Baravalle: I joined the Mothers in the first meetings in the square from the beginning of 1977 but while we were all looking for our children, I was also looking for a grandchild. Gradually I began to meet other women in my position, who were, like myself, doubly mothers, also taking the place of mothers of our disappeared grandchildren. And we could see that the work of finding our grandchildren was very different, that we had to go to different places, that we had to go to juvenile courts, orphanages, children's hospitals and to maternity hospitals where we thought they may have taken our pregnant daughters to give birth, so we decided to work together on this specific task. We began to come together as a group from about the end of 1977 with the objective of finding all our grandchildren, and, of course, all our disappeared children. In the beginning there were twelve of us, looking for twelve grandchildren. The first person we wrote to for help was the Pope. Sadly we've never had a reply.

It was very difficult to organize because public meetings were forbidden. We used to meet in cafés, pretending we were celebrating a birthday or something and when the waiter came we gave a toast to someone and when he left we planned our campaign, signed letters and organized the next meeting. Sometimes we met at bus stops and sometimes in private houses, being very careful not to draw attention to the fact that several people were meeting in one house. When the Mothers got their office they gave us a space to meet once a week.

When we heard of a case of the kidnapping of a child or a pregnant woman we tried to find out the address of the family to take details, so we could start looking for the child. We began to realize that it was something which had affected many families.

Elsa Pavón de Aguilar: Paula disappeared with her parents from Montevideo in Uruguay on 18 May 1978, one month before her second birthday. At that time I was preparing to visit them for Paula's birthday. Instead of going there to celebrate her birthday, I crossed the river to find out what had happened to the family. They said they knew nothing, that things like that didn't happen there. In Uruguay someone had told me that it was likely they had been taken as a preventive measure in the run-up to the World Cup but the event finished and I'd received no news.

When I went to La Plata I met the Grandmothers and began to work with them. I felt comfortable with them. I had never gone to the Mothers or to the square because I didn't think I had the strength to do everything the Mothers were doing. They were always being detained and persecuted and I think for this you need another kind of strength. Everyone has their own way of working. I felt comfortable with the Grandmothers. At that time I think there were about eighteen of us.

Estela de Carlotto: My daughter Laura was twenty-two, a history student at the University of La Plata and two and a half months pregnant when she was kidnapped on 26 November 1977. Like all the Mothers I did everything possible to trace her, but the reply from the police, the military, the prisons was always the same. They had no record of the event. However, periodically I received information on her whereabouts. In April 1978 a very frightened woman appeared at my husband's factory and told him she had been in a concentration camp for three weeks, that she had met Laura and that Laura had asked her to tell us that she was well and not to worry because as she was pregnant her conditions were better, that she had a mattress to sleep on and better food than the others there, that her pregnancy was going well and that the baby would be born in June. She'd said that if it was a boy she was going to call him Guido after her father, and that I should look for the child in the orphanages. Until then I had believed that Laura was already dead. When I heard this news my hopes were raised. At the time I was the head of a primary school. I left work in order to bring up the child Laura said I would find in an orphanage. I started knitting clothes for the baby and in June I started to search.

On 25 August 1978 we received a telegram from the police asking us to go immediately to a police station about sixty kilometres from my home. We went, my husband, a brother and I, thinking that perhaps something terrible had happened or perhaps, something wonderful. That she was free, that we would see Laura and her baby. But also thinking that Laura would be there, but dead. When I went into the police station I could see by their faces that something dreadful had happened. They asked if we knew Laura Carlotto. We told them we were her parents and he said, 'I'm sorry to have to tell you that Laura is dead.' When I asked why, he said she was killed in an *enfrentamiento*. I lost control and shouted 'Murderers!' and 'Criminals!' and when I saw the crucifix above the desk I shouted out that God would punish them for the crimes they were committing. They said they had nothing to do with it, that they were just carrying out the order to return the body to the family. This was something very unusual, they almost never returned a body. I think Bignone gave the order and that when I went to see him nine months earlier he knew she was alive and that one day she would be killed.

She was killed at half past one on the morning of 25 August. They said she had been in a car with a young man, that they had refused to stop for a police patrol. My husband went in to identify her body, which was lying next to the body of the young man. Half her face was destroyed by bullets and they had shot open her womb. It was impossible to know whether the baby had been born.

By about May 1978 I had become aware of the existence of the Grandmothers. I approached them and began to work with them to recover our grandchildren. At this time I didn't know whether the baby had been born, I didn't know the date of the birth, whether it was fair or dark, whether it was a boy or a girl.

Marta de Baravalle: It was a very hard struggle. We were threatened and intimidated. They tried to frighten us off. And we were working with few results because at that time it wasn't easy to get information. You had to have a lot of patience. We began to make dossiers on each case based on the testimony of the grandmother and with photographs of the child. We took these dossiers to the juvenile courts, to orphanages, to the Ministry of the Interior, to the government. We went to check the registration of adoptions in the courts and while we knew that many had been falsified, we couldn't prove anything. We knew the judges, with a few exceptions, were lying and accomplices of the military regime. Some told us our children were terrorists and that they didn't know how to bring up their children and didn't have the right to bring them up and that now they were in the hands of decent people who knew how to educate children in a way that we didn't.

The women became known as the *Abuelas de Plaza de Mayo* [Grandmothers of Plaza de Mayo] and, like the Mothers, they found support for their campaign abroad, particularly in Europe and Canada.

The first breakthrough came in 1979. Anatole Julien Grisonas, aged three, and his one-year-old sister Victoria both disappeared from the province of Buenos Aires after their parents were kidnapped by security forces in September 1976. Three years later CLAMOR, the Committee for the Defence of Human Rights in the Southern Cone, in São Paulo, Brazil, located the children in Chile, adopted by a family who had found them abandoned in the streets of the Chilean city of Valparaíso in December 1977. Both had false birth certificates which registered their place of birth as Chile. This was the first hard evidence to support the Grandmothers' accusation that the military were involved in the trafficking of children. By 1980 their own, painstaking efforts were beginning to bring results.

Elsa Pavón de Aguilar: In 1980 Chicha [the nickname of María Isabel de Mariani, the Grandmothers' president] brought me three photographs of a child believed to be Paula. The photographs had been taken to a woman in Montevideo by a friend from Buenos Aires together with the name, address and telephone number of the family the child was living with. This friend had overheard an argument during which the wife had shouted something about her husband killing the child's parents. The woman in Montevideo took the information to CLAMOR in Brazil and Chicha had gone to collect it.

It was very difficult for me to accept that the little girl in the photographs was Paula. Everyone said it was her, but I wasn't convinced and spent hours studying them and comparing them with the photos I had of my granddaughter. To accept this was my grandchild meant I had to give up any hope that they were all alive and together somewhere.

When I was finally convinced we began to visit the address we'd been given. We had to be very careful not to draw attention to ourselves. We had to try not to look suspicious because it was a place where many military and police lived and it was 1980 when they were still taking people. The area was expensive so we had to be careful about our clothes, so we didn't look out of place there. It was very difficult because there were no bus stops or bars nearby so I had to keep walking. In all the times I went there I only saw her once, from behind, but I no longer had any doubts that this was my granddaughter. The next time I went back they had moved. We couldn't find out where they'd gone. The only thing I knew was that the man she was with had been a police officer and now worked in security for Mercedes Benz and that it was likely she was in the hands of the same person who'd kidnapped her parents.

Estela de Carlotto: In 1980 we were contacted by a doctor concerned about one of his patients who was suffering from grief after the disappearance of her son, his wife and their two young daughters. The doctor already knew of us as two of his own children had disappeared. We went to see the grandmother at her home. She was suspicious at first but she gradually got to trust us and we began to accompany her to the juvenile courts in the area where her son and his family had lived. She was too old and ill to travel alone. Finally, after insisting that the judges investigate the case, we discovered information about two children given to a couple without the proper adoption papers around the time of the disappearance. Then we traced the judge who'd authorized the adoption.

The children had been found alone, wandering in the streets, and had been taken into care where they had been separated and listed as NNs [identities unknown]. A couple with no children who wanted to adopt saw the youngest who was just three months old and when they were told she had a four-year-old sister they wanted her too, because they wanted to keep them together. They had no idea that they were children of a disappeared couple. When they were informed of the truth by the judge they suffered a lot because they had looked after the sisters for three years and they obviously loved them. As they were innocent the children were left with them and today they're still with them. The grandmother visited them frequently but sadly she died soon after. She was very ill. That was why she left the children with them.

In 1980 the *Abuelas* also went to Brazil. Whenever we went abroad we made a habit of searching out Argentine exiles to take testimonies from those who had been freed from concentration camps. In São Paulo we met a couple who told us that they had seen pregnant women inside their camp, but that they had all been freed. 'For example,' they said, – 'there was a Rita from La Plata whose father had a paint factory who was freed on the night of 24 August 1978.' When I heard those words I thought I was going to die – Rita was a pseudonym used by my daughter and all the other information fitted too. I showed them a photo of Laura and they recognized her immediately. They'd been in La Cacha which was a concentration camp in a big shed between the male and female sections of a prison in La Plata. Laura had been there all the time. I'd gone everywhere looking for her but I'd never imagined that she was so close to us.

They told me that she'd given birth to her baby, that it was a boy, that he had been born on 26 June 1978 and that she'd named him Guido. The baby had been taken away from her and she believed that he'd been given to me. She'd been told that they'd brought the baby to my house and that I'd turned him away, saying I wanted nothing more to do with my daughter, but she hadn't believed them. She'd told them that I would never forgive them and that I wouldn't rest until they had been brought to justice – I realized then that my daughter knew me better than I knew myself.

The couple told me that she spent another two months in the camp and that they were with her until the night of 24 August when she was told she was going to be released. They'd told her she was going to meet her family and her baby. She had a bath, put on some nice clothes and make-up. When she saw that she was going to be taken with the other boy she realized she was going to be killed. This is what she told the couple but they couldn't believe she would be killed. They didn't know Laura was dead. But now I knew that the child had been born and that he was a boy.

The Grandmothers faced an enormously difficult task. Thirty per cent of the *desaparecidos* are estimated to be female, 3% pregnant women. The military had gone to extraordinary lengths to conceal the births of the children of detainees. Those who did not give birth in the secrecy of the camps were taken to hospitals where wards were specially converted into extensions of the detention centres. Prisoners in an advanced stage of pregnancy were kept blindfolded and guarded throughout labour. In most cases they were subjected to Caesarean operations, after which the mothers were separated from their babies and never seen again.

The admission of these prisoners was either not recorded in the hospital registers or they were listed as NNs. Staff who expressed concern about their condition were liable to disappear themselves. In a hospital in Quilmes one midwife, after hearing a prisoner shout out her name, wrote to her parents informing them that their grandchild had been born. When the relatives came to the hospital the birth was denied. The midwife, together with a nurse who had made enquiries about the prisoner, were both kidnapped and disappeared.[6] Despite the difficulties and the grave dangers they faced, the Grandmothers of Plaza de Mayo, like the Mothers, were determined to persist with the search for the *desaparecidos*.

Return to the Square

The thirteen women who met in Plaza de Mayo on 30 April 1977 had never imagined that three years later they would still be fighting for the truth about the disappearances. The Mothers were now a legally constituted organization with offices in Buenos Aires, branches developing in the provinces and an extensive network of support outside Argentina, but their conviction that it was a battle which had to be fought on the streets remained. Their strength had always been based on their willingness to use direct action. In 1980 they felt confident enough to return to Plaza de Mayo.

María del Rosario: At the end of 1979 we decided that even if they took us prisoner, even if they killed us, we would return to the square on the first Thursday of the New Year. The first time the police didn't react. We'd taken them by surprise. The second week they were waiting. They detained a lot of us but they had to let us go because we were already well known abroad. They held us until two or three in the morning and then released us one at a time in deserted places to frighten us, but, well, you have to get over all that. The beatings and the threats continued, but that year we returned to the square and they were never able to stop us again. They pulled our hair, they stopped buses and dragged us inside, but the next Thursday we went back again. And we brought foreign journalists, so they could see what was happening.

Aída de Suárez: For the Mothers the square signifies the best of our lives because the square is the place of our children. Because one day my son said to me, 'If one day I don't come back, don't cry, go to the Mothers in Plaza de Mayo. They'll help you.' The square is the most important thing left to the Mothers. The square and the House. We never stopped our marches. In some way we were always there. If there were twenty of us, there were twenty. If there were fifty, there were fifty. From 30 April 1977 we've always been there because this square is ours. On Thursdays at half past three this square belongs to us.

Notes

1. See Bousequet, Jean-Pierre, 1980, Chapter X, for a description of the events leading up to the closure of the square.
2. Reproduced from Tiffenberg Goldferb, Ernesto David, 1984.
3. Three collections of poetry were later published under the name of *Cantos de Vida, Amor y Libertad*, March 1985.
4. The Ecumenical Movement for Human Rights, led by the Bishop of Quilmes, Mgr Novak, received no support from the church as a whole.
5. Quoted in *Madres de Plaza de Mayo*, No. 8, July 1985.
6. See National Commission on Disappeared People, 1986, pp. 286–300, for accounts of the disappearances of children and pregnant women and for the cases of the midwife, María Luisa Martínez de González and the nurse, Genoveva Fratassi. See also Nosiglia, Julio E., 1985, for a history of the Grandmothers and testimonies of the kidnapping of children and pregnant women.

6.   The Fall of the Military Government

We have 30,000 *desaparecidos* today because the leadership of the Church and the unions, as much as the political leadership, allowed it.

Hebe de Bonafini[1]

Economic Collapse and the Emergence of Protest

Elsa de Becerra: The military's economic policies had a terrible effect on Mendoza. They paralysed a huge number of estates and factories, closed businesses and brought misery to thousands of people. Before the coup this was one of the few provinces in the country which had a budget surplus and Martínez de Hoz dictated that these surpluses should go to the national treasury, so that Mendoza couldn't continue to grow. The worst damage was done by the financial corruption, with the famous rates of interest which were so high that people began to think exclusively about speculation, about the interest that their little bit of capital could bring them, not about production. There were people who sold up their houses to take advantage of the interest rates and who were left with nothing, without house or money, because there were a lot of financiers who robbed people. Moreover the external debt had increased alarmingly and nothing had been invested inside the country. Under Martínez de Hoz all the money went abroad. This, together with the persecution of industry, the corruption, the high cost of living and the damage done to the public services, brought misery to thousands of families in Mendoza. You could see people living off what their family and friends could give them because they had been left with nothing.

It was the military's economic record, not human rights, which became the focus for the first mass resistance to the rule of the juntas. In 1980 four of the country's most important financial institutions collapsed as crippled industrialists failed to meet their repayment obligations and depositors transferred their funds abroad, plunging the military's monetarist policies into crisis. High domestic interest rates combined with the overvaluation of the peso made it impossible for national industry to compete with foreign producers in the shrinking home market. By 1979 imports were growing three times faster than exports and a multitude of small and medium-sized producers fell victim to what was effectively a policy of deindustrialization.[2] Between 1979 and 1980 the number of bankruptcies and receiving orders increased by 74%. Even the larger corporations were not immune: Sasetru, the largest grain and food-producing group in Argentina, went out of business in 1980 and many foreign firms, such as General Motors, Fiat and Olivetti also closed or reduced their operations in Argentina.[3] The expected injection of foreign investment failed to promote economic development. Ninety per cent of foreign funds went into short-term deposits as opposed to fixed investment, taking advantage of the high rates of interest to make a quick profit. With foreign credit relatively cheap, financial speculation had flourished as those institutions with access to international money markets, and in particular the military itself, obtained credit abroad and recycled it in local financial markets. One of the most remarkable results of the military's monetary policy was the spiralling of the foreign debt. Standing at $19 billion at the beginning of 1980, it was $30 billion by the end of the year and $39 billion by 1982.[4]

The alliance of interests which had maintained the military in power was beginning to crumble under the strain of the economic collapse. The sacking of Martínez de Hoz by the new President, General Viola, could not defuse the impending political crisis and representatives of the productive sectors began to unite against finance capital. In 1981 the *Sociedad Rural Argentina* (Argentine Rural Society) publicly protested over the economic plight of Argentine firms and the Argentine Industrial Union called for measures to halt the destruction of the productive apparatus. There was a wave of protest from the hard-hit regional producers. The era of *plata dulce* came to an abrupt end and with it middle-class acceptance of a regime they were prepared to tolerate just as long as they were able to satisfy their taste for conspicuous consumption. Intellectuals and professionals began to question many aspects of official policy. The crisis also brought criticism from within the armed forces. In March 1982 a document was drawn up and endorsed by a large number of high-ranking officers which referred to the 'failure' of the *proceso*'s economic plan which 'has gravely affected' the credibility of the armed forces.[5] Even the church was beginning to distance itself from the regime.

At the forefront of the protest movement against the government was the working class whose wages and jobs were the price for the military's monetarist experiment. After 1980 unemployment soared and real wages fell dramatically.[6] Workers at factory level had from the start practised discreet forms of protest against the regime, through go-slows or work-to-rules, but from 1979 these were replaced by strike action culminating in April 1979 in the first general strike since the coup. Two years later the CGT, the national trade union organization whose dissolution under the Process of National Reorganization had been upheld by a new labour law passed in November 1979, began to be reconstituted by the Peronist union bureaucracy. In Buenos Aires alone one and a half million workers participated in the general strike in June 1981 and on 7 November 50,000 white- and blue-collar workers joined a demonstration calling for 'Peace, Bread and Work'.

In the midst of the discontent the issue of the disappearances was, for the first time, being raised outside the narrow circle of human rights organizations. In August 1980 the newspaper *Clarín* had published an advertisement signed by personalities representing diverse sectors of Argentine society demanding information on the *desaparecidos*. The list of signatories included Jorge Luís Borges, the master of Argentine literature, and César Menotti, head of the board of selectors of the national football team.

In October came the news that an Argentine citizen, Adolfo Pérez Esquivel, whose organization *Paz y Justicia* (Peace and Justice) supported the demands of the human rights groups, had been awarded the Nobel Peace Prize.[7] The Mothers had also received a nomination, as a recognition of their struggle. As an organization, they were not eligible to receive the prize themselves.

At the same time international pressure on the junta was mounting. The United Nations was pressing for details of over 7,000 cases of disappearances and in 1980 Amnesty International published a report on the secret detention camps based on the testimonies of former detainees. The junta found it increasingly difficult to prevent news of these events reaching the general public.

Until 1981 the church, political parties and the CGT had failed to respond to the Mothers' demands that they address themselves publicly to the issue of the disappearances. In response to General Viola's proposal for a dialogue on a political transition, the country's traditional social and political agents started to take positions in the movement of resistance against military rule. The Mothers continued their campaign to press for the inclusion of human rights in the political dialogue.

The Church

Hebe de Bonafini: It was on the doors of the churches that we knocked the most frequently. We believed the church would support us, that they, more than anyone else, would defend the right to life and the security of the family. They have a lot of power in Argentina. They could have used their influence to stop what was happening. If they had spoken out this would never have happened. The church was an accomplice in the genocide. They provided the priests to bless the weapons of the military, they gave confession to the torturers. When we went to them in desperation they used our information for the support of the dictatorship. Except for a few honourable exceptions, they refused to give us masses for the *desaparecidos*, they refused to give us a place to meet. They closed their doors on the Mothers . . . they say the cross is an inverted sword.

Aída de Suárez: We always went to the church, some to the cathedral, others to local churches. They closed the doors to the churches. When we ran into the cathedral for refuge from the police who were attacking us, they brought in the police to get us out. When we asked for a mass for the *desaparecidos* they gave us a sermon on the morality of young people.[8] I was married in a church, I am baptized, I took communion, I am a Christian, all my children were baptized. My older children were married in church. It was a terrible shock for a believer like myself to go to the church for help, for support and solidarity and to have the doors closed in our faces.

In May 1981 the Conference of Argentine Bishops issued a document entitled 'Church and National Community' which pointed out the 'dangers of usury' in a reference to the regime's economic policy and which also questioned the methods used in the 'war against subversion': 'We must distinguish between the justifications for the war against subversion and the methods used in this war.'[9] Until then the ecclesiastical hierarchy had only registered any concern in private communications to the regime. Unlike the church in Chile and Brazil, they denied the families of victims of the repression any support. Rather, the Argentine church had used its powerful influence to discourage individual and collective action. Its close relationship with the military regime also enabled it to function as a channel of communication between the victims and the agents of repression. The distinction between the latter and the church itself, particularly in the case of the military chaplains, had become increasingly unclear.

Political Parties

Since the coup and the prohibition of political activity the positions of the political parties had ranged from open support or a disguised complicity to well-intentioned calls for moderation. In the main they had accepted their own powerlessness and retreated into silence. Forced to respond to the resurgence of mass action, in July 1981 some of the major political parties formed a coalition, known as the *Multipartidaria*. The politicians favoured a cautious approach to the uncertain political future. General Galtieri, the man who was to topple the President in a palace coup a few months later, publicly opposed General Viola's steps towards a political opening. In March 1981 he had declared '*Las urnas están bien guardadas*' (The ballot boxes are well guarded).[10] The *Multipartidaria* refused the Mothers' request to be included in the talks. Compared with its own modest proposals for change, the Mothers and their demands were seen to be a political liability. Its first document called for moderate changes in economic policies and a phased transition to constitutional rule. It made only a brief reference to human rights and avoided any direct reference to the *detenidos–desaparecidos*.

Dora de Bazze: We helped the political parties a lot because, thanks to us marching at the front, they were able to open a way to elections. If not, they wouldn't be where they are today, in Congress. We were the first to go out on the streets, the first to shout. We weren't afraid to do that. We went to shout in Plaza de Mayo at the most difficult time. Even if the army were there we shouted at the doors of Government House to Videla or Viola, something which no politician ever did. We were always fighting for the truth and none of them want the truth. The only thing the political parties want is power.

María del Rosario: The political parties began to take positions from 1981. All the parties joined together to form the *Multipartidaria* to call for elections. We knocked on their doors many times and they wouldn't let us in. We told them that they couldn't accept the inheritance of 30,000 *desaparecidos* because it is a crime against humanity, that they had to act responsibly and that they had to demand a reply from the military. We told them that anyone who remained silent was an accomplice of the military, because no party could claim to be a winner if it didn't demand justice for the horrendous crimes that were committed here.

We never accepted the patronage of any political party. It was an ethical and moral demand that all the political parties had to accept and that had nothing to do with electoral politics. No party could negotiate with the murderers in the armed forces. This is what we demanded and we told them that our demands would not change, whatever party was in power. In a subsequent document they mentioned the *desaparecidos*. Although it wasn't what we wanted, it was more than we had thought they would say.

Trade Unions

The trade union bureaucracy had also maintained a long silence over the disappearances, despite the fact that 54% of the *desaparecidos* were from the working class.[11] The leadership of the CGT, with one exception, had been left unscathed by the persecution. Rank and file members, however, had begun to speak out against the regime's abuses of human rights. During the OAS visit workers and employees of Mercedes Benz had published a demand for information on the fate of several workers who had disappeared from the plant. This was followed by two advertisements sponsored by *Luz y Fuerza*, the electricians' union. They also invited the Mothers to attend a mass in memory of Oscar Smith, the disappeared leader of the union. Other workers from banks, transport, construction, the ports and the car industry also expressed support for the Mothers and in February 1982 a column of workers joined the women in Plaza de Mayo.

Aída de Suárez: The union leaders never helped us. The military didn't touch the CGT. Only one union leader disappeared. It was one of the most powerful organizations in the country and it did nothing for the workers in their unions who disappeared. There were some strikes and they said the CGT was against the military but they were strikes from the grassroots, pressuring the CGT to take a position. The Mothers support the workers but the CGT never. Because it's all bureaucracy. They never fight for the working class. Not before and not today.

Carmen de Guede: The leadership of the CGT was very bad and continues to be very bad today. There are some leaders who have said they don't believe there are *desaparecidos*, even when their own members have disappeared. We've always had this bad feeling for the leaders because they've never raised their voices for the *desaparecidos*. Once they had a demonstration on a Thursday, just at the time when we were in the square. It wasn't the workers but the leaders who didn't want us to be in the square at our usual time. We almost suffocated and other people had to help us to leave the square. The leaders put themselves against the Mothers. Another time there was a demonstration which the Mothers didn't directly participate in, but we were in the square because it was a Thursday again. We stood at the edge of the square and the workers came in and every column of workers came and saluted us and stayed with us a while. We always had the support of the workers and we supported their struggle but we didn't support the leadership.

On 30 March 1982 the CGT organized nationwide demonstrations for Peace, Bread and Work to accompany the presentation of a document to Government House which incorporated a demand for information about the *desaparecidos*. The Mothers were present at the demonstrations and six of them were among those arrested after the police moved in with water cannon and tear gas to disperse the crowds trying to break through the barriers into Plaza de Mayo. The repression in Mendoza was even more severe.

Elsa de Becerra: The workers were singing the national anthem when the police fired. We were there, as *Madres de Plaza de Mayo de Mendoza*, in spite of the fact that the leaders of the CGT didn't want us there. When they saw the white headscarves they were horrified. We were singing the national anthem when the police jumped out of their jeeps, got down on their knees and fired their machine guns into the crowds. One person was killed and at least ten more were injured. This was 30 March 1982, the first time that the CGT organized a national demonstration against the dismissals and unemployment and to demand pay rises. The events in Mendoza had repercussions throughout the country. It was met with general repudiation.

The Falklands/Malvinas War

The junta did not hesitate to launch an external military diversion to defuse the internal crisis. On 2 April 1982, three days after the most serious demonstration of mass opposition to military rule, Argentine troops took possession of the South Atlantic islands which had been the subject of a prolonged dispute between Argentina and Britain. This strategy of deflecting attention away from internal difficulties had already achieved a measure of success three years earlier when the junta initiated hostilities against Chile over the issue of ownership of the Beagle Channel. Their latest objective, if accompanied by a good propaganda campaign, would be guaranteed the undivided support of the Argentine population.

The war was to validate the Mothers' fears over the limits of political commitment to the issue of the *desaparecidos* as once again they were confronted by a display of 'political realism'. One by one the trade union and political leaders lined up to voice their support for the military adventure and to announce a suspension of their demands for the duration of the hostilities. The words of Carlos Contín, the president of the Radical Party, were typical: 'Now is the hour to lay aside all domestic questions, to galvanize the unity of all Argentines.'[12] The approval was almost unanimous from the left who saw it as a war against British imperialism, a just war, regardless of the nature of the government. The majority of the political parties were represented at the swearing-in ceremony of General Menéndez as Governor of the Malvinas and many, including the CGT, sent delegates abroad to explain the actions of the military government. In the midst of the patriotic fervour which was gripping the country the Mothers, once again, found themselves isolated.

Rita de Ponce: One of my sons was doing his military service at the time of the war and he was called up to fight. For me the Malvinas meant reliving the events of the past. The military were trying to take another one of my children. But this time I was stronger and I could understand what was happening. Our sympathies were with the soldiers and the mothers of the soldiers. They took many boys from the provinces to fight the war. Many boys from Tucumán went into the navy and many died in the sinking of the Belgrano. Luckily my son never got there because the day before he was due to leave the military surrendered.

Carmen de Guede: We were opposed to the Malvinas because for us they were doing the same thing as they did to our children. They kidnapped these young soldiers as well, because they were sent out there by force. Boys who didn't know what to do with the weapon in their hands, who'd only recently been confirmed. They sent them to their deaths because their guns and equipment were useless. They were dying of hunger. The troops which came from England were much better prepared than our children. The military believed that the United States would support them but the United States is never going to support a country like Argentina against the British. We were against it because the military were using it to try to raise their prestige, to try to glorify themselves. We felt they were killing people pointlessly. They wanted to keep their hands soaked in the blood of our young people.

They organized a big campaign to raise money to send to the Malvinas and they put it all in what they called the 'Patriotic Fund'. People who had things made of gold donated them, women gave their wedding rings, but they never got to the soldiers. There were programmes on the TV which went on for hours and hours, all through the day and night, where they showed famous people donating things and where they asked people to send money to the soldiers, but all the money ended up in the hands of the military. The soldiers didn't get it. Schoolchildren were told to send boxes of chocolates to the soldiers and they used to put a little note inside the box for the soldiers to read. Once somebody bought a box of these chocolates in a shop and saw the little letter inside. They told the papers but nothing was published because the army had the press in its pocket. We always said that what was happening was one thing and what they were saying was happening was something quite different. We always said that it wasn't true that they were winning, that they were sinking all the British ships. They were all liars.

People said we were unpatriotic and that we were being paid by the English, that because we were opposed to the war we supported the English. When we went to the square during the war people threw blue and white ribbons at us. They brought people, children from the private schools, to shout at us that we were unpatriotic. They didn't only throw ribbons, they threw stones too, anything. They threatened us, but every Thursday we were in the square anyway.

Aída de Suárez: First there was the strike and the big demonstration on 30 March when thousands of police attacked the demonstrators, pulled out anyone they wanted and dragged them into vans. Then on 2 April, three days later, when they said they had taken the Malvinas and Galtieri called everyone to the square, the same people who had been beaten on 30 March went back to celebrate with the generals. People weren't conscious. Everybody went waving their little flags. The Mothers couldn't support this. There were people who said that during the war we should stop. Someone came up to me in the square and said we were unpatriotic. How wrong they were. If we really had to defend our country our children would have been in the front line because they were more patriotic than anyone.

My sister was one of those who celebrated. I said, 'How could you?' and she said, 'But they've taken the Malvinas, the Malvinas are Argentine. At last we can say they're ours!' I told her to wake up, that our country was already covered in the blood of its young people, that the military did it because the economic situation was so terrible and they were losing the support of the people.

Our people have always been badly informed. Governments never tell the truth. We knew this more than anyone. While they were losing the war, while the Argentine ships were sinking, they talked of victory. I knew they were lying because we had a very good radio. My son had paid the instalments on it by cutting down on cigarettes. And do you know what we used to do at night? I disconnected the television aerial which is very high and I fixed it to the radio and tried to find the programmes from England, the United States and Russia, because in these countries they broadcast one hour of news in Spanish. For example, at half past four in the morning we used to get the news in Spanish from Russia. So we found these stations and we listened in to the news from foreign countries and from this we found out the truth. Here, every ten minutes on the TV and radio they reported another Argentine victory over the British forces. It was all a big lie.

Graciela de Jeger: All the political parties came to tell us that we had to support them, that we had to forget our differences and join together because the nation was in danger. They told us that we should knit pullovers in the square for the soldiers. They all went to the swearing-in ceremony of General Menéndez as Governor of the Malvinas. The leaders of the CGT stood next to Galtieri and Videla. The only thing we did was to send out a statement expressing solidarity with the mothers of the soldiers.

But after the Malvinas people became more conscious. The day of the surrender I was in Buenos Aires. I went to Plaza de Mayo with a friend and we saw crowds of people shouting insults against Galtieri. They could see that the military had been lying. Relatives of missing soldiers were there and they were shouting to us, '*Madres de Plaza de Mayo*, now we understand you!' We embraced the mothers of the soldiers but we refused to support the government. History shows that an army of occupation of its own country can never win a foreign war, no matter how just the cause.

The Resurgence of Protest

The Malvinas defeat provoked a bitter power struggle in the military leadership. While the future course of military rule was being argued out in Government House different branches of the armed forces were publicly blaming each other for the outcome of the war. The politicians proved unwilling to take advantage of the political vacuum. Instead of demanding the immediate departure of the regime, the military were allowed time to attempt to restore their authority. In an effort to forestall further unrest the armed forces initiated an investigation into the conduct of the war and removed those officers most deeply compromised by it. Galtieri was replaced as President by General Bignone.

On 2 July 1982 the new junta announced its statement of intent to hold elections, although no definite date was set. Their objective was to use the intervening period to impose an agreement on the political leaders on the terms of the transition to constitutional rule, and in particular they wanted assurances that key issues including human rights and the Malvinas would not be investigated by a future civilian government.

By now, however, the components of the political agenda were being determined elsewhere. The military regime was being attacked from all directions. Ex-combatants of the war, students, housewives, the unemployed and the unions took to the streets to protest. The judiciary began challenging military control of the courts and even the press now felt able to publish critical attacks on the regime. The last months of 1982 saw an increase in militancy in the labour movement culminating in the general strike of December 1982 when nine million workers downed tools, paralysing almost the whole of industry, commerce and the service sector. The Mothers, together with the other human rights organizations, maintained a constant presence on the streets to ensure that the issue of the *desaparecidos* had a central place on the political agenda.

Rita de Krichmar: I returned to Argentina for a brief visit in 1982 and I saw that the situation was very different from 1979. There was a lot of unrest, confrontations and strikes, and people had begun to talk about human rights. Things were beginning to change and because of this we decided to return the next year. You could have demonstrations in the streets. The climate was very different from 1979, so much so that when I came back and I spoke on the telephone to my friends I was still afraid to speak to them or to say where we would meet. I was talking as if they were still persecuting me. Later I got used to it but at first if I'd forgotten my documents when I went to the shops I would come back immediately. If you went out without your documents before, anything could have happened to you. We joined a big march which had been organized by all the human rights groups. It was the first time I'd seen the Mothers carrying the huge placards with the photographs of their children. That really made an impression on me.

María del Rosario: We began the *Marcha de Resistencia* [March of Resistance] in December 1981. We marched in the square for twenty-four hours as a demonstration of civil resistance against the dictatorship. The first one took place at the time of the fall of Viola's government. We marched for twenty-four hours and in that time we had five presidents because it passed from one general to another to another until they finally agreed on Galtieri.

Just before the second march, which was on 10 December 1982, a telegram was sent to the Mothers' House asking us to go to the police station. We went, and they read us an article from the police regulations which said that public meetings were prohibited and that it was a punishable offence. We said that like all citizens we believed the Mothers had the right to protest and that since the dictatorship had violated all constitutional rights there was no legal authority we could ask for permission. They wanted us to sign a piece of paper saying that we knew it was illegal but we refused to sign anything. Four Mothers were waiting for us outside in case we didn't come out of the police station, in case they detained us. This march was repressed. They didn't let us enter Plaza de Mayo. They emptied the square and surrounded it with police on horseback and wouldn't let us through. So we decided to hold it in Avenida de Mayo, the main avenue which goes off the square.

Elisa de Landin: The second *Marcha de Resistencia*, in the December after the Malvinas war, was the best one we ever had. Thousands of people joined us over the twenty-four hours. The hotels and cafés in Avenida de Mayo left their toilets open for us, they let us use their fridges to keep our food fresh, many left out chairs in the street for us to sit down and rest. People invited us into their homes to take a shower, to have a drink, because it was the middle of summer and very hot, and others brought us food. There was a great feeling of solidarity, in spite of the fact that we still had the military in power. There was a continual stream of supporters coming all through the night. It was a very emotional demonstration for us because it showed that people were ready to take a stand against the military government.

María del Rosario: *La Marcha por la Vida* [The March for Life] was organized by all the human rights groups to call for an investigation into the disappearances and of course the Mothers participated. It was a march which was supposed to end up at Government House but we never got there because the police were trying to send us off in another direction. The organizations at the head of the march followed the police diversion, but the Mothers decided to break the police circle surrounding the square and go through. And we got through, between the hooves of the horses, but the rest didn't follow so we decided to return. There are very dramatic photographs of us breaking through the barrier. It was a very big demonstration. Groups like the *Asamblea* could mobilize a lot of people because their membership included a lot of political figures.

Marta de Baravalle: The first real breakthrough the Grandmothers had was in 1982 with the *Marcha por la Vida*. We went with placards with photographs of our disappeared grandchildren. This had a great impact on the public because it showed the exact dimensions of what had happened, that they hadn't only taken adults, but also little children. After this people began to approach us, very timidly at first, and they began to give us information about children they knew of who had arrived in a family in a strange way. Perhaps the couple couldn't have children and suddenly they had a child, or the father was a colonel or a general or a policeman and they began to think that perhaps these could be children we were looking for.

La Marcha por la Vida was the turning-point. They couldn't contain the reaction and the public began to come forward. We took out advertisements in the press. It took a lot of effort, not only financial effort but also to persuade newspapers to accept the advertisements, but by the beginning of 1983 some magazines began publishing the photographs of our grand-children. It was then that we began to see the real possibility of recovering them. In April we located Pablo Moyano and in June, Tamara and three others, all of whom were kidnapped when they were babies. Tamara's mother had been arrested by the police when she was leaving the factory where she worked. The police had passed her to the military and after nearly six years in concentration camps and then as a legal prisoner she was deported and went to live in Switzerland. Tamara had been left by the security forces with a neighbouring family. Her mother supplied us with photographs and details of the child and the area where they'd lived and we began the search for her. Finally a man came forward with information on her whereabouts.

Pablo Moyano's parents were taken when he was one year old and photographs of the child at this age were published in a magazine. As a result a man contacted us with information. Also, in this case, the grandmother had taken an imprint of his foot when he was born, so this was another clue. We had to trace his history to be able to prove to the courts that it was Pablo. Locating a disappeared child is only one part of the battle. Then another battle begins to get the child returned to its legitimate family.

We have to work hard to get all the evidence the court requires and the legal process is very slow. It wasn't until 1985 that Pablo returned home. That same year we also located Martín, Eduardo and Paula.

Elsa Pavón de Aguilar: Between 1980 and 1983 we hadn't managed to find any new information about Paula. Then in July 1983, after we had covered the walls of the city with the photographs of the missing grandchildren, a relative of mine received a phone call from a man who said he knew where she was. He had recognized her from a poster in the street, even though she was only twenty-three months when the photo was taken and in 1983 she was already seven. He gave us the address and the name of the family who had her. We went to see if it was really her. We had to proceed very carefully, to find out who this person was, what he did, where he worked, where the child was, what school she went to, how she had arrived in their hands. We had to know for certain that this was Paula before we could begin legal action. We had to find her and follow her, we had to speak to a lot of people. One of my daughters had to help me because my eyesight isn't very good. When I saw her I knew for certain it was Paula. She's very similar to her mother and my husband managed to speak to her while she was playing in a park and she stared at him as if she recognized him. She looked as if she couldn't remember where she'd seen him before. We decided to wait until after the military had gone before starting legal proceedings, as a form of security for the child. We began legal action the day after the constitutional government took power.

Human Rights on the Political Agenda

Despite their efforts, the military were unable to prevent human rights emerging as one of the key issues in the protest movement. In September 1982 the junta had issued a decree prohibiting the press, television and radio from broadcasting any further reports on human rights violations, the Malvinas and the alleged corruption of military officers. Sections of the armed forces became nervous and threatened to reverse the political opening and withdraw their promise of elections but the momentum of events was no longer in their control.

On the evening of 16 December 1982 the *Multipartidaria* and the union federations organized a March for Democracy on the streets of Buenos Aires. The Mothers were among the 200,000 people who gathered in front of Government House chanting:

> *Milicos, muy mal paridos,*
> *Qué es lo que han hecho con los desaparecidos?*
> *La deuda externa, la corrupcion,*
> *Son la peor mierda que he tenido la nación.*

(Military bastards, what have you done with the disappeared? The foreign debt, the corruption have put the country in the worst shit it's ever been in.)

One person was killed and more than 60 people were injured as the police moved in to break up the demonstration. In the following months the pressure mounted for the junta to set a date for their departure. Finally, in February they announced that elections would be held on 30 October 1983 and that the new civilian president would be inaugurated ninety days later.

The Mothers' Demands

While the political parties were selecting candidates in preparation for the election campaign, the Mothers were formulating their own election strategy. They had to convert the general principles laid down in their Articles of Association into a series of concrete proposals which could be put to the political parties. The result was a programme around which all the human rights groups united:

1. The return of the *detenidos–desaparecidos* alive.
2. The restitution of kidnapped children and those born in captivity to their legitimate families.
3. The immediate release of all those detained for political and trade union reasons.
4. An investigation into the burials of the unidentified bodies.
5. Trial for those responsible for the disappearances, torture and murders.
6. The lifting of the State of Siege.
7. The repeal of anti-democratic legislation and the dismantling of political repression.
8. The rejection of any type of amnesty.

Las Madres de Plaza de Mayo, who began a movement of resistance during this inhuman dictatorship and who do not permit any negotiation of the points stated above, ask the men and women who inhabit this country that they be consistent when it comes to Human Dignity, because over and above ideologies and beliefs, there is life, a sacred privilege, which all humanity should respect. We will fight on tirelessly because as mothers we are the centre of the human species and our only goal is that the birth of a child isn't converted into irreparable pain.[13]

Their demands represented a reaffirmation of the most fundamental rights of men and women. It followed that they were not the special preserve of any one political party. All parties had an equal moral responsibility to protect these rights. The Mothers would take a neutral position in the election campaign. This was consistent with Article 1d of the Statute of the Association of the Mothers of Plaza de Mayo:

To avoid the interference or influence of political or sectoral interests which would pervert the exclusively humanitarian nature of the Association and which would divorce us from the objectives expressed in our declaration of principles.[14]

Juanita de Pargament: We've never been involved with any one party. Of course some Mothers have sympathies with certain parties and we've never stopped any Mother from supporting the one of her choice, but as a movement we were neutral. We wanted to make our demands an obligation of all the parties. This doesn't mean that our opponents haven't tried to look for connections. When you attack the Radicals, everyone says you're a Peronist and when you attack the Peronists, everyone says you're manipulated by the Radicals. When we attack the priests, they say we're communists and when we attack the communists they say we're being used by the church. There have always been people who've said the Mothers are very religious and others who've said we're all communists.

The Junta's Response

Having failed to obtain the assurances it had sought from the political parties, the junta made a final attempt to perpetuate its impunity. In May 1983 the military's 'Final Document on the War against Subversion' was broadcast on nationwide television. This was followed in September by the Law of National Pacification which exonerated all members of the armed forces who had operated within the institutional framework of any criminal responsibility for their actions.

Elsa de Becerra: It was only in 1983 that the junta first admitted that there were *desaparecidos*. They put out this programme on television where they justified their actions in terms of a war against subversion, saying that the *desaparecidos* were all dead and that they were all terrorists. They said they would do the same again if they thought it was necessary and that the nation owed them a debt for ridding the country of terrorism.

They always speak of a 'war' and of 'terrorism', but I believe that the people have more honesty and more intelligence. There were those who had arms but they were very few in number and they had the entire armed forces against them and they were destroyed. The *detenidos–desaparecidos* were taken by force, no one has said who took them, they had no weapons and it can't be said they were terrorists. They took defenceless unarmed people from their homes, tortured and raped them and then massacred them. This is the reality and they didn't have the courage to accuse them in a court of law because they knew they didn't have a case. So they did everything secretly, all three branches of the armed forces together, with the collaboration of many civilians – the church, those with economic power, judges, doctors were all implicated.

The human rights organizations mobilized 45,000 people to protest at the military's attempt at self-amnesty. Only those sectors most deeply compromised in the 'dirty war' failed to condemn the law outright. The church called it a 'questionable document' while the political parties reserved their repudiations to official declarations. Neither the three principal constitutents of the *Multipartidaria* nor the two wings of the CGT responded to the invitation to join the demonstration.

Positions of the Political Parties

As the election moved towards a confrontation between Argentina's two historic parties, the Peronists and the Radicals, neither had emerged with a clear line on the issue of the *desaparecidos*. The Peronist manifesto was based on a moderate change in economic policies and avoided any explicit mention of the disappeared. They were opposed to an investigation into the activities of the armed and security forces and referred only to vague statements about the redressing of individual grievances in the courts. In the closing stages of the campaign the Peronist presidential candidate, Italo Luder, announced that he would honour the military's amnesty law. The Peronist leaders had found themselves in a contradictory position. Many of the *desaparecidos* were from the left of their own party who had destabilized their own government and some of the leadership had themselves engaged in para-military activity against these groups. Moreover, Luder had been a signatory to the decree passed in 1975 authorizing the military to take over the 'war against subversion'. The Peronists' election campaign failed to conceal these contradictions.

Alfonsín's victory in the mid-1983 internal elections was, in Radical terms, a move to the left. He took advantage of the opposition's dilemma by accusing leading Peronists of links with the death squads. He promised that a Radical government would launch an investigation into the disappearances and would ensure that the armed forces were made accountable to the law and elected civilian authorities. The details of his policies were, however, also imprecise. While demanding punishment for those found guilty of criminal actions, he introduced the idea of levels of responsibility very early on, drawing a distinction between those who were responsible for formulating the policy and those who implemented it.

Four days before the election the Mothers published an 'Appeal to the New Government'.

Time hasn't passed in vain. Today everyone abhors the Dictatorship, its crimes are detestable but there still exists the fear, or perhaps the compromise, that will allow them to go unpunished for their crimes. Today we are approaching the election of a constitutional government which will have to demonstrate by its actions that it is democratic . . . In order to achieve this long-awaited democracy we will participate, criticize, protest and demand and we will mobilize to secure the legitimate rights of the people. Because of this, we demand of the future elected government: *Aparición con Vida* of the *detenidos–desaparecidos*: freedom for all political prisoners and trade unionists; trial for those responsible.

They requested the immediate implementation of three measures. First, that the *detenidos–desaparecidos* be freed in the first 48 hours of the constitutional rule in order to avoid the mass murder of the survivors; secondly, the establishment of a bicameral parliamentary commission in which the Mothers and other human rights groups would be represented; and lastly, that Congress legislate immediately to enable the military to be tried and condemned by jury, trials which they did not want to be subjected to common criminal law.[15]

Against all expectations the result was a victory for the Radical Party with 52% as against the Peronists' 40%. It was the first time since the formation of the Peronist Party that the Argentine people, and in particular the industrial working class, had voted against Peronism.

Rita de Krichmar: All the political parties used the issue of the *desaparecidos*. They all said they were going to set up investigations, they were going to do everything possible to find out what happened to each one and they all promised justice. The Peronists less, but the Radicals committed themselves, saying they were going to do everything. The Peronists lost because they were very divided and people didn't want any more violence. They had various demonstrations which were very violent. When friends of mine saw the last campaign rally of the Peronists, when Herminio Iglesias [the right-wing Peronist candidate for the governorship of Buenos Aires province] set light to a coffin which bore the name of Alfonsín, they said they couldn't vote for the Peronists. And they had been Peronists all their lives. People voted for Alfonsín because he seemed honest and because they thought he would do something to find out the truth about the disappearances.

Graciela de Jeger: I had expectations that the constitutional government would fulfil its promises. Alfonsín seemed to be a serious person and he was the only politician who had signed our petitions. We had two interviews with him when he was still a candidate for the presidency. Then, just before he took power, we got another interview for a few minutes when he promised us justice and said that he would give us an answer to what had happened to each of the *desaparecidos*. But then he spoke of the three grades of responsibility. He always said they would be tried by the judges, he never spoke of a military trial. I thought it would all be very bureaucratic and a long process but I always believed he had every intention of ensuring justice.

María del Rosario: We'd met Alfonsín a few times. In 1980, forty bodies had appeared on the Atlantic beaches and we went to see Alfonsín who lived in Chacamous, near the coast, and we asked him, as a well-known politician, to go to the courts and demand an investigation. He refused. We saw him again during the election campaign when he promised us everything. All the political parties used the issue of human rights in the electoral campaign but they were always very careful about what they said. Afterwards they ignored it again. Alfonsín organized his political campaign in favour of human rights but it was forgotten the day he took power. When we saw that he received the presidential sash from the dictator General Bignone then we realized that Alfonsín had negotiated. Because if he had any dignity he wouldn't have accepted the presidential sash from a military murderer. The political parties here have always been ready to negotiate with the military. There's no other way to understand why for sixty years there has been one military coup after another.

By the last Thursday of military rule the buildings in the centre of Buenos Aires had been painted with thousands of ghostly silhouettes bearing the names of *desaparecidos*. Thirty thousand people joined the Mothers in Plaza de Mayo in an emotional gathering which reflected the mixture of happiness, sorrow and above all, hope, which the women felt as the country approached the imminent departure of the military. Hebe de Bonafini declared to the assembled crowds,

> For us the struggle isn't going to change, it's going to continue exactly the same. Instead of putting our demands to the military, we are going to put these demands to the constitutional government.[16]

Notes

1. Quoted in *Madres de Plaza de Mayo*, No. 2, January 1985.
2. Statistical evidence testifies to the extent of the deindustrialization process in Argentina. The proportion of industrial production in GNP fell from 32% in 1976 to 28% in 1983. The number of workers in manufacturing industry fell from 1,165,000 in 1975 to 740,000 in 1982. For an analysis of the transfer of resources from the productive to the financial sector, see Peralta-Ramos, Monica and Waisman, Carlos H., (eds.), 1987, Chapter 3. See also Villareal, Juan M., 'Changes in Argentine Society: the Heritage of the Dictatorship', ibid., Chapter 4, where it is argued that the military's plan had a political, rather than economic objective: the concentration of economic power was intended to centralize and strengthen the political power of the ruling class to enable them to halt the advance of the radicalized sectors of society which had taken place under populist governments.
3. From Dabat, Alejandro and Lorenzano, Luis, 1984, Chapter 3.
4. Latin American Bureau, 1982.
5. Quoted in Pion-Berlin, David, 1985.
6. Real wages fell from US$217 in 1974 to $109 in 1978 see Villareal, Juan M., in Peralta-Ramos, Monica and Waisman, Carlos H., (eds.), 1987. Official figures admit to an unemployment rate of 4–8%, depending on the region, for the period 1980–81. One study by multinational companies found 15% of the urban labour force unemployed. Labour spokesmen argue that the reduction in working hours for those in employment was the equivalent of another 8%. See Monteon, Michael, 'Can Argentina's Democracy Survive Economic Disaster?' in ibid., Chapter 2.
7. Adolfo Pérez Esquivel was one of the founding members of the Permanent Assembly for Human Rights and of the Service for Peace and Justice. According to Pérez Esquivel, *Paz y Justicia* is 'a Christian movement which has a commitment to the whole continent: to live the Gospel, with preferential concern for the poor and the most needy.' He was arrested in 1977 when he went to the police station to renew his passport and was held for 14 months without being brought to trial. This was followed by another 14 months of 'supervised freedom'.
8. This is a reference to a service held in the Basílica de San Francisco in December 1978

which coincided with the thirtieth anniversary of the Declaration of Human Rights. The Mothers expected comfort and support. Instead the priest gave a sermon on the dangers of young people associating with bad company, drugs and guerrillas.

9. Dabat, Alejandro and Lorenzano, Luis, 1984.

10. Quoted in Pion-Berlin, David, 1985.

11. The Mothers' estimate, based on their own records.

12. Quoted in Dabat, Alejandro and Lorenzano, Luis, 1984.

13. Madres de Plaza de Mayo, *Boletín Informativo*, No. 3, March 1983.

14. 'Estatuto de las Madres de Plaza de Mayo', taken from Madres de Plaza de Mayo, *Boletín Informativo*, No. 7, August 1981.

15. 'Exhortación al Nuevo Gobierno', 26 October 1983, taken from Madres de Plaza de Mayo, *Boletín Informativo*, No. 11, November 1983. The Mothers wanted the charge to be one of genocide. A 1946 Resolution of the UN General Assembly included political groups along with racial, national, ethnic and religious ones as potential victims of the crime of genocide.

16. Quoted in Goldferb Tiffenberg, Ernesto David, 1984, Chapter 4.

7. Democracy

When Alfonsín took power he had everything in his favour. He had the support of all the people who didn't want the military any more. Everyone was happy with the civilian government. Nobody thought the Radicals were going to win and it was a great relief to many people. He had the opportunity to act immediately but he didn't do it because, I believe, he'd already made a pact with the armed forces.

Beatriz de Rubinstein

Investigations

Within days of taking office President Alfonsín announced his government's intention to open an investigation into the disappearances and to initiate criminal proceedings against the nine members of the first three military juntas. The doors of the barracks, however, remained closed and the uncertainty over the fate of the *desaparecidos* turned to desperation.

Alive or Dead

In the months following the installation of the civilian government several families received letters and telephone calls which suggested that some of their disappeared children were still alive. At the same time courts were ordering the exhumation of corpses from unnamed graves in an attempt to identify what were presumed to be the remains of *desaparecidos*. Photographs of the hundreds of bodies which were being discovered in cemeteries throughout the country, together with accounts of kidnapping, torture and murder, filled the pages of the newspapers. In the light of the evidence which seemed to indicate that the *desaparecidos* were dead, the Mothers' demand for *aparición con vida*, the return of their children alive, seemed contradictory.

Carmen de Guede: When the constitutional government took power one of the Grandmothers received a series of phone calls from her daughter, who had disappeared many years before. She said there were other *desaparecidos* alive. They made a recording of the voice and gave it to Pérez Esquivel who gave it, in confidence, to the Ministry of the Interior. The Minister made it public and from then on the voice was never heard again.[1] I think if they'd handled it properly at least this *desaparecida* and those with her would be alive today. We always said that if just one appeared it would be a joy for all the Mothers. Whoever it is.

There are some Mothers who still have the hope that their children are alive, that they are in a mental hospital somewhere, so badly tortured that they've lost their memories. Others say that the *desaparecidos* could have been moved to Paraguay, in the lorries carrying the grain, because Paraguay is like a big prison, you never know what terrible things are happening there. But the truth is, we know they've killed them. *Aparición con vida* means that although the majority of them are dead, no one has taken responsibility for their deaths, because no one has said who killed them, who gave the order. Some Mothers have been sent the body of their child and they've been told they were killed in '*enfrentamientos*'. The majority have never had any news about them. We are fighting for all the disappeared and it's for this reason we continue demanding *aparición con vida*.

Graciela de Jeger: According to those who've been freed from the camps, who've told us about the dreadful tortures they suffered there, we knew it was very unlikely that our children were alive. At first we were hopeful, but now we can see it's impossible. But we don't want to assume responsibility for their deaths ourselves. We want them to say who killed them. This is why we speak of our children in the present tense. *Aparición con vida* is the most controversial of our slogans because a lot of people support us, but say *aparición con vida*, no. You're mad . . .

We already know that thousands of *desaparecidos* were secretly murdered and buried. The exhumations don't tell us anything we don't already know. In a cemetery in Tucumán there were many days when they wouldn't let visitors in. In 1983 I went there with a group of people because a friend was being buried and we saw about seventy crosses, all white, all the same, like in a war cemetery, with no names. We went back on All Souls' Day and we noticed that nobody was putting flowers on these graves. I asked an attendant who was buried there and he said 'children', but it seemed strange to me that a mother wouldn't put up a plaque with the name of her child. We began to suspect that these were the graves of *desaparecidos*. The next time we went we took flowers and a workman told us, 'Listen, they're not there, they're somewhere else. They put those crosses there to deceive you.' Later, under court instructions, they dug up some bodies which they found, not under a cross, but underneath a pathway. There were three bodies, two in the same box and one with the head decapitated and placed in reverse. Also, at the end of the cemetery there is a small square and a gravedigger confirmed to us that during the time of the repression there had been a big well there and helicopters used to come at night and throw in bodies.

Alfonsín took power on 10 December. On the 11th the spades and shovels were ready to exhume bodies in cemeteries all over the country. They brought a very important forensic specialist from the United States who worked with a very special method, like on an archaeological dig, moving the earth carefully, with little spoons. Argentine students of medicine were working with him and told us it was terrible, paralysing. Moreover, when Alfonsín took power the sensationalist press began the 'show'. People were saturated with horror and they didn't want to know any more about it, because horror has its limits. That was the intention.

We don't agree with the exhumation of the bodies. With the exhumations they want to eradicate the problem of the disappearances, because then there are no more *desaparecidos*, only dead people. From what the Mothers of Mar del Plata have told us they have returned people who disappeared from the street, or from their houses, saying they'd died in '*enfrentamientos*'. If you accept this, in your desperation to have the remains of your loved one, you lose all your rights. We don't want the names of the victims. We know who they are. We want the names of the murderers. We want them to tell us what happened. They have to explain what they don't want to explain. This is the meaning of *aparición con vida*. We respect those Mothers who want the exhumations of course, but we don't, as an organization, agree with it.

Beatriz de Rubinstein: The exhumations were another part of the government's strategy. It's very difficult for a mother who has received the remains of her child to go on fighting. In Mar del Plata there have been many exhumations. Once they came very early in the morning and told nobody what they were doing. They'd been sent by the courts to dig up three graves. We found out by accident and we went to the cemetery. Two families had given their permission and one mother, who is a *Madre de Plaza de Mayo*, said no. We saw lawyers and judges to try to get it stopped but they exhumed the body anyway. They used a team which had come from the United States to identify the remains. The bones don't interest us. What are we going to do with the bones? To receive the bodies before knowing who is responsible is a form of *punto final* [literally, 'full stop', and see p. 146] all the more unjust when you consider how many mothers will never receive the bodies – all those who were thrown into the sea by the navy and air force, dynamited, incinerated, who are never going to be found. Exhumations have nothing to do with justice.

Elisa de Landin: On 22 June 1983 we opened the newspaper and we read a statement from the Supreme Court which said that there had been no procedural irregularities in the judicial morgue. Underneath was a list of people killed in '*enfrentamientos*' and my son was on the list. It said he was killed on 7 February 1977. I calculate that the date of his disappearance was 20 January and by 7 February he was already dead. We organized a press conference in the Mothers' House, because everyone said how could it be possible that no one told me this before. As I come from a German family I went to the German Embassy with all the documentation and the ambassador wrote to me, expressing his condolences and saying he couldn't understand how I hadn't been informed. The Organization of American

States said the same thing. Why wasn't I told if for years I'd been reporting him as disappeared, searching for him, and he was already dead? I'd presented writs of habeas corpus and they'd all been rejected. I have letters from the Ministry of the Interior saying they had no knowledge of his whereabouts.

Later we discovered my son's body had been lying in the judicial morgue for four months and they never told us. When I went to claim the body I discovered the morgue had sent eight telegrams to the police station to inform them. In the police station I asked who was responsible for not telling me and they said the order came from above that they weren't to let me know.

Really, the Mothers were right not to want the bodies, because in spite of the fact I had my son's grave exhumed, I don't know it's my son. I think it's my son, but I don't know who killed him. All I know for sure is that my son isn't here. Why did they kidnap him? Why did they kill him? So the Mothers continue to say that they're not going to recognize bodies until they know who is responsible. In spite of the fact I got mine, one of mine – until today I've found out nothing about Horacio – I've never found out why Martín was killed and who killed him.

The National Commission on Disappeared People

There was general agreement between the government and the human rights groups on the necessity for an impartial enquiry to determine exactly what had transpired during the period of military rule. However, President Alfonsín rejected the Mothers' call for a bicameral parliamentary commission with power to subpoena all those military officers implicated in the human rights abuses. Instead he created a presidential commission, appointed by and answerable to himself, whose objective was to clarify the events relating to the disappearances and to investigate the fate of the *desaparecidos*. Its brief did not extend to determining responsibility but any evidence that crimes had been committed was to be passed to the courts whose task it would be to determine guilt or innocence. The investigations of the National Commission on Disappeared People (CONADEP) were to be based on testimonies offered voluntarily and it could not, therefore, expect the co-operation of the military. It had no powers of subpoena to help it to uncover a structure of repression specifically designed to guarantee the impunity of those responsible.

Much of the evidence of the clandestine operations, including detention centres and documentation relating to the 'dirty war', had already been destroyed by the late 1970s as the junta became increasingly worried about international criticism of its rule. In 1983, before the constitutional government assumed power, General Bignone had secretly ordered the destruction of documents relating to those detained under PEN and in the weeks before the new government took power the federal police had burnt all evidence relating to its anti-subversive operations.[2] The Commission's report had to confine itself to descriptions of kidnappings, torture and murders and to an investigation of the 340 secret detention centres.[3]

Hebe de Bonafini: We had many arguments in this House when a group of Mothers wanted to accept CONADEP. We didn't accept it because we realized why they organized it. We wanted a bicameral parliamentary investigation composed of members of all the parties, composed of those elected by the people, not a commission chosen by the President. We wanted a commission whose purpose would be to investigate who was responsible, not the victims. They set up CONADEP to avoid a bicameral investigation and the confrontation with the military this would have meant. If they'd formed a bicameral commission Alfonsín wouldn't have been able to hide behind 50,000 sheets of paper like he did.

Graciela de Jeger: We asked the government for a bicameral parliamentary commission to investigate and they gave us CONADEP. Many people who had never dared to come to the human rights organizations assisted this Commission, thinking it was a national organization, presidential. But it had very limited power. They weren't allowed to enter intelligence centres and seize documents. This documentation existed. Each detainee was given a number and had a file somewhere. When the dictatorship ended a group of students occupied the house of the university rector here in Tucumán and found some documents. Not many, because the most important had already been removed or destroyed after they'd been microfilmed. They found some papers which were stamped 'not suitable for microfilm'. To organize such a massive repressive structure there had to be some written orders.

Fundamentally CONADEP took declarations which had already been made by the human rights organizations. They published their findings in the book *Nunca Más* where the introduction talks about the theory of the '*dos demonios*': that the disappearances were the result of a conflict between two evils. The book was paralysing because they describe all this horror and they don't give a way out. The assumption is that the *desaparecidos* are dead and the story is over. They didn't want to publish the list of torturers and murderers who had been named in the testimonies. But it was leaked to the press and some of the newspapers published it. They kept the report well guarded in the President's safe.

In 1984 at a meeting in Santa Fe the Mothers were divided over what to do in the face of CONADEP. So it was resolved that each Mother had the freedom to give evidence to the President's Commission, but that the *Madres de Plaza de Mayo* as an entity weren't going to have anything to do with it.

Carmen de Guede: CONADEP served to waste a year. This Commission did nothing more than reproduce all the information the human rights organizations already had. It collected together all this evidence on the kidnappings and disappearances, put it into a file and presented it to Alfonsín. Alfonsín gave it to the Minister of the Interior who returned it to the army. So after a whole year which CONADEP wasted, it ended up with the military, so it ended up in the rubbish. The only good thing we can say about CONADEP is that the book and the documentary *Nunca Más* informed the public of what had happened. It made those people who hadn't known, or who hadn't wanted to know, face the truth about the military governments.

Genetic Analysis

The Grandmothers had also called for the formation of a bicameral parliamentary commission. Only an investigation aimed at identifying those responsible for the disappearances would be able to establish the whereabouts of their disappeared grandchildren. CONADEP did not have this objective and its limited powers meant that it was able to add little to the efforts the Grandmothers were already making to recover their grandchildren.[4]

While the women now had greater access to the media and to the legal system, they still had to rely on their own methods to construct the extensive proof necessary to present a case before the courts. As time went by the information they had compiled on the grandchildren and their parents, such as photographs, physical characteristics, hobbies, and tastes, were becoming less relevant. In the case of babies born in captivity they had no evidence at all, apart from a rough idea of the expected date of birth of the child. The only possible information which could prove the biological connection between the grandparents and their grandchildren was that contained in blood.

In December 1982 they had made contact with the American Association for the Advancement of Science, based in the United States. A year later they were informed by a specialist from the Blood Center in New York that their laboratories were capable of identifying genetic markers in the blood of grandparents and grandchildren which could establish with 99.9% certainty whether or not a child belonged biologically to a particular family. When the Association arrived in Argentina at the invitation of CONADEP, in order to help determine the cause of death of bodies discovered in *NN* graves, it offered its assistance to the Grandmothers. The method was put into practice for the first time in the case of the granddaughter of Elsa Pavón de Aguilar.

Elsa Pavón de Aguilar: We started legal action to get Paula the day after the constitutional government took power. Then the battle to prove she was our granddaughter began. We had photographs of her as a baby and of our family, we had the testimonies of people who lived near the family who took her and who'd seen how she'd appeared with them and we had the results of the blood tests. My family and my son-in-law's family all had our blood analysed. The tests proved to a certainty of 99.8% that she was my granddaughter. Despite this, the judge wanted her to stay with that family until the legal process was completed but we fought this. We had to wait until 13 December 1984 before we could finally bring her home.

I think the readjustment is difficult for everyone. She didn't know her real history but I imagine she had the sensation that everything wasn't as it seemed. I don't know what the family who kidnapped her told her, but when the judge told her the truth she cried a lot, which is a logical reaction, and then she adjusted very quickly. She wasn't used to going out. She'd spent her time either at school or alone indoors. Now she's started all sorts of activities to help get her out of herself, to develop. She's asked what's happened to her parents. She wants to know the truth.

The readjustment is difficult for the family too. She was taken when she was a baby. The last time I'd seen her she was twenty-one months old and suddenly I met a child of eight and a half, a different child. She had a different surname. She was brought up in a different way. I knew her as a child who liked eating everything. She used to love cucumbers, yoghurt and sausages but when she arrived home she didn't want any of those things. Now, yes, she goes to the fridge and eats everything, but when she first came she was a child with completely different tastes from the child we knew before. She has a different way of speaking too. There's also a problem with her education because this couple registered her date of birth as two years after her real birthday, so she's lost two years of schooling. We have a child who should be in junior school but who's still in the infants.

There are still problems with the other family but all that's being settled in the courts. Paula's surname is still legally theirs and it will be another two years before the position is final. And the kidnappers still haven't been found guilty of any crime.

Doctora Ana María di Lonardo is head of the Department of Immunology at the Durand Hospital in Buenos Aires. This is the department which, at the request of the courts, carries out the blood analyses which provide crucial evidence in the legal battle to prove the identity of the disappeared grandchildren. The role of Doctora di Lonardo and her team is a purely scientific one and they have no other connection with the work of the Grandmothers.

Dra Ana María di Lonardo: In June 1984 CONADEP invited a group of forensic scientists from the American Association for the Advancement of Science from the United States to visit Argentina to assist in the identification of the corpses of *desaparecidos*. They were accompanied by a geneticist, Dr Marie-Claire King, who was asked to help in the identification of children of *desaparecidos* and to investigate how these children, who were not with their biological families, could be identified biologically and restored to their families. She was very surprised to find that our unit had all the required facilities. People had believed, including CONADEP, that it wouldn't be possible to carry out these tests in Argentina and that it would be necessary to do the work in the Blood Center in New York. This unit was established to provide compatibility tests for organ transplants and these are the same tests as those used for the identification of the grandchildren.

From June 1984 the first cases began to arrive where it was necessary to resolve scientifically conflicts between two families over the biological parentage of a child. Normally we study the presumed grandparents who are questioning the identity of the child. In all the cases we have studied so far the families who have the child have never agreed to the test. Never.

If all four grandparents aren't alive we ask to test their children, the brothers and sisters of the *desaparecidos*. In this way we try to reconstruct the genetic information of the dead grandparent. After this biological test has been carried out we use a mathematical formula to establish the probability of 'inclusion' of this child in this family. From this we arrive at a percentage of probability of 'inclusion' and we have to decide if this index is significant as proof that this particular child belongs to this family. We use four groups of distinct genetic characteristics so that if one alone doesn't say very much we have three more to increase the information available to us.[5]

These tests can also be applied to the identification of children who were born in captivity. If a grandmother has received information which leads her to believe that a particular child is her grandchild, the investigations carried out here may be the most important evidence to determine the truth of the claim. This was the position with the Gallinari–Abinet case where we carried out tests on all four grandparents and their other children. We constructed a genealogical tree and our results showed a very high probability of inclusion.

Leonor Alsonso de Abinet: On 5 September 1976 they kidnapped my daughter from her house in Caseros, in the province of Buenos Aires. In the middle of the night of 5 September, they also took me from my house. I was asleep. I woke up because I heard windows being smashed and I tried to turn on the light but the electricity had been cut. There were a lot of them, all armed. They put a gun to my face and then they covered my head with a hood. I thought it was a nightmare, waking up and finding that metal against my skin. They tortured me in a clandestine camp, in the presence of my daughter, who was seven months pregnant. They tortured my daughter too. She was in such a bad state that I didn't think my grandchild could have been born. All the same, when they released me three days later I began the search for them. I couldn't do anything publicly because they were threatening me. They said if I spoke out they would kill me. I went to all the human rights organizations in secret but I stayed with the Grandmothers because they are concerned with the grandchildren and there's still a possibility that we will find the grandchildren. The Grandmothers helped a lot. They did everything possible to recover my grandchild.

She was found in the hands of a police officer. The Grandmothers found her through reports that were made by several members of the public. She was born on 5 November 1976 and registered in the name of the police officer. We don't know where she was born. It was very easy to prove she was my granddaughter because of the blood tests. They analysed my blood, the blood of my husband and the other grandparents and they proved more than 99% positive. She was returned to me a week ago [this interview took place in April 1987], the first child born in captivity to be recovered. She is very well, very happy. I think she always knew we were looking for her. I think she was looking for us too, subconsciously.

The police officer refused to testify and he hasn't yet been charged with the kidnapping of the child.

Estela de Carlotto: We have documentation on 208 cases of disappeared grandchildren, but from other sources we know that the real figure is closer to 400. So far we have located forty-three and twenty have now been restored to their legitimate families [by December 1987]. We've found four children who were murdered. Two of them were the Lanouscou children, aged five and six, murdered together with their parents after their house had been raided by the security forces. The only one to survive was a baby girl who the military have always insisted is also dead. When the graves of the children were exhumed there were only two bodies and some of the clothes of the little girl to make it look as if she was buried there too. We believe that she is with one of the murderers who carried out the operation. The third child to be found dead was eleven months old when he was taken. When the security forces kidnapped the mother they left the baby in a children's hospital. He was very ill. He was a little boy with Down's syndrome who needed very special treatment, which he didn't receive, and he died in the hospital ten months later. The fourth was a child who died on the point of being born, inside his mother's womb.

As far as my case is concerned, the military had always told me that there was no baby and the military courts had also denied it. In 1985 with the arrival of the scientific team from the United States who came here to identify bodies, I asked for legal permission to have my daughter's body exhumed so that a forensic examination could determine the cause of death, to prove she wasn't killed in an *enfrentamiento*, and to determine whether or not the child had really been born. The investigation proved that Laura was shot at close range and that they'd broken her arm before killing her and the bones of the pelvis showed fissures which only women who've given birth have. So science proved that Laura had given birth to her child a short time before she was killed.

I've taken the evidence to the courts so that they can investigate the murder and try to find her murderer. I'm still looking for the child, who will be nine years old now, a boy, called Guido. Of course he'll have a different name and it's certain he'll be living with a police or military family of thieves and murderers. In all the cases of the children we've located not one of the kidnappers has been punished for the crime. Only one has served a prison sentence and that was for contempt of court.

Prosecutions

'Due Obedience' and 'Equal Application of the Law'

The question of the prosecutions of those responsible for the illegal repression formed the second component of Alfonsín's policy on human rights. The Mothers and the Grandmothers, together with the other human rights organizations, had called for trials for all those implicated in the disappearances. The influence of the human rights groups on government policy proved, however, to be slight.[6] The government's strategy was formulated almost unilaterally by the President and his advisers and with the negligible participation of Congress. The limits imposed by the armed forces were never openly admitted by the government. However, Alfonsín's decision to limit prosecutions to the members of the first three juntas and those who had carried out manifestly illicit actions and to exonerate other members of the officer corps with the concept of '*obediencia debida*', [literally 'due obedience': following orders] was widely seen as a concession to the military.

The issue of 'due obedience' had never been clear in Argentine law but in 1984 Congress approved a government bill which attempted to clarify the circumstances in which a military subordinate could be held responsible for the crimes committed in the execution of orders from a military superior. The new law stated that a subordinate was judged not responsible except when in a position to exercise discretion, when he was aware of the illegality of the action or when he was involved in carrying out illicit acts. It was to be left to the courts dealing with the cases of these officers to decide what constituted 'illicit acts'. *Obediencia debida* echoed the argument presented in the junta's final document on the disappeared in which the military chiefs assumed full responsibility for the anti-subversive operations and which asserted that junior and middle-ranking officers were only carrying out orders. Underlying the President's strategy was his concern not to create irreparable divisions between military and civil society, and his determination that the officer corps as a whole should not be held responsible for the crimes of the military governments.

The Mothers had pressed for the introduction of legislation which would enable the military to be submitted to a special trial by civilians for a crime which amounted to genocide. This proposal was also rejected by the President. He was concerned to avoid any approach which suggested that the military were being subjected to a political trial and preferred instead to apply existing law and constitutional guarantees. The nine would be charged with criminal offences established in the Penal Code, offences defined as such at the time of military rule.

According to the Code of Military Justice both military offences such as insubordination and common criminal offences committed on military premises were subject to the jurisdiction of the armed forces. Since most of the offences fell into the second category the President was forced to amend the law unless the military were to be tried exclusively in military courts. To this end a new statute was approved by Congress which, while permitting the members of the first three juntas to be tried by the highest military court, the Supreme Council of the Armed Forces, introduced two main modifications. First, any decision could be appealed against in civilian courts and second, in the case of the military courts demonstrating 'unwarranted delay' the cases would be transferred automatically to civilian jurisdiction.

Alfonsín's approach was based on his conviction that the military coup and subsequent events were a response to the actions of the armed left. It followed that the law had to be applied equally in both cases. The order for the arrest of the first three juntas was accompanied by an order for the arrest on similar charges of seven ex-members of left-wing guerrilla groups.

Elisa de Landin: When they were torturing me they were laughing among themselves. It wasn't this *obediencia debida* that they want to invent now. They might be able to make someone fight in a war, but not torture. This isn't anyone's obligation. There is no *obediencia debida* for torture. I can understand that if a soldier's in a war and he's ordered to take a hill, he doesn't know why he's going. He's ordered and he obeys. But if they order you into a house to rob, to kidnap young people and to torture and murder, this isn't *obediencia debida*. In the Military Code it says that if you don't want to obey an order, you can refuse. Here nobody refused. They were all accomplices.

Elsa de Becerra: The politicians are acting in the same way as always. When their positions are threatened by the military, they negotiate and the great victim is the Argentine people. They want to put on trial generals who are already out of the army, who no longer have power, and they're handing out amnesties to the most dangerous, the middle-ranking officers, the generals of tomorrow who have grown up with the doctrine of national security.

None of them believe they did anything wrong. All of them are absolutely convinced that they did a good job and that they would do the same thing again. Because the Argentine military share with the armed forces of all Latin America the common denominator of the doctrine of national security. They are not there to defend their countries. They are forces of occupation of their own people. It's the same all over Latin America and it's not an accident. They are there to serve the interests of the United States. As long as this isn't put right we're going to continue with the sword of Damocles over our heads. The politicians have power because the people have voted for them. They have a duty to the people and they're betraying us and they're defending the weapons that will be used against us again.

Alfonsín has promoted officers who were named as torturers in the testimonies that we, and other human rights groups, have collected. We are talking about a crime of genocide which was organized by all three of the armed forces accompanied by many civilians. The church was another accomplice. Testimonies have proved the extent of the complicity of the church and these so-called priests cannot be allowed to walk free.[7] The repression wouldn't have been possible without the co-operation of many civilians. Those with economic power, the factory owners who allowed the military to operate concentration camps on their premises;[8] the union leaders who stayed silent, the judges who rejected our writs of habeas corpus, the professionals, like the lawyers and doctors and government officials who covered the tracks of the murderers. These people mustn't continue to hold positions of responsibility in our society because they have proved they have no right to this responsibility.

Graciela de Jeger: By prosecuting the ex-members of the guerrillas they wanted to make us believe that they were the ones who were responsible for the military coup. This isn't true. The guerrillas in Tucumán were wiped out a long time before March 1976 and the other groups were paralysed. The guerrillas were the pretext. Much of the evidence they had against them was extracted from other prisoners under torture and therefore isn't reliable. But our greatest fear is that they want to imprison them as hostages, so that later they can negotiate an amnesty for the military.

Moreover, we believe that those political prisoners still in detention should be released. They were arrested in the time of the constitutional government of Isabel, this is the argument they use, but they were sentenced by the military judges in the time of the *proceso*. Almost none were caught in the act of committing a crime. The evidence against them is in the form of confessions made under torture. There were no written orders for their detention. Almost all were held in secret detention camps before being legalized. They've been in prison a long time, living in very bad conditions. According to the government there are no political prisoners in Argentina, just common criminals, even though their status is recognized by the United Nations. How can we talk about human rights and democracy when there are political prisoners in our jails?

We understood that before Alfonsín took power there had been a pact. To let the constitutional government govern there was a price – a few heads would roll, but the rest would go free. This is why Alfonsín didn't prosecute the last dictator, Bignone. They said that the army would purify itself, but of course, the military courts did nothing.

Marina de Curia: How can the military be allowed to judge themselves? How can people who have tortured and murdered judge others for the same crime? How can we have faith in this 'justice'? Until now not one military officer has admitted to condemning one single *desaparecido* to death. The reason they are *desaparecidos* is because the military didn't want to sign the death sentences. They didn't have the courage to put them on trial and the President expected justice from the military courts? They were cowards then and they continue to be cowards.

Such cowards that they searched us every time we went to the barracks for information as if they expected to find bombs, two old women, myself, with another old dear like me. Such cowards that they wouldn't accept our evidence in the military trials. The army is so *machista* that in Article 259 of the Military Code it says no woman who has led an honest public life can be obliged to give evidence in military trials. When I was called to give evidence in the army barracks I took advantage of this. If they get you alone they pressure you so I requested that they come to my house, because in your own territory you have the advantage. I told Graciela that a military judge was going to come to hear my evidence in my home and we decided that she should be there, in another room, to record the conversation. We waited for them on the agreed day. We didn't know if they would come in uniform or in civilian clothes. They never came, not in uniform or in civilian clothes. They were such cowards that they wouldn't come and take evidence from a *Madre de Plaza de Mayo*.

The military aren't sorry about anything. Now they're trying to rewrite history and make people believe that what they did wasn't so bad. They still threaten and intimidate. They haven't changed at all.

An End to Repression?

Antonio Tróccoli, the Minister of the Interior, had announced at the end of 1983 that the repressive apparatus of military rule had been dismantled.[9] The government had cut the military's share of the national budget and the command structure had been reorganized so that the President was the sole Commander-in-Chief of the armed forces with a civilian Minister of Defence beneath him in the military hierarchy. Sixty high-ranking officers were sacked or pensioned off and the number of conscripts was cut by 30%. The government had also introduced changes in personnel within the military academies in an attempt to eliminate the indoctrination of the national security doctrine.

The reorganization of the security services had proved more difficult. The problem of identifying the membership of these organizations was illustrated by the case of Raúl Guglialminetti, an agent inherited from the military regime who was appointed head of the President's security staff and later uncovered as a member of the intelligence unit of an extreme right-wing terrorist group plotting to destabilize the government. This was one of many examples which suggested that the security forces were still engaged in illegal activities. Between January and December 1984 the Mothers had documented over two hundred incidents, including kidnappings of students and militants, bomb attacks such as that on the offices of CONADEP, threats and calls by military officers for a military takeover of the government. Human rights activists, in particular, were singled out as targets.

Graciela de Jeger: The threats and the provocations didn't stop with the constitutional government. People have assaulted us at our marches. Once, at a demonstration for disappeared journalists, a man attacked us and tried to stop us marching. He was someone implicated in the case of a disappearance. The police took him away and we saw him later at the police station. He took out a string of medals and said he'd got them for killing 'leftists'. One of the Mothers was surrounded by three people while she was walking down a deserted street on the way to the shops. A woman struck her on the back of the neck. Now I always go out well-protected, wearing lots of clothes, a scarf and a polo-neck jumper. Some Mothers who were called to give evidence at the trial of an ex-chief of police were intercepted on the way to the court and threatened with death if they didn't give up the case. Our houses are still painted with slogans and many Mothers still receive threatening telephone calls.

Beatriz de Rubinstein: When we're selling our newspapers in the street they say things to us. They ask us how much we're paid to wear the headscarf or why aren't we at home washing the dishes. They call us by telephone. They send us packets which they say are bombs.

The daughter of Beatriz de Rubinstein disappeared on 7 February 1977. On 13 November 1984 she received a parcel containing human bones together with the following letter:

Mar del Plata, November 1984

Dear Madam,

As a culmination to your endless search for your daughter Patricia, we have decided to send you what's left of her, which, without any doubt, will satisfy your anxiety to meet her again earlier than was foreseen by God.

This decision was taken as a result of a long investigation into your daughter's activities with the armed guerrillas and, just in case you don't know, we will give you a synthesis of the crimes that she committed, together with her husband.

– TREASON.
– AIDING AND ABETTING THE ACTIVITIES OF THE ENEMY.
– COLLABORATING ACTIVELY WITH THE MONTONERO MURDERERS.

As a consequence of all the above we condemned her to death.
May God, our Father, have mercy on her soul.

Legion Condor – Squadron 33 – Mar Del Plata[10]

The Trial of the Juntas

The Supreme Council of the Armed Forces had been given six months to reach its conclusions on the cases of the nine members of the first three military juntas. After nine months the Federal Court requested the records of the proceedings, together with a report. In this report the Supreme Council declared its inability to give an estimate of the length of time required to complete the trial, but also anticipated its decision by suggesting that it was not possible to hold the military commanders responsible for acts committed in the 'war against subversion'.[11] The Federal Court interpreted this as 'unwarranted delay' and the date for the second trial, officially described as a 'court martial by civilians', was set for April 1985.

The nine military commanders were charged with 711 offences ranging from theft, murder, illegal detention and rape. As the date for a trial unprecedented in Latin American history approached, a wave of bomb attacks hit Argentina's principal cities. Military chiefs warned of growing unrest in the ranks and public statements were issued from all sectors of the armed forces expressing opposition to the prosecutions. Faced with an increasingly violent situation, President Alfonsín went on television to denounce the military threat of destabilization and 250,000 people gathered in Plaza de Mayo in support of the government's call to 'defend democracy'.[12]

Carmen de Guede: The trial was good in that it informed the people about what had happened. It was good they called the exiles and people who'd escaped death in the camps to give evidence but I think they should have called the Mothers to recognize that we are victims. I think the principal victims after our children are us.

It was good there was a trial but for us it was a parody of a trial. They never put the military in the dock. The people came to give evidence and the accused were never present. The defence lawyers came in their place. Any common person accused of something is required to be present. In the trials of those who they said were carrying out orders the accused officers had to be in court but Videla, Massera and the others only went to hear their sentences. In the courtroom they always referred to the accused as General someone, Admiral so and so, and the victims were always called 'terrorists' and 'subversives'. When they went to court to hear their sentences they were allowed to wear their military uniforms. We, as *Madres de Plaza de Mayo*, weren't allowed to wear our headscarves.

If you watch the television or listen to the radio, Vilas and the others on trial are referred to by their rank. Like the way they talk about 'General Vilas' who is 'being tried in Bahía Blanca for human rights abuses in the war against subversion'. In the first place for us this was not a war, because to kidnap unarmed people from the street, from their houses, from their workplace is not a war. In the second place the *desaparecidos* weren't subversives. There are no innocent and guilty victims of the repression like the government prosecutor is trying to say. There are just victims. Even under this constitutional government they continue to call the *desaparecidos* subversives. And they speak of 'excesses' and 'errors' when it's very clear that this was a well-planned operation, organized on a massive scale, and not the result of the 'excesses' and 'errors' of a few officers. So we never had any confidence in the justice of these trials.

While the judges were considering their verdicts, the President, faced by another coup plot, declared a 'state of siege'.[13] The verdicts were delivered in December. Two of the nine, Videla and Massera, both of the first junta, were sentenced to life imprisonment while its third member, Agosti, representing the air force, received four and a half years. From the second junta, Viola was sentenced to 18 years and Lambruschini to eight years. Its third representative, together with the three members of the third military junta, including Galtieri, were acquitted of all charges. Hebe de Bonafini, who was forced to leave the courtroom as the sentences were being read after refusing to remove her white headscarf, declared it 'a terrible and tragic fraud perpetrated on the Argentine people.'[14]

Juanita de Pargament: Now we don't initiate trials. From the time we realized that 90% of the judges are those who co-operated with the military government, we considered it useless. In the beginning we tried, but little was done, for the same reason, because they were the same judges who'd rejected our writs of habeas corpus. We know they won't give us a reply and that the cases will stay forgotten on their desks. We have lawyers working with us to advise us when we are threatened or if we're attacked or if they detain someone and we suspect the problem is political. But we don't take cases to the courts. With these judges it's not worth doing anything. Only when things change will we do something in the courts. Because of this we are calling for an independent judiciary. We believe that the problem of the *desaparecidos* is a political problem which requires a political solution.

Democracy?

Argentina's political leadership, however, was concerned to close this chapter of the country's history and turn the nation's attention to the future. The popular human rights movement was seen as an obstacle to the government's objective of reconciliation. Questions over the way forward under a constitutional government had also opened divisions between the human rights groups. Some had dropped the demand for *aparición con vida*. Differences also emerged within the Mothers themselves. In January 1986 elections were called for the first time since their formation which concluded with the withdrawal of six members of the founding committee from the Association.

The Mothers' insistence on the permanent exclusion of the military from politics had led them to demand a radical transformation of society. It was a position which challenged a system of political relations which had dominated Argentina's recent history and which brought them into open conflict with the constitutional government.

In attacks reminiscent of the military, the President made it clear that he saw no place for the Mothers under a constitutional government. During the first *Marcha de Resistencia* since the end of military rule President Alfonsín proclaimed he was not in agreement with the 'political objectives' of the demonstration which he considered did not 'coincide with the national interest'. In the same press conference he stated that there were no *desaparecidos* alive. Eight months later, while on an official visit to Germany, he declared to journalists who had questioned him on the *Madres de Plaza de Mayo*, 'We have serious discrepancies with the positions of the Mothers, which, in this instance, I believe are political positions. I believe that it is highly negative for democracy to think about the defence of those who caused all the terrible bloodshed in the country, with an elitist conception which leads towards subversive terrorism.[15]

The Mothers' reply, in an editorial in their newspaper, was a clear statement of the battle which still had to be fought for the achievement of democracy in Argentina.

To this president, who claims to be democratic, it is necessary to explain, once again, in case he's forgotten, what the meaning of 'national' is to us.

What is authentically national is a population who develop the wealth of this country for their own benefit; it is to receive an adequate wage, to have enough food, to have a home; it is to be able to educate our children, to have health protection, to improve our intellectual and technical capacity, to have our own culture and to have freedom of expression; it is to have armed forces to drive lorries, planes and boats which transport troops and materials to places of natural disaster, who work with the people in an efficient and rapid way; it is to have a police force which protects freedom and respects all citizens; it is to have impartial judges who guarantee justice; it is to have duties and rights which can be exercised freely; it is simply, to have the right to life, but with dignity.[16]

Carmen de Guede: Alfonsín doesn't have the power. He's governed by the military. To do anything he has to have the support of the military. For example, whenever one is put on trial they plant bombs so that for every one who's sentenced, a large number are just cautioned. You can see it in two ways. The military are angry with Alfonsín so people think he must be doing something, or the government lets it happen to remind people that there is always the threat of a coup so that they'll accept that he can't do more than he's already doing. In this way the bombs ensure that Alfonsín will be returned to power because they're making people think there is only a choice between Alfonsín and the military. They're frightening people so that they'll vote for him again. We've always said Alfonsín was controlled by the military. Since he's come to power he's hardly spoken about the *desaparecidos*. Last year he said he didn't want the Mothers to go to the square any more. When he's been abroad and journalists have asked him about the *Madres de Plaza de Mayo*, knowing that he's a member of a human rights organization himself, he told them we were 'outside democracy' and he said more or less that we were the 'mothers of terrorists'.

We've always worked in a different way from the other human rights organizations. From the beginning the Mothers went to the streets and the others worked from their offices. They were more passive. It's another system of working. If we didn't go to the square we wouldn't exist any more. In many places the other organizations have disintegrated. We've always believed in going to the streets to fight injustice and we've always said exactly what we think.

Graciela de Jeger: The numbers at our marches have fallen. This is something which is happening throughout the country. Before the enemy was very clear. Everyone could see them. When Alfonsín came to power the waters began to divide. One of the biggest factors in the demobilization was the illusion that something was being done. Some Mothers began to say that Alfonsín had good intentions, that you have to give him time. As we became more clear and combative people began to withdraw. Others left because they felt deceived and frustrated and there are people who have been badly affected psychologically. Others are old or ill and some have died.

Also, the press has remained silent about us. There is a conspiracy of silence. They never publish our communiqués and they don't mention our participation in events or cover our demonstrations. We take them information about our marches and they don't want to know anything about people who question the politics of the government. If they don't write about us, we don't exist. Once we organized a march in Tucumán, together with the other human rights organizations and youth groups, to Arsenales, to denounce it as a clandestine concentration camp. We marched seven kilometres on a very hot day, with banners and placards. Not one newspaper or television channel mentioned it. The police filmed us, but the media, no.

Juanita de Pargament: In Argentina there is still censorship from above and self-censorship amongst journalists. There are still some brave journalists and we can rely on them. Our newspaper, which we started two and a half years ago with help from our foreign supporters, is produced by the great sacrifice of our team of journalists working here. Many work on other newspapers during the day and they come here tired in the evenings to write and discuss the articles with us, so that they're always of a very high standard, with the best material possible. The Mothers contribute as well, we have reports from the Mothers from the provinces and we write the editorial. The newspaper is sold all over the world and has received foreign awards. Many journalists have been thrown out of their jobs for working on the newspaper of the *Madres de Plaza de Mayo*. Others have to use pseudonyms so they won't be thrown out. We still have to live with this.

People are still afraid today. Afraid that there will be another coup, afraid to speak, comment or give an opinion. We are fighting for 30,000 *desaparecidos*. There should be at least 10,000 people every Thursday in the square. Fifty-four per cent of the *desaparecidos* were workers, but it's not the families of workers that march with us. Why not? Because they're frightened that their other children will be taken if the military return, or that they'll be sacked or that they'll go hungry.

Elsa de Becerra: Those with economic power also have a responsibility for the crimes of the *proceso*. When Alfonsín came to power we asked him what had happened to half the external debt. These billions of dollars couldn't be accounted for because a small group of people had sent the money to their personal bank accounts abroad. There was nothing to justify that kind of debt in Argentina. The correct thing would have been to create a parliamentary commission to investigate where this money had gone. Instead the President issued a decree which made the government responsible for paying the debt, which means we, the people, are responsible for the debts of the military governments, while those who benefited, the economic powers, the financiers who robbed the people, can carry on benefiting. It's because we have to pay these debts that the government has introduced austerity measures. This is why so many people are suffering such serious economic hardship.

Beatriz de Rubinstein: People are still afraid. Many ask us if it will compromise them if they sign our petitions. After ten years there's still fear. That's how terrible what they did was. And many people are so poor they can't participate. You can't go to a *villa miseria* to talk about our struggle. They can't give us help because they need help themselves. They need food, they need to learn to read and write, their children need education. If you don't have the basics you can't understand a struggle for your rights.

We have to defend this constitutional government even if they kill us in Plaza de Mayo. We don't want another coup. We were the first to go to the streets to call for the end of military rule. But we have to defend democracy too. We have to continue to fight to ensure that they don't deliver another constitutional government into the hands of the military.

Hebe de Bonafini: We are still waiting for democracy in Argentina. The passivity of many of the political parties and unions alarms me. This government has demobilized the people, sent them back to their homes, and they try to make us believe that if we go to the streets we are against democracy. The Mothers were the first to fight for democracy. Where was Alfonsín when we were marching in Plaza de Mayo? The threat to democracy comes from the torturers and murderers who walk our streets freely, and from those who protect them.

The church hasn't changed at all. They still express the same opinions. For them the biggest threat to family life is pornography and divorce. The priests tried to stop a film being shown because it showed a virgin being raped. They were outraged about a film but they were silent when young women were being raped in the military's concentration camps. When 30,000 people disappeared they never uttered a word of outrage. They're still the accomplices of the military. The other day in Salta the priests and military officers who were calling for a coup sat side by side at some religious meeting. I always say the boots and the priests' gowns are the coups of tomorrow. They always work together to repress the people. The Pope's visit [in June 1987] and his talk of reconciliation was about the same thing.

The CGT hasn't changed either. It's still led by the same bureaucracy who are all fascists. Of course the ordinary workers have nothing to do with the leadership. We have contact with the workers' Human Rights Commission, who have nothing to do with the others. When the Ford workers occupied the factory the Mothers supported them. We support the just demands of the workers for a dignified wage, a decent home, and the right to health and education services.

The enemy isn't in the *Casa Rosada*. The torture, the murders, the genocide were for one thing only: to apply an economic plan which would bring misery to the majority of the people and those responsible, including Martínez de Hoz, are still free. It was the hands of the military that murdered but they were pushed by a class that always wants to dominate us.

This class still dominates us. Economic repression is the strongest form of repression because with the repressive apparatus intact we always have to be alert. There are so many recessions. Wages and salaries aren't enough to live on. There is unemployment. There is hunger. The economy is organized so that every day everyone earns less and the wealth of the country remains for the few. We still have the same problems that our children were fighting to change, because many people are still without houses, the *villas* are growing. We don't have salaries that allow a family to live with dignity. The state needs the repressive apparatus ready to use against us whenever necessary.

Now there's a lot of discontent so I think we are going to see repression again. Alfonsín may have the government but the armed forces still have the power. We have to fight for the armed forces to return to their barracks, but without weapons, because the weapons are only used to repress the people.

Full Stop

It was the trials of middle-ranking officers which were to provoke the greatest threat of destabilization to the constitutional government. An estimated 1,700 prosecutions had been initiated against some 700 officers for crimes committed during military rule.[17] In many of these cases the courts did not consider they had sufficient evidence to secure a verdict. After four years of constitutional government and numerous military and civilian trials, Lieutenant Astiz, for example, implicated in the disappearances of the Mothers from Santa Cruz Church, the two French nuns and the Swedish girl, Dagmar Hagelin, had not been convicted of any crime.[18]

Just after Christmas 1986, against a background of growing unrest within the officer corps, Alfonsín signed an act which became known as the '*punto final*', setting a time limit on new prosecutions of military officers. Within 60 days the courts had to decide if there was sufficient evidence to prosecute individuals, otherwise all charges were to be dropped. After this time limit had lapsed, cases could not be re-opened, even if new evidence were found. The courts responded by trying to rush through hundreds of cases against military officers before the deadline expired in April 1987. As a result, over the Easter weekend middle-ranking officers facing trials led a series of rebellions in military establishments across the country. Confronted with the refusal of other army units to move against the rebel officers, the government acceded to their main demand: an end to the prosecutions of officers on active service.

Trials of more than 20 naval officers accused of illegal detention and torture at ESMA were immediately suspended. Within weeks Congress had sanctioned the Law of *obediencia debida* which formally limited responsibility to the top generals, except in cases of rape or the abduction of children. President Alfonsín admitted that some of those who had committed serious crimes would remain unpunished.

The law was challenged by human rights lawyers on the grounds that it violated the constitution but on 23 June 1987 the Supreme Court ruled the law constitutional and ordered that charges against more than 300 officers be dropped. The Supreme Court also overruled sentences passed on three people in December 1986 who had been convicted on charges of torture and murder. *Punto final* and *obediencia debida* had opened the way for an amnesty not only for those officers awaiting trial, but also for all those, with the exception of the highest ranking military, who were already serving prison sentences after being found guilty of grave abuses of human rights.

Notes

1. This refers to Cecilia Viñas who disappeared in 1976 and telephoned her family seven times between December 1983 and April 1984. See *Madres de Plaza de Mayo*, No. 2, January 1985.

2. In its report CONADEP noted that a considerable amount of documentation had been destroyed or concealed. A card was assigned to each new detainee and in many camps prisoners were photographed and declarations obtained were tape-recorded. See Amnesty International, 1980, for reconstructions of some of the documentation used, including daily record and target application forms by which the groups of kidnappers obtained official permission from their district office to carry out a raid.

3. See National Commission on Disappeared People, 1986.

4. In 1984 the government formed two commissions, one in the Secretariat for Human and Family Development and the other in the Subsecretariat of Minors of the province of Buenos Aires, which were both involved in the search for disappeared grandchildren. It was the investigations of the latter which led to the discovery of the death of the Down's syndrome baby (p. 135) and the former located three young girls. See Abuelas de Plaza de Mayo, 1985.

5. Apart from blood groups, three other groups of distinct genetic characteristics are analysed: those contained in HL antigens, plasma proteins and restriction enzymes.

6. For an analysis of the positions of the human rights organizations, the government and the military on human rights, see Osiel, Mark, 1986.

7. Survivors of the camps testified to the presence of several prominent members of the church hierarchy. Pio Laghi, the Pope's representative in Argentina, was one of those named in the list of repressors compiled by CONADEP. The following testimony is just one example. For Christmas 1976 some prisoners held at ESMA were taken to an improvised altar where a chaplain offered mass. 'We were hooded and handcuffed with shackles on our feet. It was a surreal situation, inexplicable, and more so because throughout the proceedings we could hear the screams of those being tortured. The chaplain (can he be called this?) asked which of us was going to confess . . .' Testimony of Lisandro Raúl Cubas to Amnesty International, quoted in *Madres de Plaza de Mayo*, No. 1, December 1984.

8. There are many cases which demonstrate the co-operation between factory owners and management and the security forces. Testimonies of many Ford union delegates implicated the management of the Ford factory, see National Commission on Disappeared People, 1986, pp. 373–6. Before the coup the Acindar Company demanded photographs of their workers for new factory passes which were subsequently used by the security forces to carry out raids. An illegal detention centre operated on the premises of this factory, which was later examined by CONADEP. The junta's first Minister of the Economy, Martínez de Hoz, was director of the company at the time. See ibid., pp. 381–2. At the Ledesma sugar factory kidnappings were co-ordinated by security forces and company police. See the testimony of Olga de Arédez, Chapter 2.

9. See *Madres de Plaza de Mayo*, No. 1, December 1984 and, for an account of the human rights organizations' interview with Tróccoli, No. 7, June 1985.

10. From *Madres de Plaza de Mayo*, No. 1, December 1984.

11. See the report by Amnesty International, 1987.

12. Opinion polls carried out in Buenos Aires showed that some 80% of its population supported the prosecutions of the military juntas. The threat of conspiracy denounced by Alfonsín on television was more apparent than real. It was used by the President to help underline the government's determination to keep the political initiative. According to Jimmy Burns (1987), it was a ruse, timed to coincide with the start of the trial.

13. The State of Siege was declared in October and lifted on 10 December 1985. Twelve men accused of belonging to a right-wing conspiracy behind the bomb attacks were placed under arrest. With the lifting of the State of Siege they were freed and finally the courts considered there was not enough evidence to bring charges against them. Soon after, two of the officers named in the conspiracy were promoted which fuelled suspicions that the declaration of the State of Siege was a poorly planned ploy to bolster faltering support for the Radical Party on the eve of elections.

14. *Clarín*, 10 December 1985.

15. See *Madres de Plaza de Mayo*, No. 2, January 1985 and No. 10, September 1985.

16. Editorial, *Madres de Plaza de Mayo*, No. 2, January 1985.

17. See Osiel, Mark, 1986.

18. In March 1984 a civilian judge was prevented from initiating legal proceedings against Astiz for his role in the kidnapping of Dagmar Hagelin by the Supreme Council of the Armed Forces which unexpectedly announced that Astiz had already been acquitted on charges arising from this case in 1981. The Federal Court of Appeals instructed the Supreme Council to re-open the case and on 22 February 1985 the military court exonerated Astiz once more in the Hagelin case. In May 1985 the Federal Appeals Court nullified the ruling of the Supreme Council and overturned the 1981 decision of a naval judge. The Supreme Council was ordered to continue its investigations into the case of Dagmar Hagelin. In April 1986 the Supreme Council once again returned a verdict of not guilty for lack of evidence. The case was referred for the third time to the Federal Appeals Court who decided that it should be dropped on the grounds that the six-year statute of limitations for the crime of illegal detention had expired. Astiz was brought to trial in early 1987 together with 19 other naval officers on charges of illegal detention and torture carried out on the premises of ESMA. Aftr the Easter uprising all these cases were suspended pending the ruling on 'due obedience', which finally exonerated him of all charges. See Appendix 111 of Amnesty International, 1987. In December 1987 President Alfonsín signed a decree promoting Astiz to the rank of Captain and then ordered his retirement from the navy. This decree was later rescinded and in a series of government concessions to notorious military figures, Astiz was promoted to the rank of Commander and allowed to remain on active service.

8. The Future

The fight for justice can't be compromised. Our struggle is for ever.

Hebe de Bonafini

María del Rosario: We began to understand and strengthen our struggle, to discover the purpose of our struggle in stages. Because when you go out to the street like that you don't have a clear motive, you have the anxiety of the loss of a child, the desperation, and when you begin to fight you realize the struggle isn't about a child, it's about a system which destroys everyone who thinks, everyone who disagrees. So one child is converted into thousands of children and the struggle takes on a different meaning.

First we each put the name of our own child on the headscarves and then we changed it to all the *desaparecidos*, because now we aren't fighting for just one, but for all of them. And not only for all the *desaparecidos*, but for all young people who aren't satisfied with this system, who want change, the possibility of a better life. Because many of our young people are badly paid, they can't study, they don't have homes, they don't have a future. What can they do when they find all the doors shut in their faces because the factories have all been closed down?

We didn't recognize the change at the time. We entered the abyss in a violent, rapid way. When you have everything, not material things, but your family, work, health and a family life, sometimes you become egotistical. You don't realize there are others suffering injustices. This to some degree was the case with all of us. You are concerned that your children can study, that they live well, that they have everything they need and you live and work focusing on your nuclear family and you don't think about what's happening outside your home. This is because of the education we're given. In spite of the fact many of us are the daughters of immigrants and we knew what our parents had lived through, in Spain with the Civil War, for example, the Second World War, the brutality of the Nazis. We knew about all this, but here it was like an island apart. One of the first things we learnt was that there could be no resistance without solidarity. Here we have professionals standing side by side with cleaners – there are no differences.

It's only now that I think – I used to be different. I used to be able to spend the whole afternoon shopping for a pair of shoes. These things don't make sense anymore. It doesn't make sense to spend ages getting ready for a party. Now these things seem superficial. Now I have to know what the papers say, what the government is doing, what the judges are talking about. Now I'm conscious of the world around me.

It's a struggle which is a school and which not all mothers have been able to follow, because not all have realized that now we are fighting for something more than we were in the beginning. Many have destroyed themselves thinking about their own child, a child who still hasn't come back and isn't going to come back. But we are not destroyed. The opposite, because we are fighting for the children who are still growing up and for the children of the future. We are determined to continue fighting until the last day, even though we know there is no hope of our children returning. So it's become a very profound sense of struggle.

For us there is only one future, to continue the struggle until the day we die, so that justice will be the guarantee of life in the Republic of Argentina. If there is no justice there is no right to life. We live in a country where the police kill without a second thought and where all rights are trampled on. The right to liberty, to health, to work, the rights of workers all depend on the right to life. We won't have the right to life until the torturers and murderers are in prison. There is no other solution.

We have to fight to stop the politicians who are trying to make deals with murderers and torturers. The leadership of the political parties and powers like the church, the industrialists and important sectors in the country always negotiate with the military because they need their weapons to repress the people who demand their rights. Ours is a fight without barracks, a struggle that doesn't have an end. It's a fight to the death because what happened in this country, this genocide, is without precedent and we won't allow it to be forgotten. We will continue protesting and demanding justice and the struggle will go on after we're all dead.

I always say that our struggle is like a branch that always has new leaves because after we've gone the young people who work with us will continue the battle.

Beatriz de Rubinstein: In the beginning we were just like everyone else. Maybe we could see what was happening was wrong, but we still believed in Argentine justice, in the church, in the institutions. We weren't conscious. It was our children that fought injustice then. We didn't become conscious until it affected our own families. We had no political experience. We learnt along the way. In the beginning we vacillated. We didn't know how to organize ourselves, but little by little we learnt. We learnt not to trust anyone and not to negotiate what we believed was right with anyone.

Some people have tried to say that we only want vengeance. The church itself has said, 'Enough of this vengeance', but it's not vengeance we want. We want to make sure that this is not a country where torturers and murderers go unpunished because we want to make sure this never happens again. Our struggle is for the *desaparecidos*, but we are also fighting for the same things our children were fighting for. We have taken on our children's battle for decent wages, a decent home, education and health.

I don't believe we're feminists. I believe that women in Argentina are oppressed, by the church and by our laws, and I consider that women are equal to men but I believe that this country has a lot of problems that affect men and women. You have to learn a lot of things before you can understand feminism. Many of us have had problems with our husbands. The men have given up. They've resigned themselves to the fact that the children aren't going to come back. There are many women who have been left widows. Many husbands have died of grief. It seems that men have less capacity to deal with something like this. Many believe it's all finished and some of them don't want us to go to the square any more. We go anyway. In that sense we're feminists!

We try to balance the demands of our husbands and children and grandchildren, of our work and of the struggle. But fundamentally it's the struggle that's important. The struggle goes beyond the lives of our children. It's about the future of our country.

Juanita de Pargament: The reason we're all sane today is because we are still fighting. We come here, to the Mothers' House, to talk together, to work, make banners, write, to attend to people. We have committee meetings every week, meetings with journalists and lawyers. Every Tuesday and Thursday the Mothers have lunch together and we discuss and plan our activities. Every three months we have a national meeting of all our affiliates when we assess the last three months' work and plan for the next three months. There are a thousand things to do every day and working together like this is a collective therapy.

In this respect the psychology team who work with us have been very important. During the time of the worst repression, when any of us could have disappeared, when people were disappearing every day, when they followed us in the street and broke into our homes, we always had people from this team by our sides. Now the team has grown a lot. They've had to create new concepts to deal with the psychological effect of disappearances. It's been very good for us because mothers who have lost the meaning of the struggle have returned here to take it up again. They consider that a mother who has suffered such a terrible shock isn't a sick person, but a person affected by a particular problem. They have had to modify their theories of pain.[1] Why? Because disappearance is something new in Argentina and new ways have to be found of helping people to live with it. They don't only treat the mothers, but also fathers and brothers and sisters of *desaparecidos* and the children of disappeared parents who are now being brought up by another member of the family. They do it because they believe in our struggle. They're not paid. No one who works in this House is paid.

We also have a sub-committee which helps children with disappeared parents, who are being brought up by their grandparents or other members of the family. These children are now beginning secondary school and the grandmothers may be old and in need of economic help. We receive money from abroad, from Mme Mitterrand's charity in France, from Italy, Sweden, Spain and Holland. It's only a little, but it's a help. It allows them to study and to have the opportunities their parents wanted them to have. We also receive other assistance, such as second-hand clothes, which we distribute among the families of *desaparecidos* who are in need. If a family has a broken door or no roof on their house, we help them with the repairs in whatever way we can. We feel honoured to be able to help them.

We weren't afraid to fight during the dictatorship and we're not afraid now. We have grown and we will continue to grow when people realize we're fighting for them, for the new generation, so that this doesn't happen again – when people see that we are fighting for a better country, when they lose their fear.

We are fighting so that it won't be forgotten, because to forget the past, to have no memory, is a danger for the country, because what happened will happen again. The Mothers have this memory, this pain, and we are working for the future so that the new generations won't live through what we've lived through, so people won't disappear, aren't tortured or kidnapped. We are working so that what our children wanted will become a reality. Our children wanted every family to have a decent home, enough food and clothing, and they wanted every child to have the opportunity to go to school. Because our country can give all this and has to give this. Our children worked in the *villas* as doctors, building homes, teaching. When people understand why they were taken, what they wanted, they are going to understand us and we'll have something better.

There is repression all over Latin America. All the dictatorships worked together. They kidnapped people in Bolivia and brought them here, Argentines and Bolivians. They took Argentines in Uruguay and brought them here. All the dictators worked together to repress the people. All this has to change in Latin America. Governments have to be in the hands of civilians because they are the only ones who understand the people. The Mothers have influenced women all over Latin America. The mothers of Chile wear a black headscarf to represent their dead children because in Chile there were less disappearances, more murders. The mothers of Uruguay who began in the time of the dictatorship didn't wear a white headscarf but a placard across their chest with the photographs of their children and they march with us. The mothers in El Salvador wear white headscarves. We know that mothers in many parts of Latin America wear white headscarves. We have been an important example of struggle and perseverance to the world.

Carmen de Guede: Now I come to work in the Mothers' House to help out with the campaigns and to attend to people. I don't have a specific role here. Four years ago we formed an affiliate group in Quilmes and when there are national meetings I represent it. Sometimes I have to go to conferences and discussions to speak for the Mothers which was difficult at first, but you get used to it. Last year I represented the Mothers in Brazil at a conference of a group called Torture – Never Again. There was a mistake with the ticket and I arrived four hours late but they all waited for me. It was a very nice experience for me. The people I met there still write to me and send me articles from the newspaper.

There are men who work here too. Some of the lawyers and journalists are men but the committee is made up only of Mothers. In this House it's the women who make the decisions. I think that women are stronger than men. The men who've stayed with us are more passive. They stay at home. When this government came to power, the fathers, like the Mothers, believed that things were going to change but when we saw what was happening we continued to go to the streets and the men stayed at home. There are cases of husbands who don't want their wives to go to the square. The Mothers still come, but they have a lot of problems at home. We know we're not going to find our children by going to the square but it's an obligation we have to all the *desaparecidos*.

The Mothers will continue the struggle. We always say that we're going to continue as long as our bodies allow us. We are going to lose some Mothers on the way, some who can't walk because they're too old or because they're too ill to carry on. But as long as there is some life left in us we'll continue marching in Plaza de Mayo.

Marta de Baravalle: I have four children, including Ana María, the *desaparecida*. We had a beautiful family, a large family. On Saturdays or Sundays there were eleven or twelve of us around the table and now I'm alone. My children have left home and my husband died the day of the World Cup, 25 June 1978. He died of grief for Ana María.

My daughter was concerned about injustice, like all the *desaparecidos*. Like all of them she used to give her clothes to people who needed them more than her. She couldn't imagine this world of other people or why they had to live this life with no help. She liked to help people. She helped in times of floods and disasters. She couldn't understand why the government did nothing to help the people, to alleviate their suffering, why children were living without enough food or clothes. All the *desaparecidos* were like this. She used to write a lot. When she disappeared I found a letter among her things and it gives me strength when I read what she wrote in that letter. She did what she had to do.

We can't let all these human qualities of love and tenderness that were taken from all the young people be lost. We take our strength to go on from them. When they came to my house I remembered how strong my daughter was and this made me stronger. It was then I realized, now I die or I fight. Before, perhaps, I'd been egotistical because I didn't want to sacrifice my daughter. I didn't want her to get up early and go to the *villas* to look after and bathe the children. Now I'm fighting to recover this idealism.

The Grandmothers speak out against the government, perhaps quietly, but with the conviction that what we're saying is the truth. We've denounced the *punto final* and *obediencia debida*, which mean impunity for all those who have murdered and tortured. We'll continue to denounce injustice. I never thought I'd have to confront these public situations. It's difficult but you manage it because you know you have truth on your side. It's a terrible reality that has touched our lives and that we are still living and don't know how long for. Because the other children are still alive. I have nephews and nieces who know what happened. We have to make sure it never happens to them. And the Grandmothers have to continue the search for the grandchildren.

We are optimistic we will find them. The law of the Genetic Bank means that all those grandparents who have disappeared grandchildren and who still haven't found them have the right, by this law, to ask the unit at the Durand Hospital to make all the tests, the results of which go on to a computer. They store the genetic data of all the families with disappeared grandchildren so that at any time in the future a child who has doubts about his background can ask to have his blood tested and compared with the information on the computer. Even after the grandparents are dead, this information will be there to allow children to reclaim their true identity. With the restoration to her family of the first baby born in captivity we are hopeful about the others.

Estela de Carlotto: Now we've been transformed into detectives. First we receive a report from a member of the public saying that in such-and-such a house in such-and-such a street a couple who'd never been able to have a child suddenly appeared with a baby. Then we begin an investigation to collect all the evidence we need to take the case to court. This can take three or four years. We work together with groups of lawyers, doctors, psychologists and experts in genetics. The psychologists help with the process of adjustment after a child is restored to its family. The child needs to be treated for many years to ensure that no trauma is suffered. They also help the grandmother and her family and we have some cases where they help the family who had the child before, if this family was innocent. These are the people who didn't know the child was a child of a disappeared couple and who hand them over when we tell them the truth. They also suffer pain and we offer our psychologists to help them overcome the grief. In these cases a larger family is formed. The grandchild visits the family who brought him up and the family visits the child.

People bring us information every day. We've got more than 5000 details which have been brought in by the public. We have found all the children as a result of information given by the public. Now we have an office, a telephone, an address, people come here every day and give us some new piece of information so we can begin the search. We have to visit the house where the child was seen, take photographs, search for birth and adoption papers. We have to do everything with a lot of discretion and respect because we don't want to create anxiety in the child population. We don't want children who have been legally adopted to feel persecuted or uncomfortable. When we are carrying out our investigations nobody realizes because we do it very quietly and we take a lot of precautions.

One day mine will come, somebody will bring me evidence about my grandson I'll be able to investigate and I'll be able to find him in the same way as we've found the forty-three other grandchildren. It's a struggle that goes on for ever. It isn't something personal now. I'm looking for my own in the same way I'm looking for all the disappeared grandchildren.

Graciela de Jeger: The Mothers aren't out to get political power. We are unusual in that we're not associated with any one political party, nor with any one social class. What political party meets every week, rain or shine, no matter whether it's New Year or Christmas? What political party has four national congresses every year to discuss their political line? Some will say you can't change a society without power, but I believe that the young people who work with us, when they enter society, will spread our ideas to many people.

The Mothers are always in demand. People come and ask us to speak at meetings, discussions and demonstrations. Many people with problems come to us to ask for support, because we support all the oppressed sectors. Homeless people who occupied an empty building came to the square in Tucumán and we went to show our solidarity. We support the political prisoners in the fight against injustice and we support people fighting oppression all over Latin America. We believe in the liberation of men and women. Clearly women are doubly oppressed, especially in Catholic–Hispanic countries. We are oppressed as workers in a dependent capitalist country, because women work in the lowest paid, least qualified work and we also have the housework to do. This makes it more difficult for women to take part in the struggle.

The pain is still there. At first we used to imagine the exact minute they died, how they were tortured, how many times. Then we had to compile our files, watch films, lead discussions and we had to draw a curtain over the details of their suffering. But the pain will always be there. There is always something that brings back that pain. For me, it's the photographs. I still can't look at the photographs of the *desaparecidos* in our files.

We have to fight so that this genocide isn't forgotten and so that it never happens again. In Tucumán there were thirty-three concentration camps in operation, including the first, and it's the only place in the country where there hasn't been one single trial of a military officer for human rights abuses. We all have to fight, from the provinces and from the cities, the whole of Latin America, for the day when our people will suffer no more repression.

Margarita de Oro: It surprises me when I see what I am today. Before I was shy, a cry-baby. I had no political consciousness. I didn't have any kind of consciousness. All that interested me was that my children were well. I was one of those mothers who went everywhere with their children. If they organized dances at the school to collect money, I was the one who was selling the tickets. I was involved in everything my children did. You only become conscious when you lose something. When the Mothers first met we used to cry a lot and then we began to shout and demand, and nothing mattered any more, except that we should find our children. Now I fight, I shout, I push and if I have to, I kick but I still wonder to myself how I could have gone inside those military buildings searching for my son with all those guns pointed at my head.

I've learnt a lot of things through this struggle. I was brought up a Catholic. My mother was very religious. After all this I lost my faith. The church was the biggest accomplice in the repression. I've learnt that there is repression all over Latin America. In Chile, for example. There are a lot of Chileans living in Mendoza and we also work with them. Once some of the Mothers went to a big demonstration in Santiago de Chile and they were sent home. They weren't allowed off the plane. Another time we were invited to the Argentine–Chilean border to a meeting of youth groups from the two countries. It was wonderful. The young Chileans took away some of our headscarves and they gave us flowers and some little birds which had been carved from bone by the political prisoners.

Some people say I have to resign myself to the situation, that I have to forget about the past, think about my grandson and start again. I can resign myself to the death of my husband because it's a law of nature, you grow old and you die. But how can you resign yourself to something like this? Without an explanation? They have to say what happened, who killed them and why, and those responsible have to be punished so that this never happens again in Argentina.

I have to think about the future of my grandchild and all the other children in Argentina. They talk about human rights now in the schools. They're talking about everything Sasha has lived through. Once a child asked him what he thought about the madwomen in Plaza de Mayo. He said to him, 'Haven't you got anyone disappeared?' and the boy said, 'No, because they're all subversives.' How can they teach human rights when murderers and torturers are still walking the streets?

Now I'm alone with Sasha. We survive with the help of my daughters and with the money that the *Madres de Plaza de Mayo* give us from the donations which come from abroad to help the women who are bringing up their grandchildren. Some of my family have tried to control me. They say if you stop going to the square, you're one of us again. My family now are the *Madres de Plaza de Mayo*.

Elisa de Landin: Here we are, Jews and Catholics, all religions and all classes and we all work together as one. We all respect each other and this is something wonderful. Recently we were saying what could be better than to be together like this. A family celebration can't give us more than we have here every day. Because we each have the same pain, we each understand how the other feels, we can understand each other's problems. When one weakens or gets disheartened there's always someone standing by her side to give her strength. A Mother who comes to the House can find the strength to continue the struggle. It's the one who stays at home, who only comes occasionally to the square, who give up. Here in this House there's always work to be done, always a reason to be on our toes. Together we give each other a strength which I think is unique in the world.

Now I'm a member of the committee. I've been to various places to speak in public. Sometimes it's difficult, you feel like you did when you had to take an exam at school, your heart beats fast, but when you begin it all goes away. At the last meeting it was decided that all Mothers without passports should get one because there are lots of trips coming up. I got mine only yesterday. Being here you are always learning. There are some Mothers who are very clever. They have a very good political sense and every day you learn more.

Some people say that the *Madres de Plaza de Mayo* are asking too much. When we went to see Alfonsín in Government House soon after he became President he said, 'What do you want, señoras? Do you want us to torture them like they tortured your children?' He was already being pressured. I had expectations that the constitutional government would fulfil their promises but now I realize that we have a long battle in front of us to make these promises a reality.

This is a permanent struggle. We believe that when we're all dead, the young people who work here with us and our children will continue with our demands. The *desaparecidos* can never be allowed to be forgotten. What happened to our children must never be allowed to happen to another generation of young people.

Hebe de Bonafini: To me the Mothers are women who have broken with many aspects of this system we live in. First, because we went to the streets to confront the dictatorship, because we were capable of doing things that men couldn't do. We've broken with the system because we aren't a political party and yet we still have political influence. We continue in the same way as before. I think this is what's difficult to understand. We are listened to much more than if we had become a political party. I think that without being a political party we have a political line, not party political, but we have a political line which is resolute. Without wanting to be deputies or senators, we are the opposition to the government, the opposition this country doesn't have.

We're always invited to speak at conferences, to open meetings. We are supported by a lot of people in the world. We have lots of groups of young people who come here to help us with our campaigns. The groups in solidarity with the *Madres de Plaza de Mayo* are growing inside and outside the country and they have to support whatever we are doing, things that sometimes seem crazy, like covering Government House with headscarves to show we are a barrier against injustice and the military '*no pasarán*'[2]. It's a very different way of fighting but it's a way which has influenced women in Uruguay, Chile, Colombia, El Salvador and in all the countries where there are *desaparecidos*. I believe that every country should find its own form of struggle to suit its situation. We have built our own defences and antibodies to defend ourselves against our enemies.

I think we are an organization fighting for life and freedom. The fight for life isn't just about words. The words 'peace', 'freedom', 'human rights' are so over-used that they've become dead words. We have learnt that in reality, life and peace and freedom are rarely defended in this world. We try to share with people what we have learnt over these ten years, what the streets and the struggle have taught us, which is to defend life, even with our own lives if necessary.

I don't think the Mothers are feminists, but we point a way forward for the liberation of women. We support the struggle of women against this *machista* world and sometimes this means we have to fight against men. But we also have to work together with men to change this society. We aren't feminists because I think feminism, when it's taken too far, is the same as *machismo*. So yes, we want to say that we agree that women should have the same place as men, not above or below, but equal, and we have pointed a very clear way forward to this. I think we have also raised some new possibilities for women, the most important of which is the possibility of the socialization of motherhood. This is something very new.

The woman I was before gave me the preparation, the maternal feelings and the tenderness to be the woman I am today, because in spite of the fact that I'm a very tough person, some people say like a 'warm rock', we never separate our feelings, our tenderness, the human part, from the politics. I believe this is very important. It's there the 'two women' come together: this 'warm rock' that they say I am today and the tenderness of having been a mother and of having been brought up in a small working-class community, which I believe is a beautiful thing which few people can experience now.

I've always had to continue with the housework, to wash, iron, cook, clean. I'm not a rich person. Now I live alone with my daughter and we continue doing these things. I believe the most difficult thing is to continue being the person you've always been and to keep your feet on the ground. I cook here for everyone. For me cooking for twenty is the same as cooking for one, and we like to eat together because this is also a part of our struggle and our militancy. I want to continue being the person I've always been. Sometimes I'm criticized for wearing a housecoat and slippers in public but I'm not going to change. Of course my life is different. I still receive threats, I'm still followed. That's always in the background, but the other thing is much more powerful, what you have to do for those who are not here.

We're going to continue in the same way because we still haven't got justice. They've tried to convert us into the mothers of dead children and put an end to the problem of the *desaparecidos*. We will never accept they are dead until those responsible are punished. If we accepted that, we would be accepting that murderers and torturers can live freely in Argentina. They can't negotiate with the blood of our children. The *Madres de Plaza de Mayo* are never going to permit that.

Notes

1. See Kordon, Diana, et al., 1986.
2. To mark the tenth anniversary of the Mothers' first meeting in Plaza de Mayo white headscarves signed by supporters from all over the world were hung around the square. '*No pasarán*' (They will not pass) is the slogan used by Nicaraguan supporters of the Sandinista government.

Bibliography

Newspapers

Boletines de las Madres de Plaza de Mayo, August 1981–September 1984, published by Madres de Plaza de Mayo.
Madres de Plaza de Mayo, December 1984–June 1987, published by Madres de Plaza de Mayo, Hipólito Yrigoyen 1442, 1089 Capital Federal, Argentina.
Informaciones Nos. 1–12, published by the Abuelas de Plaza de Mayo, Corrientes 3284 4°H, 1173 Capital Federal, Argentina.
Buenos Aires Herald
Clarín
Gente
La Nación
La Opinión
La Prensa

Secondary Source Material

Abuelas de Plaza de Mayo, *Niños Desaparecidos en la Argentina desde 1976*, Buenos Aires (1985).
Amnesty International *Extracts from the Report of an Amnesty International Mission to Argentina 6–15 November 1976* (1977).
———— *Testimony on Secret Detention Camps in Argentina* (1980).
———— 'Disappearances', a Workbook, New York (1981).
———— *Argentina, the Military Juntas and Human Rights, Report of the Trial of the Former Junta Members, 1985* (1987).
Andreas, C., 'The Chilean Woman: Reform, Reaction and Resistance', *Latin American Perspectives*, Vol. IV, No. 4 (1977).
de Bonafini, Hebe, *Historia de Vida*, Fraterna/Del Nuevo Extremo, Buenos Aires (1985).
Boserup, E., *Women's Role in Economic Development*, Allen & Unwin, London (1970).
Bousquet, Jean-Pierre, *Las Locas de la Plaza de Mayo*, El Cid Editor, Buenos Aires (1980).
Bronstein, Audrey, *The Triple Struggle, Latin American Peasant Women*, WOW Campaigns Ltd., London (1982).
Burns, Jimmy, *The Land that Lost its Heroes*, Bloomsbury Press, London (1987).

Canitrot, A., 'Discipline as the Central Objective of Economic Policy: An Essay in the Economic Programme of the Argentine Government since 1976', *World Development*, Vol. 8 (1980).

———— 'Teoría Práctica del Liberalismo', *Desarrollo Económico*, Vol. 21, No. 82 (1981).

Catholic Institute for International Relations, *Some Considerations About the Role Played by the Roman Catholic Church in Argentina and in particular its Episcopate in Relation to the Violations of Human Rights which have taken place under the Present Circumstances*, Buenos Aires (1978).

———— *Death and Violence in Argentina*, a report by a group of priests in Argentina, London (1980).

CEPAL, *Mujeres en América Latina: Aportes para una discusión*, (1975).

Chaney, E., *Supermadre: Women in Politics in Latin America*, University of Texas Press, Austin (1979).

Dabat, Alejandro, & Lorenzano, Luís, *Argentina, the Malvinas and the End of Military Rule*, Verso Editions, London (1984).

Di Tella, Guido, *Argentina under Perón 1973–76, the Nation's Experience under a Labour-Based Government*, Macmillan, London (1982).

Ferrer, Aldo, 'The Argentine Economy 1976–9', *Journal of Inter-American Studies and World Affairs*, Vol. 22, No. 2, May 1980.

Gillespie, Richard, *Soldiers of Perón: Argentina's Montoneros,* Oxford University Press (1982).

Graham-Yooll, Andrew, *The Press in Argentina 1973–8*, Writers and Scholars Educational Trust, London (1979).

Hodges, D.C., *Argentina 1943–76: The National Revolution and Resistance*, University of New Mexico Press, Albuquerque (1976).

Hoffman, Stanley, *Duties Beyond Borders*, Syracuse (1981).

Hollander, Nancy Caro, 'Si Evita Viviera', *Latin American Perspectives*, Vol. I, No. 3, (1974).

———— 'Women Workers and the Class Struggle: The Case of Argentina', *Latin American Perspectives*, Vol. IV, No. 1/2 (1977).

James, Daniel, 'The Peronist Left 1955–75', *Journal of Latin American Studies*, Vol. 8, No. 16 (1976).

Jaquette, Jane S., 'Women in Revolutionary Movements in Latin America', *Journal of Marriage and the Family*, Vol. 35, No. 2, May 1973.

Jelin, Elizabeth, 'Conflicts under the Second Peronist Regime 1973–76', *Development and Change*, Vol. 10, No. 2, April 1979.

Kordon, Diana, et al., *Efectos Psicológicos de la Represión Política*, (a collection of essays by the psychology team working with the Mothers), Sud Americana/Planeta, Buenos Aires (1986).

Latin American and Caribbean Women's Collective, *Slave of Slaves – the Challenge of Latin American Women*, Zed Press, London (1980).

Latin American Bureau, *Falklands/Malvinas: Whose Crisis?*, Latin American Bureau (1982).

Lewis Paul H., 'The Female Vote in Argentina 1958–65', *Comparative Political Studies*, Vol. 3, No. 4, (1971).

Little, Cynthia Jeffress, 'Education, Philanthropy and Feminism: Components of Argentine Womanhood 1860–1926', in Lavrin, Asunción (ed.), *Latin American Women*, Greenwood Press, Westport, USA (1978).

Little, Walter, 'Civil and Military Relations in Contemporary Argentina', *Government and Opposition*, Vol. 19, No. 2, Spring 1984.

Lowenthal, Abraham F., *Armies and Politics in Latin America*, Holmes & Meier, London (1976).

Madres de Plaza de Mayo, *Cantos de Vida, Amor y Libertad* 1,2,3, Buenos Aires (1985).

Mainwaring, Scott, 'Authoritarianism and Democracy in Argentina', *Journal of Inter-American Studies*, Vol. 26, No. 3, August 1984.

Marini, A., 'Women in Contemporary Argentina', *Latin American Perspectives*, Vol. IV, No. 4 (1977).

Minority Rights Group, *Report No. 57, Latin American Women*, MRG, 36 Craven St., London WC2N 5NG (1983).

Molyneux, Maxine, 'Anarchist Feminism in Nineteenth Century Argentina', *Latin American Perspectives*, Vol. 13, No. 1 (1986).

Munck, Ronaldo, *Politics and Dependency in the Third World: The Case of Latin America*, Zed Press, London (1984).

Nash, J. & Safa, H. I., (eds.), *Sex and Class in Latin America*, J. F. Bergin Publishers, New York (1980).

———— *Women and Change in Latin America*, Bergin & Garvey, New York (1985).

National Commission on Disappeared People, *Nunca Más (Never Again)*, Faber & Faber, London (1986).

North American Congress on Latin America (NACLA), *Argentina in the Hour of the Furnaces*, New York (1975).

Nosiglia, Julio E., *Botín de Guerra*, Tierra Fértil, Buenos Aires (1985).

Organization of American States, Inter-American Commission on Human Rights, *Report on the Situation of Human Rights in Argentina*, Washington (1980).

Osiel, Mark, 'The Making of Human Rights Policy in Argentina: The Impact of Ideas and Interests on a Legal Conflict', *Journal of Latin American Studies*, Vol. 18, Part 1, May 1986.

Partnoy, Alicia, *The Little School: Tales of Disappearance and Survival in Argentina*, Virago Press, London (1985).

Peralta-Ramos, Monica and Waisman, Carlos H., (eds.), *From Military Rule to Liberal Democracy in Argentina*, Westview Press, Boulder and London (1987).

Pescatello, A., (ed.), *Female and Male in Latin America: Essays*, Pittsburgh Press (1973).

Pion-Berlin, David, 'The Fall of Military Rule in Argentina 1976–83', *Journal of Inter-American Studies and World Affairs*, Vol. 27, No. 2, Summer 1985.

Potash, R., *The Army and Politics in Latin America in 1945–62: Perón to Frondizi*, Athlone Press, London (1980).

Randall, M., *Sandino's Daughters: Testimonies of Nicaraguan Women in Struggle*, Zed Press, London (1982).

Recchini de Lattes, Zulma, *La Participación Femenina en la Argentina desde la Segunda Guerra hasta 1970*, Cuaderno del CENEP, No. 11,

———— *Dynamics of the Female Labour Force in Argentina*, UNESCO (1983).

———— & Wainerman, Catalina H., 'Marital Status and Women's Work in Argentina', *Genus*, Vol. XXXIV, No. 3–4 (1978).

Rendel, M., (ed.), *Women, Power and Political Systems*, Croom Helm, London (1981).

Rock, David, *Argentina 1516–1982: From Spanish Colonisation to the Falklands War*, I. B. Taurus, London (1986).

Rouquié, Alain, (ed.), *Argentina Hoy*, Siglo XXI, Mexico (1982).

———— *Poder Militar y Sociedad Política en la Argentina, II, 1943–73*, Emece, (1982).

———— 'Argentina: The Departure of the Military – End of a Political Cycle or just Another Episode?', *International Affairs*, Vol. 59, No. 4, Autumn 1983.

Safa, H. I., 'The Changing Composition of the Female Labour Force in Latin America', *Latin American Perspectives*, Vol. IV, No. 4 (1977).

Saffiotti, H. B., *Women in Class Society*, New York (1978).

Schoultz, Lars, *Human Rights and U.S. Policy towards Latin America*, Princeton University Press (1981).

Selser, Gregorio, *El Onganiato, la Espada y el Hisopo*, Carlos Samonta Editor, Buenos Aires (1973).

Seoane, María & Ruiz Núñez, Héctor, *La Noche de los Lápices*, Contrapunto, Buenos Aires (1986).

Simpson, John & Bennett, Jana, *The Disappeared: Voices from a Secret War*, Robson Books, London (1985).

Snow, Peter G., *Political Forces in Argentina*, Praeger, New York (1979).

Sobel, L. A., *Argentina and Perón 1970–5*, Facts on File Inc., New York (1976).

Tabak, Fanny, *Autoritarismo e Participação Política de Mulher*, Edições Graal, Rio de Janeiro (1983).

Tiffenberg Goldferb, Ernesto David, 'Surgimiento y Evolución del Movimiento de Madres de Plaza de Mayo en el Contexto de los Neuves Movimientos Sociales', unpublished thesis, Universidad Autónoma de México (1984).

Timerman, Jacobo, *Prisoner Without a Name, Cell Without a Number*, Penguin, Harmondsworth (1982).

Torre, Juan Carlos, 'The Meaning of the Current Workers' Struggles', *Latin American Perspectives*, Vol. II, No. 3 (1974).

Verbitsky, Horacio, *La Ultima Batalla de la Tercera Guerra Mundial*, Nueva Información/Legasa, Buenos Aires (1985).

Vogelgesang, Sandy, *American Dream, Global Nightmare, The Dilemma of U.S. Human Rights Policy*, Norton, New York (1980).

Wainerman, Catalina H., 'La Mujer y el Trabajo en la Argentina desde la Perspectiva de la Iglesia Católica a Mediados del Siglo', *Desarrolo Económico*, Vol. 21, No. 81, April–June 1981.

Walsh, Rodolfo, 'Open Letter from Rodolfo Walsh to the Military Junta, 24th March 1977', The Committee to Save Rodolfo Walsh, 9 Poland St., London W1V 3DG, July 1977.

Wynia, G. W., *Argentina in the Post-War Era: Politics and Economic Policy-making in a Divided Society*, University of Mexico Press, Albuquerque (1978).

Index of Mothers

Index